THEY

WILL

HAVE

TO DIE

NOW

THEY
WILL
HAVE
TO DIE
NOW

MOSUL AND THE FALL OF THE CALIPHATE

JAMES VERINI

W. W. NORTON & COMPANY
Independent Publishers Since 1923

For information about permission to reproduce selections from this book, write to
Permissions, W. W. Norton & Company, Inc., 500 Fifth Avenue, New York, NY 10110

For information about bulk purchases, please contact W. W. Norton Special Sales at
specialsales@wwnorton.com or 800-233-4830

Manufacturing by LSC Communications, Harrisonburg
Book design by Chris Welch
Production manager: Beth Steidle

Library of Congress Cataloging-in-Publication Data

Names: Verini, James, author.
Title: They will have to die now : Mosul and the fall of the caliphate / James Verini.
Description: First edition. | New York : W. W. Norton & Company, Inc., [2019]
Identifiers: LCCN 2019014781 | ISBN 9780393652475 (hardcover)
Subjects: LCSH: IS (Organization) | Mosul (Iraq)—Politics and government—21st century. |
    Iraq—Politics and government—2003-
Classification: LCC DS79.9.M6 V47 2019 | DDC 956.7044/342—dc23
LC record available at https://lccn.loc.gov/2019014781

W. W. Norton & Company, Inc., 500 Fifth Avenue, New York, N.Y. 10110
www.wwnorton.com

W. W. Norton & Company Ltd., 15 Carlisle Street, London W1D 3BS

1 2 3 4 5 6 7 8 9 0

To Aya, Amina, Maha, Zainab, Zina, Clementine, and Vivian.
I'm sorry for the world we're giving you.
Please help us make it better.

And to Christopher Hitchens.
You were wrong about Iraq, but right about
most everything else.

Of course he has a knife. He always has a knife. We all have knives. It is eleven eighty-three and we're barbarians. How clear we make it. Oh, my piglets, we're the origins of war. Not history's forces nor the times nor justice nor the lack of it nor causes nor religions nor ideas nor kinds of government nor any other thing. We are the killers: we breed war. We carry it, like syphilis, inside.

—ELEANOR OF AQUITAINE IN *The Lion in Winter*

CONTENTS

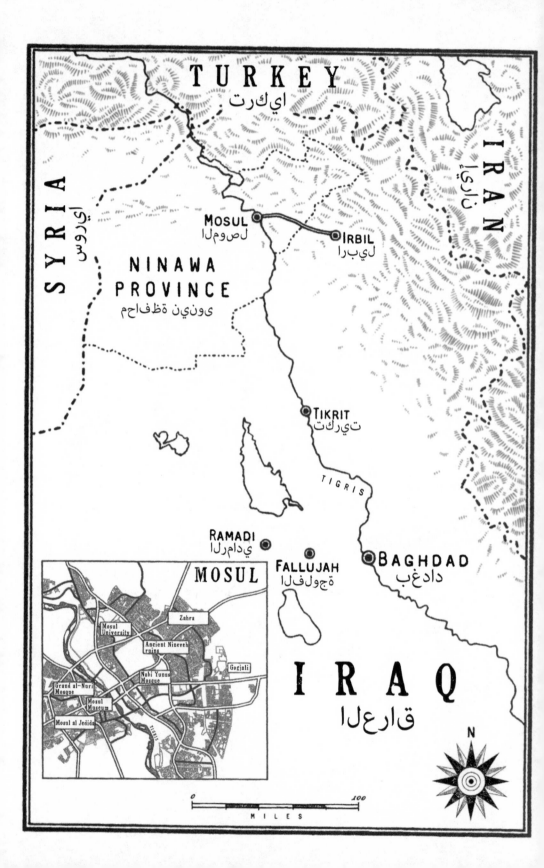

I

ZAHRA

I have come forth alive from the land of purple and poison and glamour,
Where the charm is strong as the torture, being chosen to change the mind

—G.K. CHESTERTON

Two weeks into ground operations to recapture Mosul, Iraqi troops breached the city limits, fighting their way in through a series of suburbs and neighborhoods in the southeast. But for another few weeks after that they could go no farther on the main access road into east Mosul than a hill on the city's outer rim. On the crest of the hill, astride the road, Islamic State fighters had lathered an embankment of rubble and scrap. By the time you noticed the embankment and its impassibility, bullets were already flying overhead. Then you noticed, between you and the embankment, a panorama of what would happen if you insisted on continuing forward. To the right of the access road was the apartment building from which the bullets flew and, to its left, a cemetery.

It was the fall of 2016, and the jihadis had been fighting on the back foot long enough that they knew a good defensive position when they saw one. They were understandably reluctant to give up the apartment building, really more of a complex of buildings, as you learned when you got a better look at it, and as perfect in its quiet ugly menace as it was in its situation. It overlooked not just the access road but some of the districts into which the troops were trying to push. From the buildings' many exterior planes of sickly pebbledash and rust-stained stucco protruded balconies and roofs, a dealer's choice of positions in which the Islamic State fighters set up machine-gun emplacements and snipers' nests. The Iraqi troops would hose down the outside of an apartment with 50-caliber fire, or send a grenade into a window, and then another jihadi would appear in another window returning fire. The Islamic State had been in fighting retreat for over a year, had ceded most of its ground in Iraq, and yet here the jihadis still were, popping up, shooting back when not shooting first. If you couldn't admire their pluck, you had to marvel at it.

Why those buildings weren't reduced to rubble with ordnance I never learned. The international coalition backing the Iraqi ground forces was flying sorties day and night over Mosul and a constellation of artillery firebases surrounded the city. Some mornings the strikes were constant, making the whole city quake, the atmosphere pulse and bellow. Most likely the jihadis were keeping the apartments stocked with civilians. They did this. When they couldn't get enough Moslawis to serve as human insulation and cannon fodder they imported them from surrounding villages, and the invisible presence of who knew how many innocents inside the apartment complex added to its menace. The place was ominous in the literal sense. It issued omens of an extensive, filthy, many-angled fight. It was the sort of frowning pile you had to see only once to think 'Well *of course* armed zealots would be shooting at me from there.'

The Iraqi troops had, with great effort and bloodshed, established a small headland of control in a district to the north of the access road, beyond the reach of the gunmen in the apartments. To get to this district their convoys took a right off the road about a hundred meters downhill from the embankment, onto a partially paved side street that quickly degenerated into a dirt track. The neighborhood into which they drove, Gogjali, was as poor as Mosul got. About four hundred miles north of Baghdad, Mosul is the capital of the governate of Nineveh, the agricultural heartland of Iraq. On the Tigris, which bisects Mosul into its eastern and western halves, and near the borders of Turkey and Syria, the city has been a hub of trade, licit and illicit, for centuries. The results can be seen in Mosul's many mansions and its beautiful marble-and-tile mosques. Gogjali's mosque was a cinderblock box, its narrow streets unpaved, the privacy walls of its one-story houses still mudbrick. It had been one of the first neighborhoods seduced by the jihadis, you heard. When the Islamic State's clandestine recruiters had started approaching Moslawis, whispering about an impending takeover, they had made short work of winning over people here. *Look at those big houses down the hill nearer the river. You can live in one of those if you join us.*

Gogjali was now the beginning of the rear on the eastern front, the only battle front in Mosul where the fighting was steady. The Iraqi 9th Division, armored and stodgy and questionable, was probing tentatively about the city's southeastern edge, and the better but not entirely dependable 16th was somewhere closer by, while the federal police and paramilitary forces were stirring around. But it was here in the east that the special forces formation leading the invasion of Mosul, the Counter-Terrorism Service, had put the first real puncture in the Islamic State's defenses. It was through this puncture that the main part of the Iraqi infantry, ten thousand strong, was trickling and would soon pour. The Islamic State had started life as an insurgency, using insurgent tactics, but now it was a regime, a government, even, in its way; it held territory, it had in Mosul Iraq's second or third most populous city (depending on who did the counting), and now it would have to fight a conventional battle over territory, one government versus another.

Gogjali was also home to what, in those early days of the battle, was the Iraqi troops' only frontline triage station. What few CTS medics there were had taken over an abandoned home and an adjoining vacant lot. Every morning they set up shop in the lot, carrying out their gurneys and rolls of gauze and squeeze bottles of iodine and IV kits, most of it donated by foreign charities.

Early one morning, the front line was just beyond the triage station. The pounding of airstrikes and artillery and the chatter of gunfire reverberated through the pall of dust and smoke and moist haze—the rainy season was beginning. The procession of casualties into the lot was already incessant. I arrived as a civilian caught in a shelling was carried in. He was put on a gurney. In moments, he was dead. His brother collapsed onto the body, weeping and hollering. He flung himself to the ground, still weeping and hollering and now smacking himself.

A CTS squad had been ambushed. A pair of bloodied soldiers lay on stretchers, too dazed to take note of the mourner writhing in the dirt beside them. A major was carried in by his limbs by four of his men as blood pumped from a gunshot wound in the rear of his thigh. Though clearly in excruciating pain, when a medic went to roll up the major's sleeve in order to put in an IV, the major got it in his mind the man was trying to lift his watch and he sat up, wheezing and flailing his arms in protest. In the late morning, the fighting quieted as the jihadis went to mosque. This happened every day, but on Fridays the lull was longer and particularly inauspicious. On Fridays the Islamic State imams gave sermons.

'On Fridays, Daesh fights well,' a soldier watching the scene with me said, using the Arabic term for the group.

In the early afternoon, the firefights resumed. An enemy sniper set to work. Like most Islamic State snipers, he was good. A soldier was brought in with half his jaw shot off. He was followed by a man with a long, shallow red groove through his pate, and he by two more men with head shots, both close to death. The Humvees skidded into the lot one after another, sending up a dust cloud that hung among the medics and patients.

Journalists gathered. The writers hung on the periphery but the photographers swarmed around the gurneys. The Iraqi troops hated having their casualties photographed. A photographer approached a wounded man. A soldier told the photographer, calmly, 'Take that picture and I will burn your vehicles.'

In came a Humvee full of soldiers whose torsos and legs were punctured with shrapnel from an RPG; a man with a sucking chest wound; another with his left hand blown off, the shattered fibula jutting from the shreds of his wrist.

'When we move forward, they fight. But this number of injured, for going forward, this is nothing. We're doing good,' said the soldier watching with me. Like many CTS soldiers, who were trained by Americans, he spoke English, and like most of them he had an excellent and dark sense of humor. His name was Ali.

'Fuck this imam,' Ali added. He said it without anger. It was more of a tactical suggestion.

Young and reedy, with glinting blue eyes, Ali made no more pretense of helping with the wounded than I did. There was nothing to be done, but still you felt useless. We reclined against a wall, on a quilt, smoking the thin Turkish cigarettes the troops favored, looking on at the carnage. A bemused grin suggested itself on the corners of Ali's mouth with each new load of casualties.

'How do you think the battle's going?' I asked him.

'For me? Nothing. I don't care,' he said. 'Just I care about my family. I don't care about Iraq. It didn't give me anything.'

Looking at the refugees filing past the triage station, I pointed out that he at least had a job. The stupidity of this occurred to me only as the words left my mouth. It was like saying, 'Well you've got your health.'

'Because they don't have anyone else to employ in this fucking job!' he said. 'But we die every day, like five times.'

Bad but salvageable cases were carried from the lot into the carport of the home, where an American medic worked on them. Many Americans had, in the past few years, volunteered to help the militias fighting the jihadis in the rural border regions of Iraq and Syria, and now a few had found their way into Mosul. The volunteers included soldiers of fortune, Evangelical Christians, thrill-seekers, lost souls, even some combat veterans, and very occasionally—the only ones of any real use—medics. Some had taken a course, invested a lot of money in tourniquets, and flown over. A few really knew what they were doing. The American medic in Gogjali knew what he was doing. Like most of the volunteers, he was a loud buffoon, whom you could find by night drunkenly mouthing off in the hotel bars back in the Kurdish city of Irbil, where the journalists and aid workers and the other hangers-on lived, but he was a large-hearted, loud buffoon, and devoted, and he saved a lot of lives in that carport.

This didn't make the Iraqi military's attitude toward its wounded any less careless by the coalition's standards. There were far too few Iraqi corpsmen to attach them to individual combat platoons, or even companies, and anyway the idea would have been superfluous, almost laughable. The Iraqi philosophy, stated often, was: people die in war. That's what war is for. Anyone not ready to die shouldn't be here. This wasn't just the predictably callous philosophy of the high command; infantrymen held it too, and especially the infantrymen of CTS, who had been through enough that, though you doubted their judgment, you couldn't question the sincerity of their fatalism. Since the Islamic State had begun seizing land in Iraq, in the first days of 2014, over twenty thousand Iraqi troops had died.

A week earlier, Ali told me, his company had been ambushed. Four dead, thirty-five injured, twelve Humvees totaled. They were pinned down all night. The jihadis who had them surrounded never let up yelling what they'd do to the soldiers once they were caught. At 3 a.m., the company ran out of ammunition. Ali wasn't scared of dying, he said, but 'I was scared of them taking me alive. So I spared a bullet. I call it—we call it, all of us—a bullet mercy. A mercy bullet. When you are surrounded, you kill yourself.'

They were finally rescued the next afternoon. The Americans had been no help, he complained. Here were, at the very least, a detachment of the 101st Airborne, planes, helicopters, drones, god only knew how many Special Forces commandos, and none of them had come to his company's aid. What had we given him? A mouthy amateur surgeon in a carport.

'Why you didn't shoot them?' he asked me. 'You just watching. You say I want to fight them. Why you don't fight them?'

'I don't know,' was all I could think to say. Ali shrugged.

As we talked, Moslawis in their hundreds walked by the triage station. Families, groups of families, whole city blocks' worth of families. They were leaving the neighborhoods where the fighting was heaviest, where ordnance was tearing apart the buildings and pavement and bullets and grenades everything else. As they walked they were trailed by shell bursts—enemy artillerists considered them fair game for abandoning the Caliphate. I looked down a dirt road. Behind a fleeing group, a mortar round came in with that unmistakable quick, high whistle. As the shell burst cracked the air and an earthen plume surged up, the refugees didn't scatter, didn't even cower much, but just accelerated into a trot, and then, a few seconds later, the violence spent, the plume descending, slowed back to a walk.

The men dragged trolley bags and carried on their backs grain sacks they'd turned into rucksacks. The women clutched bursting handbags. They waved halved broomsticks and lengths of plastic piping tied with white cloths to signal to the soldiers their docility. The old and sick were in wheelchairs and wheelbarrows, carried on backs. The dead were pushed on handcarts and donkey wagons, laid out on their backs and wrapped in quilts. Not just calm, many of these refugees were serene, somehow, particularly the children, who smiled, skipped, pulled at their parents' hands as though a giant playground were in sight. Maybe they were euphoric with safety, maybe they were enjoying the adventure. It was an astonishing sight and impossible to see without immediately admiring—no, revering—their resilience.

I asked Ali why he stayed, if he didn't care about the war.

'Just to feed my family. And sometimes, sometimes when I see civilians, I say to myself, my job is good. I say, I'm doing good, I'm saving lives. In Qayara, I just cried. I saw they were happy and I thought, I'm saving these fucking lives, goddamnit. But only sometimes. If I had the chance, I'd leave Iraq.'

'Where would you go?'

'Everywhere.'

I pointed out that none of the wounded soldiers being brought into the triage station were wearing flak jackets or helmets. Nor was Ali. Well-trained and experienced though CTS was, its men had no interest in protective gear. It was the same attitude that made them disregard medical care. God decided your fate, not you, not your materiel. If it was your day, it was your day.

'This,' he said, poking my flak jacket with a finger as though it were as meaningful as a satin sleep mask. 'This can't help you.'

Ingresses into Gogjali were few, and almost every vehicle that passed in—every Humvee, every tank, every armored personnel carrier and mine-resistant ambush-protected vehicle, every freight truck, bull-dozer, pickup, earthmover, gas tanker, flatbed—had to rumble along that same track off the access road, shaking the mudbrick walls and the shoddy homes behind them. All day every day, children rushed from courtyards up to the vehicles to wave and cheer the troops on. One girl, who appeared to live with a gaggle of siblings and cousins, was particularly enthusiastic. She was maybe five years old, under-nourished but sturdy, a terrific bouncer, with brave, matted hair and a purple turtleneck whose plush material did fascinating things with the dust thrown up from the wheels, which were taller than she and which she got much too close to for my liking. I would wave and smile and then put my hand flat and still, imploring her to not get so near our truck, with no effect.

What did she know of what was happening to her city, to her country? Did it matter? She was alive. She was smiling. She became a kind of lucky mascot for me and my colleagues. 'There she is,' we'd say, happy to see that her family's house still hadn't been shelled and that she still had all her limbs.

From the vehicle windows, soldiers tossed to her and the other children sleeves of crackers, tinned sardines, bottled water, canned cheese (which exists), sometimes whole ration boxes with all of those things and cooking oil and sugar besides. The most common present, though, was *khubz*, the dense white bread that Iraqis eat with most meals and that poorer Iraqis, and now the refugees walking out of Mosul, and likely too the jihadis, took as their only meals. Some days it seemed the whole war was fueled by khubz. The loaves were as ubiquitous as ammunition. They materialized on the battlefield every noon, folded, steaming in plastic bags that sprang up like mush-room patches on command-post sofas, in Humvee seats, on curbsides, stairwell treads, wall copings. Alongside the invasion of men, an inva-sion of bread. When the troops pulled out from a position you'd see khubz crusts everywhere, hardened, moldering, wet with rain or urine, doing low duty with the shell casings and cinderblock shards.

On maps of Iraq, the access road into east Mosul is Highway 2. It existed long before acquiring that label. With reasonable confidence we can say it has been there since the sixth millennium before Christ. Mosul encompasses the remains of ancient Nineveh, the last capital of the Assyrian empire, the largest and most populous empire of its day—the early first millennium B.C.—and, thanks to the Hebrew Bible, among history's most indelible villains. Highway 2 was then an imperial road connecting Nineveh to the Zagros Mountains of what is today Iraqi Kurdistan. The Assyrian warrior-kings rode it in order to worship at the temple city that Irbil then was, consecrated to Ishtar, goddess of war and love, or to hunt the lions and elephants that once dwelt in the Zagros foothills and the Nineveh plain, or to murder and enslave the mountain peoples from whom the Kurds descend. Later, Babylonian troops marched down it. They were followed by the armies of Alexander the Great—some ancient historians have the Macedonian conqueror defeating the Persians in Nineveh, others in Irbil. Alexander may be buried in northern Iraq. After Greeks, Romans. A millennium on, Saladin came this way to do battle with the Crusaders, and he was followed by the Mongol hordes. Then Suleiman the Magnificent, and Marco Polo, who mistakenly believed Mosul was still a great imperial capital, and Lawrence of Arabia, and the pilots of Hermann Göring's Fliegerführer Irak, and General David Petraeus.

In the approach to the battle against the jihadis for Mosul, which would lay waste that city like nothing since the Old Testament, Iraqi forces fought their way along Highway 2, taking it back mile by mile; once they breached the city, they were driven up and down Highway 2 on their way to and from the front lines. Just how many of these soldiers knew of the history they ferried over I could not say. I believed—at any rate I liked to tell myself, with the bad conscience of a man whose country was once again inserting itself into history it did not understand—they were more than, say, my friends in Brooklyn who know in which generals' footsteps they follow when they go down Bedford Avenue. The older Iraqi soldiers, always eager to discuss history with me, history of any sort—Iraq's, America's, whosoever's—they would have at one time known quite a lot, even if they'd since forgotten. They had been educated in the Baath era, when Saddam Hussein made Iraq one of the most literate countries in the world. He'd renovated ancient temples and palaces, too, and Iraqi schoolchildren were steeped in the glories of Mesopotamia, and alone in the world in that they read about the invention of cities and law and government and written language and then got to visit the places where these things were invented.

As for the younger soldiers, it was anyone's guess. They had grown up during the occupation, the American era. In school they might have studied the 2005 constitution, written in haste as the country descended into civil war. They might even remember its rousing preamble:

> We, the people of Mesopotamia, the homeland of the apostles and prophets, resting place of the virtuous imams, cradle of civilization, crafters of writing, and home of numeration. Upon our land the first law made by man was passed, and the oldest pact of just governance was inscribed, and upon our soil the saints and companions of the Prophet prayed, philosophers and scientists theorized, and writers and poets excelled.

But that was only if they'd gone to school. Some had a few years, some none at all. Some, uprooted by the occupation or the civil war, when more than two-and-a-half-million Iraqis fled the country and another two million were internally displaced, had daydreamed as they listened to foreign do-gooders reciting from donated textbooks under the white tarpaulins of refugee camps. Some had spent their childhoods just wandering.

As far as I could see, what knowledge the younger soldiers did have of Mosul and its history came from their cellphones. Facebook prophecies, WhatsApp conspiracy threads. History as conspiracy. The realest thing in this phone-world may have been the execution videos, uploaded and shared not just by jihadis and civilians but by soldiers, too—they were as prurient as everyone else watching this war, including me. Thanks to their phones, they did at least have a thorough understanding of Mosul's geography, courtesy of a stupendously precise satellite mapping application that was updated daily by the command. They may have known nothing of what lay beneath the dirt and cobblestones on which they trod and onto which their blood spilled, but they could track their progress meter by meter.

And it was by mere meters that the battle was progressing. The combat had begun October 16. It was the second week of November now. The battle map at CTS field headquarters, a wall-sized, more detailed version of the phone map, contained two very small polygons near the floor, corresponding to where you stood as you looked at it, in Mosul's southeast corner. The polygons were crosshatched in blue, green, and red marker strokes, the colors corresponding to the sectors that had been seized by CTS, the 16th and 9th. The rest of the map, stretching to the top of the wall, showed the remainder of Mosul's two hundred fifty-one neighborhoods. These sectors were still the charcoals, ashes, and nickels of satellite photography—a grayscale of entirely hostile terrain. Solid Caliphate.

The battle plan was no secret: turn gray into color. The troops would take east Mosul, expanding out from Gogjali, clearing and occupying neighborhood by neighborhood, until they reached the Tigris. Then they would cross the Tigris and do the same thing in west Mosul. They would do this with small Humvee columns, armored personnel carriers and some tanks, but mostly on foot. Once they got into the city's original neighborhoods, medieval-laned warrens, they would have to move entirely on foot.

The command estimated the combat would take four to six months. Some commanders told me it could be done much faster— CTS had seized Fallujah in thirty-four days over the summer—and perhaps it could have been if the troops had treated all civilians as militants. Certainly there were commanders and men who wanted to take this approach. For them, every Moslawi was a jihadi and a traitor. Others told me clearing Mosul could require years. They pointed out it had taken eighteen months to dislodge the enemy from Ramadi, a city not half Mosul's size.

In addition to the military dead, almost thirty thousand Iraqi civilians had died in the war against the Islamic State, which at its height held most of northwestern Iraq, thousands of square miles. Three million people had been displaced. Whole swaths of country-side and whole cities lay in ruin. Fallujah was a ghost town. Ramadi was shattered. Long before it was over the war was being called Iraq's second civil war, the first having been that of the mid-2000s. But this time around it was more complicated. This was a mongrel conflict, both civil war and invasion.

What all the commanders could agree on, what every Iraqi knew, what the world knew by the time it began, was that the battle for Mosul would be that war's climax. The city's recapture would effec-tively mean the end of the Caliphate as a place if not the Islamic State as an idea. Mosul was the Caliphate's prize possession, with between a million and two million inhabitants, wealthy, cosmopoli-tan, layered with history, beautiful in parts, home to one of Iraq's most prestigious military academies and one of the region's best universities. It had not been startling when the Islamic State had seized Raqqa, its self-proclaimed capital in Syria, a country in the midst of a civil war where several such groups claimed territory. When, in June of 2014, the jihadis had seized Mosul, however, a city at least five times the size of Raqqa, it was astonishing. We had entered a new epoch of war, just as surely as we had on September 11 thirteen years before. In Mosul, it was obvious, the jihadis would make their grand last stand. Smaller fights would follow, but this would be the show-stopper. It would be not just the biggest and most devastating battle of this war, but the biggest battle, in a sense the culminating battle, of what was once known as the War on Terror. When it was only half done, a Pentagon spokesman would call the fighting in Mosul 'the most significant urban combat since WWII.'

I was in Mosul when I read that. I had gone to Iraq for the first time in the summer of 2016 on assignment for *National Geographic,* to write about life in the Islamic State's wake. I got a month-long visa. I ended up staying the better part of a year. Only later did I understand why. It wasn't just to see the jihadis up close or to cover a war or to prove my mettle. No, the main impulse, I realized, many months into the battle, was a certain guilt. Shame, even. Though I never said it aloud to an editor or anyone else, maybe never so much as thought it explicitly, I knew I had to do penance. I had to do penance for being a coward and a hypocrite. I lived in New York in 2001, just out of college, and, at my first real newspaper job, I covered the destruction of the World Trade Center. I should have found a way to go to Afghanistan after that. I wanted to. A braver voice in me did, anyway. But I was too scared. Two years later, after attending one antiwar rally and writing some faintly damning things about the Bush administration, I watched American troops roll into Baghdad and Mosul from the comfort of my living room. Americans and

Iraqis died in the hundreds, then the thousands, then the tens of thousands, as Iraq was torn apart and tore itself apart. I was still a journalist, a conscience-stricken one, I liked to think, and I could have, I should have, gone to Iraq, but didn't. Later, I took to reporting on war and conflict in other parts of the world, but still I avoided Iraq. Maybe I was still too scared, maybe too embarrassed about what my country had done there. But how do you write about war as an American and not write about the American war of your time? As an American writer of my age, how do you not face Iraq?

So I went. I went to tell the stories of Iraqis, a people whom my people had invaded, had very nearly ruined, indeed had ruined in ways, as I would find; a people—civilians, soldiers, jihadis—now living and dying in a new and blacker war, a war with a foe at whose core was a death cult, yes, a war that emerged from centuries of history, yes, but a war that nevertheless would not be happening, at least not in this way, if not for the American war that preceded it. I had to write about this country whose story had been entwined with my country's story for a generation now, for most of my life, so entwined that neither place any longer made sense without the other. That is what I tried to do in the pages of *National Geographic* and then *The New York Times Magazine*. And that is what I've tried to do in this book.

A week after I met Ali at the triage station in Gogjali, I found myself late one night about a half-mile farther into Mosul, with a CTS company. CTS is made up of three roughly brigade-sized units of elite light infantry, each with several battalions and intelligence and support elements. The company I was with had fought its way into the neighborhood where we were now, Zahra, killing or driving out the jihadis and setting up a command post and barracks in a group of requisitioned homes surrounding Zahra's central plaza. Most of the modest rowhouses in this lower-middle-class district of shopkeepers and pharmacists and taxi drivers had made it out of the fighting intact; others were crumpled but salvageable; others mere rubble. In the plaza were a mosque and a park, or what had been a park—now it was a stretch of mud where Humvees, an Abrams tank, an armored bulldozer, and a fuel tanker were parked.

I should point out that while my articles and this book are composed of scenes, the experience of war is not. Experientially, war is mainly sound. In the news, in a movie, you see a war, but once amid a war, you mostly hear it. You listen to projectiles all day and night, but only rarely do you watch them leave a muzzle and even more rarely do you see impact. You're usually sitting in some house or truck or squatting behind some berm, listening to the destruction. War is loud. Loud and listless. Quite dull, in fact. The scenes you'll read in this book made up a miniscule portion of the time I spent in Mosul. The rest of the time I spent waiting. War consists largely of waiting for war, as it turns out, a fact that probably doesn't come as news to you. The secret has been out at least since Troy, where a decade of bickering kings and lamb roasts amounted to a few weeks of fighting. 'Big Mars seems bankrupt in their beggar'd host,' the French at Agincourt whinged while waiting on Henry V, 'The horsemen sit like fixed candlesticks.' Or take Orwell: 'Today or tomorrow or the day after you were going back to the line, and maybe next week a shell would blow you to potted meat, but that wasn't so bad as the ghastly boredom of the war stretching out forever.' Empty hours must cook off, years, to distill a few seconds of movement. The imbalance of inaction over action, of meaninglessness over meaning, is grievous, somehow, a kind of temporal wound. 'Even deep in the bush, where you could die any number of ways, the war was nakedly and aggressively boring,' Tim O'Brien said of Vietnam. 'It was boredom with a twist that caused stomach disorders.' And if the temporal imbalance of war sickens time, the sensory imbalance, the imbalance of sound over sight, at the same time robs it, telescopes it, collapses it. A half-second of half-consciousness carries the completion of another life. You barely catch the momentary wiping out of lineages. You're a pointless prophet, overhearing enormities you can't hope to understand.

That night in Zahra, I stood in the plaza, listening as a polyphony of firefights came together around me. First was the reliable dialogue of the troops' M-4s and the jihadis' AKs. That was overlaid with the jihadis' louder PKCs and the last-word metallic clangor of the troops' Humvee-mounted 50-cals. Over the guns came the curt percussive peals of rocket-propelled grenades.

I climbed to a roof, ducked below the parapet so as not to create a silhouette for the enemy snipers, who had night-vision equipment but were good enough not to need it, and peeked over. Mosul is situated in a riverine basin and a high perch can give you a view over much of it. Tracer bullets arced over the roofs. Fires burned around the city in a necklace of throbbing orange-red. There was little moonlight and the edges of the buildings were revealed by incandescence. Looking onto this hellish cityscape, Bosch's *Last Judgment*, with its fiery twilight tortures, came inevitably to mind. Then the mind leapt to the images that had led to this war, the art of this surpassingly artistic enemy, its own scenes of torture so minutely and stylishly documented and instantaneously broadcast to the world, videos much worse than viral, of firing squads and beheadings and dismemberments and forced drownings and burnings-alive, of sex slaves, of triumphant city-taking columns, black banners fluttering across the landscape, images that outraged the world almost as much as they titillated and petrified it.

A ghoulish chorale crept into the gunfire. The jihadis were baying from mosque loudspeakers.

'Allahu Akbar! Allahu Akbar!'

Others shouted the phrase from the streets. From more loud-speakers came a *nasheed*, an Islamic State anthem. I asked a soldier how it was that the same song was coming from different places in perfect unison. He pulled from his fatigues a pocket radio. He tuned it to 92.5 FM and turned up the volume. The nasheed played.

'Daesh's radio station,' he explained.

I awoke with the troops before dawn. Their mission this morning was to assist in the assault on an enemy-held neighborhood to the north. The company commander, a major, had found a house whose roof afforded a good vantage onto the route in. On the floor of the main room were what appeared in the darkness to be long bolts of fabric. Only when the major daintily stepped around them, indicating with his hand not to talk, did I see this was in fact the family who lived here, huddled under layers of quilts, sleeping together in the center of the house so as to be as far as possible from the exterior walls and windows should they be blown out during the night.

The major's company had distinguished itself fighting the Islamic State in Ramadi and Fallujah. He had become a celebrity on nightly newscasts and a folk hero on YouTube, and was afforded certain perks by the high command, including the use of a small surveillance drone. It was so small that it could be carried in a backpack by a sergeant who, after sustaining one injury too many, had decided he could be of more use as the major's adjutant. On the roof, the sergeant, Karim, removed the drone, an insect-like quadcopter, from the backpack and explained to me that the machine used to belong to the Islamic State. The company had found it. Karim had never used a drone but was a hand with computers and gadgetry and soon mastered it. Once he had it hovering above us, he handed the controller to the major. As ash dangled from his cigarette, falling and collecting in the fold of a pantleg, the major minutely moved the knob of the controller, flying the drone slowly northward and studying the feed from its camera on the small screen. He saw that the enemy had put up roadblocks.

The sunrise was threaded through with black smoke from the car fires the jihadis had lit to try to obscure their positions from surveillance. The futility of this could be heard and felt every few minutes, as a jet dove in to drop a bomb or an artillery shell found its target, with a sky-consuming shriek and a thunderous, intestine-seizing impact. Yet the jihadis set the cars ablaze every day.

On the street below, the Abrams tank and the armored bulldozer were parked ahead of two Humvee columns. Locals emerged from their houses, at first tentatively, then more confidently, as they found the fighting was not hard upon them, as it had been the day before, but sounding out from nearby. Parents sent their children to make tea for the soldiers. They brought bread, sweets, whatever they could spare. The soldiers shared their cigarettes, still a precious commodity in newly liberated parts.

A lieutenant smoked with a man as they sat on the low wall outside the man's home.

'Maybe I can join the army or police one day,' the man said.

'How old are you?' asked the lieutenant.

'I was born in 1983.'

'I think you're too old. They wouldn't make you an officer. Three years to become an officer in the police, two for the army.'

'When Saddam was here, the system was different.'

A Humvee pulled up to the curbside. A general stepped from it and ascended to the roof. The major briefed him. The general gave the order to move. The engines coughed to life. The columns would have to cross a wide boulevard to access Tahrir, the neighborhood coming under assault. The general had learned the hard way that unless he took precautions, the jihadis could easily steer their vehicle-born improvised explosive devices—mobile car bombs, essentially, driven by soon-to-be-suicides—into his columns. The columns were particularly vulnerable on wide throughways like this boulevard.

But the detritus of destruction was also the means of protection. The boulevard's lanes were covered over with downed streetlamps, shop awnings, power lines, wrecked cars, and endless supplies of loose cinderblock. The bulldozer driver had pushed together three cars and a freight truck on its side, grills to bumpers, creating a barrier on one side of the intersection. On the other he'd piled up a rubble berm. Now the columns could not get directly sideswiped by a vehicle-borne improvised explosive device, at least. That is, assuming the device in question was not itself a bulldozer. The jihadis had those.

The columns made it across and merged to fit into a narrow street. The fighting was close. A boy stepped from a doorway. A soldier yelled at him from a Humvee, 'Go back inside!' The column came to one of the roadblocks the major had noticed on the drone feed: impudently straddling the street, blocking our progress, was the cab of a freight truck. The column snaked into a series of increasingly narrow streets. It came to a halt before a soccer pitch. On the pitch's far side was an avenue from which the gunfire rang out—the front line, or one of them. On the avenue was a mosque and next to that a minaret. The minaret was about seven stories high, overlooking Tahrir. Mosques, in addition to whatever divine protection they might afford, were havens from airstrikes, like apartment complexes full of civilians. As a matter of cultural respect and public relations, mosques were targeted only when it was absolutely necessary. The jihadis of course knew this. Gazing up at this minaret, you could entertain only one thought: *perfect perch for a sniper.*

The general stepped from his Humvee and glanced at the minaret with lack of interest. Encouraged by the sounds of the soldiers, a man opened the front gate of his home. His wife and daughter peeked out.

The general walked up to them. He was entirely in the open, in full view of the minaret, wearing no flak jacket or helmet.

He shook the father's hand, patted the girl's head, accepted a kiss from the wife, who said 'God bless you.' As she did a shard of pavement popped up near the general's feet. It was followed by a half-second's hiss and a faint snap. Then something ricocheted off the hood of the Humvee behind him, with another hiss and snap. The family disappeared back behind the gate. Soldiers leapt from the street. The general glanced over his right shoulder at the minaret with scarcely more interest, shrugged his left shoulder, turned on his heel, walked with his rear to the minaret, unhurried, still fully exposed, inviting a bullet in the back, and finally sidestepped behind a Humvee, flashing a grin.

The sniper kept firing. He put a round into the turret of the Humvee in which I sat, just above my head. The next went into the windscreen of the Humvee behind mine. A third pierced the side mirror of the one alongside. The minaret was about a hundred meters away, and this marksman apparently intended to showcase his expertise for us, picking apart the vehicles while he waited for someone to stumble into his sites. One turret gunner peppered the minaret with 50-cal fire and another climbed into the turret above me and, with an Mk 19 launcher, pumped out 40-millimeter grenades, each discharge coming with a decisive, satisfying *thrumppp*, like the clearing of some collective sinus, and rocking the vehicle. The minaret's noble terra-cotta façade crumbled and smoked. It was another Friday, as it happened, the day of prayer and rest in Islam, the most appalling possible day to be shooting up a place of worship, and the enemy, perhaps taking this engagement as sacrilege, loosed a wave of mortar fire onto our position.

I took cover in a house. I found the major on the roof, with Karim, sitting beneath a clothesline, smoking and drinking a Red

Bull and monitoring the action on the drone feed. Another column was advancing some blocks to the north, and over a radio the major directed it. 'You're doing good. Keep going. Now go to the left. At the next street, block the way with your Humvee.' A vehicle-borne improvised explosive device detonated, shaking the entire neighborhood and sending the clothesline shuddering and the ash falling from the major's cigarette into his pants.

'They are good fighters,' the major told me. He was speaking of the Islamic State. 'I respect them. People need to die. They have the loyalty for that. I know their loyalty is in the wrong place, but most of their fighters we've found, they have that loyalty. It's difficult, in an army, to find a fighter who's ready to blow himself up, to fight until he's dead.'

Like most Iraqi soldiers I met, he was willing to give credit where credit was due. Whatever else they might be—lunatics, half-wits, junkies, fake Muslims, pawns of the Saudis, of Washington, of Israel, there were as many theories as soldiers—the jihadis were not cowards. 'They want to die,' someone said every day. It was rarely meant as an insult and never became cliché.

As the major spoke, an enemy propagandist somewhere nearby, probably in another mosque, got on a loudspeaker.

'Fight the infidels!' he could be heard to bellow. 'Fight them because they are American agents! They are Israeli agents!'

In coalition parlance, the jihadi tactics were known as 'harassing fire,' a dependable source of amusement to the Iraqi soldiers whose English was sufficient to appreciate the term's insufficiencies. The Islamic State's harassers included expert snipers, ingenious bomb-makers, mobile mortar teams, and, perhaps most harassing of all, the suicide-drivers of the vehicle-borne improvised explosive devices, or VBIEDs.

In the battles for Ramadi and Fallujah, the biggest before Mosul, the Islamic State had relied on mines and improvised explosive devices. That their skill with these was impressive only stood to reason—the organization included in its ranks not just longtime jihadis but military veterans from Iraq and elsewhere. In those cities, I saw streets whose pavement was gouged in neat zigzag patterns, the result of expertly laid line-charges. One string can disable a whole column. The Iraqi troops had become just as good at spotting and disarming the bombs. They learned to recognize the signs— bulges in the dirt, solitary bits of scrap, closed doors in abandoned houses. The jihadis realized that, in Mosul, they would have to raise the ante. The Islamic State's bombmakers had experimented with some VBIED designs in Ramadi and Fallujah and had got good results. To prepare for the battle of Mosul, they began producing them on an industrial scale. The vehicles ranged in size from freight trucks to tiny two-door compacts. They were armored with metal sheeting, drywall, plywood, anything that could absorb rounds and send off shrapnel. Their interiors were gutted and filled with explosive. Sometimes the driver was welded inside. You can go online to see how it was done. The Islamic State's propaganda arm, al-Hayat Media Center, put out how-to videos, which look like very sinister episodes of the old MTV show *Pimp My Ride*.

Al-Hayat had also put out videos to celebrate the joining of battle in Mosul. These included a new execution video showing kneeling prisoners in the signature orange jumpsuits, their foreheads being spray-painted with script, presumably the Islamic State motto No God but God, before they are shot in their heads point blank with a shotgun—while a nasheed plays, of course. But the centerpiece was *The Ignition of War*, a twenty-minute-long mess of occasionally dramatic footage from the prelude skirmishes outside Mosul. Jihadis fire rifles and rockets and mortar pieces and even blow up a tank.

The biggest explosions in the video are caused by VBIED attacks. That weapon would prove the Caliphate's deadliest in Mosul, and it slowed down operations considerably. The troops carried AT-4 shoulder-fired antitank rockets to counter the VBIEDs, but not enough of them, and the attacks usually came out of nowhere. The Caliphate had the horrid things deployed in garages around the city, waiting to strike; the time between when the driver turned over the engine and when he detonated could be a matter of seconds. Many days, the troops could take only a few blocks. Even the most basic maneuvers, like the Humvee columns crossing that boulevard from Zahra into Tahrir, had to be guarded and perfectly coordinated. Barriers had to be built. Tanks had to face down avenues of approach. But the VBIEDs kept coming. You heard their unmistakable, booming detonations throughout the day. Looking up, you saw the distinctive VBIED smoke plume, with its high, thin stem and budding cap, so eerily like an early-model nuclear mushroom cloud. Some days they seemed as frequent as the airstrikes. They were the jihadis' answer to airstrikes, kamikazes on wheels.

Into Mosul the Islamic State also introduced something entirely new to insurgent warfare—a drone fleet. Its ever-resourceful procurement branch managed to smuggle in untold numbers of the small cheap machines, the kind of thing you can buy in a shopping mall hobby shop or on Amazon, such as the quadcopter Karim carried in his backpack, and jihadi engineers built more rudimentary winged versions.

On his phone, Karim showed me video from an enemy quadcopter. The jihadis used the drones not just to target strikes but also to record them. When an attack was successful, they would edit the video and upload it online, part of the steady diet of near-real-time footage from this battle they'd been feeding onto the Internet. The jihadis valued the VBIEDs for this purpose because their explosions registered so well on the drone cameras, their plumes rising high into the sky. The clip Karim showed me, from a few days before, saw a VBIED attacking a CTS position not far from where we stood now.

'Those are ours,' Karim said, playing the video and pointing to the Humvees on the screen. The car bomb crashed into a Humvee and exploded. The screen turned a ghostly gray, as though overcome with some digital stain. As it cleared, a lone Humvee sped from the scene while the other two went up in flames.

'I was injured,' he said, lifting up his sweatshirt to reveal a scar. 'No, wait, this is from something else.'

It was hard to keep track. Karim had been wounded five times since CTS had started fighting in Anbar in 2015. In Ramadi, he was hit with shrapnel twice. Later he was on patrol when he noticed a pillow in the road.

'My friend said don't touch it. I told him, "It's nothing." I kicked it. It just exploded.'

In Fallujah, an SPG-9 rocket skivered the Humvee in which Karim was serving as gunner. It was the scar from that which he'd wanted to show me, a discolored, sunken patch below his ribcage. Looking down at it, he said, sounding disappointed, 'It was a big hole before.' He was not accorded any special sympathy for five wounds. Plenty of his friends had been wounded as many times, some more.

We were standing in the front courtyard of one of the requisitioned homes on the plaza in Zahra. It was a mercifully quiet afternoon. The company wasn't pushing forward today, and the jihadis were planning who knew what, or perhaps were resting like the soldiers. Another sergeant major, Ali (not the Ali I'd met at the triage station), watched the video with us. He had also been at the scene of the attack but had avoided injury. A minute before the car bomb arrived, he'd jumped from his Humvee to go around the corner and relieve himself.

Karim, who was in his twenties, had full, rosy cheeks and a shaved head. He had left off gunning after the rocket incident in Fallujah to become the major's aide-de-camp, and the absence of combat had pushed his belly over his fatigues. Ali, in his mid-thirties, had the trim, ready bearing of a born soldier and wore a proud crescent of a mustache that hung, with the slightest jauntiness, over his lip. You got the sense it may not have been luck but some battlefield canniness of the bladder that pulled him from the Humvee that day, though he too had been wounded repeatedly in the last two years.

Another man joined us. He was a sergeant major as well, the highest rank for noncommissioned officers, and like Ali was in his thirties. Even with its casualty rates, CTS was a highly sought-after posting. For Iraqi men who wanted to see action, nothing else in the security forces vaguely compared. And it came with a good salary. Officers and enlisted men alike tended to stay. CTS had been created by the Bush administration to pursue high-value terrorist targets. Already suspicious of the new Iraqi government, Bush ensured that the formation was put under the authority of Iraq's national security council, and not that of the prime minister or defense minister— 'so that its targets would not be politicized,' as a retired American general who oversaw training of Iraqi military told me. CTS was tasked with hunting all insurgents, Sunni, Shia, and otherwise. It quickly became the force in which American generals had the most confidence—one of the few, in fact, in which they had any confidence at all—and in the war against the Islamic State, CTS worked in lockstep with the Americans. It was the only unit with a direct line to air support and artillery. But not even the Americans denied CTS had never been meant for a conflict like this. Its operations were supposed to last hours, maybe a few days, not months and years. The retired American general told me, 'One of the things that the CTS has developed into, that we did not envision, and that I think is not healthy, is they are now the shock infantry.'

The sergeant major who joined us, Rasul, was very tall and had improbably long, copious hair, important-seeming hair.

'The people here are nice, but they've been damaged by Daesh,' he told me. 'Before, the people in Mosul didn't like the Iraqi army. The army was bad to them. But now, they've said to the army, "Welcome, please help us."'

'In Mosul, the army left everything to Daesh,' Ali said, meaning that the troops had abandoned the city to the jihadis in 2014. 'We don't know what happened. I think al Qaeda, they made a plan with other countries. Maybe the Iraqi government was involved. You know, the borders of Iraq—with Turkey, Saudi Arabia, Syria—they're all open.' The Islamic State's tactics were so good, he believed, because the Turkish or Saudi or Syrian armies, or perhaps all of them, had trained the jihadis.

'You should write something that makes Trump kick the Saudis' ass,' Rasul said. 'The Arabs are all with Daesh. We think Trump is going to be better than Obama. Obama supports Daesh.'

Almost every Iraqi soldier I'd met claimed to be eagerly awaiting the tenure of the newly elected Donald Trump. Some hoped he would attack the Islamic State with more obvious brutality than Barack Obama had, others that he would go after Iran, others Saudi Arabia. (Trump had pledged to do all three.) Most of all, though, they seemed to look forward to an American president who fit the mold of what they thought an American president ought to be. As far as I could tell, this meant a belligerent and nostalgic white man.

'Obama doesn't help us,' Ali said. 'He doesn't like us. We were waiting for Obama to do something, but he did nothing.'

I told them that some soldiers I'd met, like the other Ali at the triage station, professed not to care much about Mosul. They considered it too mired in Iraq's past, too mutinous, too Arab. While Ali and Karim weighed the idea—no doubt they'd heard it many times themselves, if they hadn't actually voiced it—Rasul seemed to take offense. He said 'Mosul is also Iraq. We have to care about it. We have to control it. That's why this operation is taking so long. There are many civilians here, and we are here to help them. If Daesh came to America and took control of one of the states, would the government or the army care about it, or just leave it? This is our country. For the first time in this operation, the Iraqi army and the Kurdish peshmerga have worked together. Many peshmerga have died. Mosul is our city. We have to kill the Daesh people in it. We have one flag.'

Ali told me that his wife, who taught painting at a girl's school in Baghdad, often begged him to leave the military. 'She says, "Ali please leave your job." I say "No." If I leave my job, I'll fight Daesh as a civilian. I love Iraq. But there is no future in Iraq. There is no future because the government is a motherfucker. I have a home. I have a car. I have a job. My salary's good. But no safety. No future. The government doesn't care about the people. I'm sure that somehow the government supports Daesh.' He apologized for his English, which he thought inadequate, because it wasn't as good as Karim's.

'When I drink, I speak English one hundred percent,' Ali explained.

Another man approached with his phone outstretched. He showed me a Facebook conversation he was having with an American woman, or someone alleging to be an American woman. She'd befriended him. He spoke no English and she no Arabic, so he was responding to her professions of admiration with emojis. It worked. With every laughing-crying face and thumbs-up, the woman grew more attached, it appeared. He asked me to text her and learn more, though he knew he was already smitten.

'I will open my heart to her,' he said.

I started laughing. I stopped when he looked confused. He was entirely sincere.

'I will buy her a nice house in Baghdad,' he said.

Although there wasn't a medic among them, the company had set up a small medical storeroom in one of the commandeered houses. It was full with boxes of medicine whose use the soldiers didn't know and it served mostly to buoy the spirits of the locals. Some intrepid residents had reopened a market nearby and the Islamic State was shelling it insistently. This kind of attack was known in coalition parlance as 'indirect fire,' a term even more misleading than 'harassing fire.' It felt direct enough to the adults and children caught with shrapnel. They were rushed in to be bandaged. If their wounds were very bad they were driven in a Humvee out of Zahra to the triage station in Gogjali. Others came in with dormant prescriptions or complaining of headaches. A girl arrived having swallowed her chewing gum, the look of terror in her eyes worse than what I'd seen in children who'd been shot.

Oftentimes, the locals who showed up just wanted an outsider to speak to, someone on whose face the nightmarish details of the last two years might register. An old man arrived with an empty medicine box in hand and a boy, the child of neighbors, at his side. He wasn't sure what the medicine was but he knew his wife needed to take it every day and that she hadn't taken it in five days. As a soldier rooted among the small white boxes, the man explained that he owned a women's clothing shop. The Caliphate allowed him to keep it open under certain conditions. He was forbidden to sell underwear—not to the men of Zahra, and *certainly* not to the women—and he had to restock to meet the increasingly strict dress codes. By the end, women could only wear loose black abayas, black burqas and chadors, black gloves and black shoes. No skin could show and no body parts could be suggested aside from the shoulders and head. By then, very few people had the money to keep up with the requirements.

'Seventy-three years I've lived in Mosul, and never have I seen life as bad as it was under the Islamic State,' he told me. 'They came to kill people and steal our money. At first they were nice with the people. They never asked to grow beards or not to smoke. But then they changed.' He looked at the boy. 'Here in Zahra, I saw many kids with the jihadis. They trained them. Just before the army came in, I saw two of them, two boys, with rifles. They were scared. They said, "Please pray for us. We need to kill the Iraqi army because they came here to kill us and kill you, too. Please join us. Help us."'

'One of my friends, he joined them,' the boy said. 'He came to me and he said, "Let me give you some advice. Join us. You'll get money. They bring girls to us at night."'

The soldier told the old man he couldn't find the right medicine.

CTS had spilt a lot of its own blood to capture Zahra, and the jihadis were shelling the troops' positions at every opportunity. They were also staging the occasional counterassault on foot and dispatching VBIEDs. Still, there was little security on the plaza: no roadblocks, no regular sentries. The soldiers just kind of kept an eye out when they felt like it. Between missions, they had little to do. The residents had even less to do, and, bored of sitting in their houses, they gathered in the street to talk and perambulate, though the jihadis were shelling the streets. Then, again, they were also shelling the houses, so what the hell. They would slowly walk about, usually ending up back at the command post, asking the soldiers for the third time that day how the battle was going, whether there was news on when the electricity and water might be turned on, what was happening with the refugees and the prisoners.

I met a man outside his small pharmacy. He'd owned it for thirty-two years. He had no stock and none of his neighbors could have afforded medicine if he had, but he needed something to occupy his mind, so he'd reopened the shop. Now he stood outside it, patiently waiting for business to resume. He too had been allowed to stay open in the Islamic State, and he was even allowed to continue selling Viagra, a favorite in good times and bad. But no condoms. The jihadis asked for painkillers and some amphetamine-like drug whose name he'd forgot.

'It made them crazy,' he said.

I spoke with a taxi driver. Before 2014, he'd made his best money taking people to nearby cities like Kirkuk and Tal Afar. He couldn't do that after Mosul was taken, and Moslawis, broke, stopped taking taxis, so what few fares he got were jihadis, higher-ups, he sensed. He didn't dare engage in the normal chit-chat—he didn't ask where they were from, for instance. But their appearances and accented Arabic suggested they came from all over, Europe, Asia, America, beyond. He noticed that they often lived in nice neighborhoods, where they'd commandeered the nicest houses. Still, he said, 'They were cheap, gypsies.'

A jihadi would always do the same thing when he got in the taxi. First, he would check what frequency the radio was on, to make sure it wasn't one the Caliphate used to communicate. They were convinced everyone was a spy. Next, he'd check the car for weapons. Then he'd inspect the ashtray to see if the driver had been smoking. Finally, he'd lean toward the driver and sniff, trying to detect tobacco. The driver stopped smoking in his taxi, instead stopping for furtive cigarette breaks in alleyways, after which he'd spritz himself with cologne and put in a piece of chewing gum. One day he felt bold and asked a jihadi passenger a question.

'Why have you guys smashed everything in Mosul?' he asked.

'Never you mind,' the jihadi replied.

At a house near where the taxi driver sat, the green façade and exterior wall were newly pitted by shrapnel and frag. A white-bearded man stood in front.

'I don't know what happened, exactly,' he told me. 'We were inside. We heard a big bomb. Two, three bombs.' He pointed to the holes in the stucco. 'My wife and kids wanted to see what had happened. They came outside. Another bomb came. All of my children were killed, along with my wife.'

He shuffled to an adjoining empty plot, where he'd at first buried them. Later, soldiers helped him disinter the bodies and bring them to the graveyard south of Highway 2, where he gave them a proper burial. I asked him if he blamed the Islamic State for their deaths.

'I don't know. This happened.'

He shuffled to the infirmary with his wife's death certificate, where he found Karim. The man had heard he could be compensated for his dead family. Karim brought him inside, to a portable printer which he carried from position to position for just such grim administrative occasions. Karim explained that he would make copies of the certificate and send them to Baghdad. If the man wanted to be compensated for his whole family, he would need to get a death certificate for each of his dead children. Someone in a ministry would inspect the documents and, hopefully, stamp them. Then he'd be paid. At least, that was how it was supposed to work. Karim described the process three times, but the old man didn't follow.

'Will the government pay me?' he asked.

'Yes, but, father, believe me, the stamp you need is in Baghdad, not here,' Karim said.

'Please, I need it stamped.'

'Father, do you think we're Daesh?' another soldier cut in. 'That we're going to kill you? We must send the certificate to Baghdad.'

'Please, I need your help. I'm very tired. I'm an old man.'

'I swear, there's nothing more I can do for you,' Karim said. 'I am just a soldier here.'

I spent that night with an assault team, in a commandeered house behind the avenue on which the menacing minaret stood. It was still the front line. We slept side by side, foot to head, I with my flak jacket and boots on and my helmet next to my head. The closest Islamic State position on the avenue was maybe a hundred feet away.

The soldiers awoke at dawn in good spirits. Early mornings before the call to move were an essential interlude, a chance to do nothing and do it stylishly. They gathered around a gas burner on the floor to warm themselves and fry eggs, which they scooped from the pan with pieces of khubz. One man lovingly prepared a hookah with double-apple-flavor tobacco, the company favorite. Another put on a blue trilby hat and purple scarf. I asked if he'd found these accessories in the house. He looked almost insulted.

'I wouldn't take another person's clothing,' he said.

He carried them in his rucksack. This was his leisure wear.

'I fucked your sister last night,' the hookah-preparer informed him.

'No, excuse me, I fucked *your* sister last night.'

The call came in and they climbed into their Humvees. We drove down a street, in partial view of the minaret. Soldiers walked alongside. We were moving only a matter of seconds when one went down. The sniper's bullet went into his back, below the shoulder blade. It must have been obscenely painful, but the soldier barely reacted. He kneeled, like an athlete who's had the wind knocked out of him. He lurched to a curbside and sat down. He looked nothing so much as disappointed.

Firefights rang out from the avenue. The assault team moved from house to house, looking for jihadis, or, failing that, for positions from which to shoot at jihadis. Occasionally they kicked in a door, but usually they didn't have to bother. They just knocked. Most of the homes were occupied with their owners or refugees or both. Some cowered in back rooms. Others sat around in their dens and kitchens, bizarrely placid. Some were laconic, others so relieved to see the soldiers they couldn't stop talking.

The team went into a house where two brothers lived. They had a butcher shop, they explained as they brought the soldiers into the backyard. The jihadis ate a lot of lamb. They wanted the good cuts and always demanded a discount.

'They were cheap like gypsies,' one brother said.

'We're scared,' the other said. 'After they've declared the Daesh gone, what if they come back again? Or a militia? Terrorists. Something like that?'

There was no way from their yard to the house on the avenue, so the soldiers moved to the next home, where they found a retired English teacher and his wife, more eager to help.

'Tell them about the mosque,' she said to her husband.

'In the mosque around the corner,' he said, 'they stored weapons.'

They brought the soldiers a stepladder to get them over the back wall of their yard and into an empty house facing the avenue. The soldiers quietly ascended to the roof. Ducking below the parapet, they put a hole in its base with a sledgehammer and chisel. A sniper took up a position on his stomach, inched his rifle barrel into the hole, and looked down his scope.

The team continued on. They came to a house where five families had been holed up for weeks. The children—there must have been two dozen of them—sat lined up on either wall of a hallway, quiet as the grave. In the next house, they found a family who'd taken in their neighbors. They too warned the soldiers about the mosque with the weapons in it, as a man recounted being harassed by the Hizbah, the Caliphate's dread religious police.

'They said "Why have you shaved?" I told them I hadn't shaved, I just can't grow a beard. They didn't believe me. They said "Are you playing with us? Who gave you permission to shave?" I told them "I swear I haven't shaved." They took my ID.'

His brother picked up the narration.

'I couldn't even buy underwear for my wife. They didn't like the pictures advertising the underwear. They said these pictures came from the devil. You couldn't buy anything, even perfume. They didn't like the perfume pictures, either.'

The soldiers came to the last home on the block. If they could set up in the house behind it, on an intersection on the avenue, they would have good firing lines in three directions. The metal front door was set against a backplate and dead-bolted. For fifteen minutes, they took turns pounding at the bolt with the sledgehammer. Hearing the ruckus, more men came in to the entranceway to take turns, until it was full of panting soldiers. A burly young man stepped up and, with a tremendous whack, sent the bolt flying.

'Is there anything else I can do for you?' he said, and took his exit.

Inside, they found the signs of a hasty departure. Moslawis knew the jihadis were looting homes. (It was said soldiers were, too, though I never saw this.) The flat-screen television had been removed from its wall mount and stashed somewhere. An ornate display case with the family silverware had been turned to face a wall and draped over with a bedsheet. The refrigerator was empty save for four ramekins of pudding, as though the family had made one final meal and decamped before dessert.

Another half-hour was needed for the soldiers to break through a gate inside and to climb into the house they wanted to get to, on the far corner, only to find it had no windows facing onto the avenue. It was useless. As we came downstairs, an immense explosion shook the house. The walls quavered and masonry hurtled to the floor. I got in the hunch-shouldered crouch, like a bad surfer, that explosions seem to necessitate of the initiate. I remained on my feet, but I couldn't prevent the sound from entering my ears. It was, to that point, the closest I'd ever been to a bomb of that size, and I'll never forget the sound.

It was a VBIED. The driver had steered into the military-controlled sector of Tahrir and rammed a Humvee. The explosion killed a gunner. He was a popular man with a nom de guerre that was the most benign and yet the most memorable I ever heard in Mosul: SpongeBob, his comrades called him. His young son had given him the name. A journalist with *VICE*, Ayman Oghanna (the best videographer to work in Mosul), had got to know the gunner, and told me his story. SpongeBob had once saved Ayman's life, in fact, shooting a VBIED driver with this 50-cal before the man could ram the Humvee he and Ayman were in.

Like just about everyone else in CTS, SpongeBob had been injured several times. In his case, the injuries had started long before this war. In Baghdad, where he was from, during the civil war of the 2000s, he had been abducted by Shia militiamen. CTS hunted all insurgents, regardless of sect. He was Shia, but his abductors didn't care. They tortured him. They drove nails through his palms and pulled out his fingernails with pliers. They shot him, five times. Believing he was dead, they left him in a garbage dump. That's where a stranger, a Sunni man, found him, and carried him to a hospital.

The VBIED that hit SpongeBob's Humvee was so laden with explosive, nothing was left of him.

2

The families fleeing Zahra, Tahrir and the other neighborhoods of east Mosul were corralled at a way station in Gogjali, across a dirt road from the triage station, a half-built home whose gate had been shelled away. Men and boys stood about in the courtyard, women and girls sat on the unfinished cement floors within. Knowing jihadis had been sneaking out of Mosul in the waves of refugees, an intelligence officer attempted to question the men, but there were far too many of them, and they were too reticent and unnerved, for the interrogations to get anywhere. In front of the house was parked a row of open-top freight trucks. Once their trailers were packed with human cargo, they would drive to a refugee camp. There were by now nearly a hundred camps around Iraq.

For the most part the refugees were too frightened to speak with me, too. But one day a stout man in a fraying sweater and sweatpants, his face unevenly shaved, approached me. He was eager to speak. He was from Zahra. Ahmed, or Abu Omar as he was known, was with his two daughters and was in need of information. Where would they be taken? When could they return? How could he seek compensation if his house was damaged? His eyes were laughing and frantic behind dirty wire-rim glasses. They seemed to ask—demand—'Can you believe this place?'

I and every other journalist got these questions. When Moslawis saw a foreign face, particularly a white one, they assumed it belonged to someone of authority. And if they learned you were American, well then their expectations made you feel really pointless. Americans could and did do anything they liked, you were informed.

'Take any Moslawi, from the ignorant man who doesn't know how to write or read to the professor of history,' a lawyer from a prominent old Mosul family told me. 'Ask him one question: Who has all the keys to what's going on in your city? They will answer you: the United States of America.'

I got Abu Omar's phone number before he left the way station and found him and his daughters some weeks later in a refugee camp known as Khazer. An hour's drive east of Mosul on Highway 2, in Iraqi Kurdistan, it was on a hillside next to a river. The bucolic scenery wasn't visible from inside the camp, where the atmosphere was humid with suspicion. It was presided over by Kurdish soldiers and intelligence agents, many of whom had fought the jihadis. Their general attitude was that every Moslawi was a jihadi at heart. If they'd wanted to escape Mosul, with its countless egresses, the thinking went, they could have. They'd stayed because they liked the Caliphate. Abu Omar was told, 'You Moslawis are all Daesh.'

His tent, half-barrel in shape and about three meters by five in size, was between a storm fence and the toilet that serviced his section of the camp—four floor holes in a prefab shed for perhaps fifty families. For washing and cooking there was a water tank with a few unenthusiastic spigots. The winter rains had started, and there was mud everywhere. Rats roamed at night. Abu Omar had been given sleeping mats, blankets, a solar-powered lamp, and a propane stove. Food distribution was erratic. A small market had sprung up outside the perimeter fence—but where was he to get the money? He'd worked as a security guard at a cellular tower in Mosul and was barely getting by even before he was laid off when the Islamic State cut the mobile networks.

'We thought the government would take care of us after we lived under Daesh for so long,' he said. 'But it's the same crap here. It's like a jail.'

There hadn't been regular water service in Mosul for months before they left, he went on, ushering me through the entry flap into the tent, and he hadn't prayed in he didn't know how long. He felt guilty. 'But to pray, you must be clean. Islam is clean.' (He understood some English, but we spoke with the help of an interpreter.) However, the real problem was that the Islamic State had soured him on the whole idea. 'God forgive me for saying it, but now I don't even like to hear the call to prayer. I hate it because of them. God forgive me. On Fridays, their preaching was all instigating people to kill, to deceive one another, to pillage. This is not our religion.'

I asked if he was married. He explained that, in 2005, his wife was kidnapped. Her body was left in the street. He believes she was killed by al Qaeda, though accidentally, confused for their neighbor, a woman with the same name who was running for local office. The neighbor was later killed when her house was bombed.

His three children were with him. His son, Omar, had been seven when his mother died and his older daughter, Aya, two. His youngest daughter, Amina, was the child of a short-lived second marriage. Unable to care for the children, he put them in an orphanage. The experience had taken its toll. Amina was anemic, and, Abu Omar confided, lowering his voice, though not so low that anyone could miss it, 'Aya has a mental disorder.' Aya, a sweet-natured girl who at fifteen looked both older and younger than her years, with a woman's body and a child's face, but who did not have a mental disorder I ever noticed aside from shyness, looked down at her knees as he said this. Amina smiled apologetically. As for Omar, he might be big—at nineteen, he looked like an unfinished sculptor's stone, with tremendous shoulders and a heavy, bowing head—but he had 'the brain of a child.' When he heard his father say this, Omar, who had been in the corner of the tent praying, smiled mildly. This was not the first time Abu Omar had insulted him like this in front of a stranger, I got the sense. Omar had not been at the way station in Mosul, his father explained, because he'd been detained by military intelligence. This was pro forma for young Sunni men these days.

'The ones who had some connection with the Daesh, they beat them very badly and took them away,' Abu Omar said. 'Those who had nothing to do with them were kept for a few days, then brought here.'

'They blindfolded all of the guys with me, but they didn't blindfold me,' Omar said boastfully. It was unclear whether he wanted to impress his father or me or both of us. 'I was the supervisor of all the other prisoners.'

'Because he was not involved with Daesh,' his father said.

This wasn't the first war Abu Omar had lived through. It was the fifth. In the 1980s he had been drafted into Saddam Hussein's army and sent to fight in Iran. When he refused to send a grenade into a house with a family in it, he told me, he was put in the brig. But what had really stuck with him was the sight of the so-called Mahdi Brigades, the swarms of Iranian men and boys who were made to run into the Iraqi minefields armed only with plastic keys dangling from their necks. The Ayatollah had handed them out, assuring their bearers the keys would gain them entry to heaven. Mosul wasn't bombed in that war, which would go on for nine years, as Baghdad and Basra were, but it suffered in a different and arguably more profound way, Abu Omar recalled. A large majority of the Iraqi officer corps, slaughtered in Iran, came from Mosul, many from its oldest and most venerable families, who could trace their roots in Mosul back to Ottoman times.

Abu Omar wasn't of that genteel warrior caste. Though his family went back generations in Mosul, they were working class Sunnis, Saddam's natural constituency. After the war with Iran he was chosen to serve in the Fedayeen Saddam, one of the dictator's notorious internal security organs. In 1990, he was ordered to the border with Kuwait. No one was told why they were there until, one morning, they were told to invade the country. Like all his comrades, he thought the invasion insane, but he dared not disobey. Twelve years of increasing hardship followed, as international sanctions and Saddam's megalomania sapped Iraq. When the Americans arrived in Mosul, in April of 2003, Abu Omar said, 'We felt happy. But if we had known things would turn out this way, of course we would've wished to stay under Saddam.'

His house was near the mosque from whose minaret the sniper had shot at the CTS general. In fact, it was to that mosque, al-Nuaimi, that Abu Omar and his son Omar had repaired on Friday afternoons for years before the Islamic State took over Mosul. The jihadis installed in all the city's mosques loyalist imams. Some were foreigners, others Moslawis who'd sided with the group. At al-Nuaimi, the imam who took over was one of the latter. He called himself Abu Bakr.

The local residents whom I spoke with remembered the imam Abu Bakr well, though their memories differed. He'd lived in the neighborhood for years, and he used to occasionally worship and preach at the smaller mosque on the plaza in Zahra that CTS commandeered. Some residents remembered him as easygoing, not a troublemaker. Others remembered his diatribes against the Iraqi government, which were not rare—antigovernment sentiment in Mosul ran high after 2003. But others told me they knew for a fact Abu Bakr had been furtively recruiting the young men of Zahra to the Islamic State before the takeover. Once the Islamic State was in control, and Abu Bakr took over al-Nuaimi, their memories merged. The imam's sermons at the mosque were infamous. He told children to attack their parents if they objected to jihad, wives to slit the throats of their husbands if they kept them from joining the movement. He railed at the men of Zahra, calling them cowards. As the troops closed on Mosul, he hollered from the minbar, 'Kill the Iraqi army! Kill whoever wears the uniform!'

Omar went every week.

'Oh, I never missed one of his sermons,' he told me.

Abu Bakr always wore a rifle slung over his shoulder, including when preaching. He told Omar and his friends they were apocalyptic warriors in waiting. They would help deliver the world from unbelief. Many of Omar's friends joined up, either because they were 'brainwashed,' as he put it to me, or because they were threatened, or needed the money, or were bored, or because they wanted a cause to belong to. One friend was sent to Syria to fight. When he got back he showed Omar a video on his phone that he'd made on the front line. A comrade stands on a hilltop. Suddenly he drops to the ground, shot. Omar's friend races to him. He's dead.

'The dead man had a big smile on his face,' Omar, smiling, told me. 'He was pointing his finger like this'—he extended his index finger, an expression of the unity of Allah—'and the first thing I said was, "I wish I was him, I envy him." My friend said "Then why don't you go and bomb yourself, become a martyr?" I told him, "I can't. My family needs me."'

Abu Omar said he was constantly warning his son about Abu Bakr and the Islamic State. He tried to forbid Omar hanging out with jihadi friends. Omar didn't have the native mental equipment to counter their arguments on his own, his father believed, nor did he have the education. He had come up in the American era and spent much of his youth in the orphanage. Abu Omar could see the deceit in the imam's ideas more easily. He had been conscripted into Saddam's wars, yes, but he had also been a beneficiary of Saddam's saner policies, of the revamping of the country's education system and the literacy drives. Abu Omar had learned in school of Mosul's long history. Some Moslawis considered that history glorious, others accursed, and probably it was both, but there was no question, he understood, that Mosul's history was essential to Iraq's history—and to the world's.

It's unknown who first settled Mosul, but if the city didn't start life as a fortress it soon enough became one. The first signs of habitation in that spot on the western bank of the Tigris, thirty miles north of where the river meets the Greater Zab, come from the fourth millennium B.C. The settlement there, absorbed into the Akkadian empire, would come to be called *muswila*, meaning 'Western fortress.' The eastern fortress in question was the larger and more famous one across the river, Nineveh, whose ruins present-day Mosul encompasses and which gives its name to the governate of which Mosul city is today the seat.

Under the Akkadians, Nineveh was a temple city. The Assyrians seized it sometime in the fourteenth century B.C. The great Assyrian kings were in the habit of establishing new capitals to glorify themselves and their favorite gods, and around 700 B.C. Sennacherib made Nineveh his capital, dedicating it to Ishtar. Under Sennacherib, archaeologists believe, Nineveh became the most populous and advanced city of its day, and the Assyrian Empire the largest on earth, with outposts and tributaries stretching as far north as the Caucasus and as far south as Sudan, to Persia in the east and Cyprus in the west. It took in Asia Minor, Egypt, and the Levant. There is evidence, too, that Nineveh, or possibly the smaller settlement on the far bank, contained a significant Hebrew population. After the Assyrians conquered part of Israel, refugees appear to have made a home at one or both of the dual citadels on the Tigris. The ancient Aramaic name for Mosul, ʿebrāya ʿA, means Hebrew fortress.

The immensity of the Assyrian compass was not just geographic but historic. Nineveh was a repository of the discoveries and cultural objects of all the Near East. That is, of culture itself. It is of course in the land between the two rivers—the literal meaning of Mesopotamia—and its environs that we find our first evidence of cities, of mass agriculture, of law, writing, temples, monumental art. King Ashurbanipal's library at Nineveh was the greatest ancient center of learning before Alexandria, containing thousands of tablets on those subjects and more. These achievements may have existed elsewhere, but if they did, we have no record of them yet, possibly because there was nothing to record, or possibly, one imagines, reflecting on the Assyrian war machine, because the messengers and messages of the past were murdered, dismembered, splintered, smashed, and ground to dust beneath the heels and horse hooves and chariot wheels of Sennacherib and his line, who, in addition to being great creators and collectors of culture, were lusty eradicators of it.

The Israelites were but a minor bump in the road for the Assyrians, who also trampled the Hittites, Babylonians, Egyptians, Nubians, Phoenicians, Canaanites, Medes, dozens of lesser-known peoples, and history only knows how many forgotten ones. These savage victories were described in cuneiform inscriptions. Here is one from Sennacherib on what he did to the people of Elam:

> I cut their throats like lambs. I cut off their precious lives as one cuts a string. Like the many waters of a storm, I made their gullets and entrails run down upon the wide earth. My prancing steeds harnessed for my riding, I plunged into the streams of

their blood as into a river. The wheels of my war chariot, which brings low the wicked and the evil, were bespattered with their blood and filth. With the bodies of their warriors I filled the plain like grass. Testicles I cut off and tore out their genitals like the seeds of cucumbers.

Here, later, his grandson, Ashurbanipal, still annoyed with the Elamites, on what he did to their remains:

I pulled down and destroyed the tombs of their earlier and later kings, who had not revered the deities Ashur and Ishtar, my lords . . . and I exposed them to the sun. I took away their bones to Assyria, I put restlessness on their ghosts . . . I left his fields empty of the voice of mankind.

And in that family, mind you, Sennacherib was known as the voice of reason, Ashurbanipal as the maniac, not just the bibliomaniac, so vicious that the Assyriologist H. W. F. Saggs, who broke his back in the Second World War, lamented, 'Ashurbanipal gave war a bad name.' But neither king could claim to have invented any cruelty. For centuries their forebears had been at it, as had, of course, every other empire in the region and beyond.

For their warmaking and mutilation the Assyrian kings offered the most unanswerable of justifications—the original justification, you might say: *The gods bade us do it.* In the Assyrian creation myth the *Enuma Elish*, which was much the same for the Babylonians, from whom the Assyrians filched their cosmology and much else, the universe begins in war. Aššur, the god for whom the civilization is named, goes to battle with the monstrous goddess of the sea, Tiamat, and her army. He suffocates Tiamat, shoots arrows into her stomach, tramples her, brains her with a mace, and opens her veins.

The other gods calm him down. Aššur gets riled up again. He bifurcates Tiamat. One half of her carcass brings forth heaven, the other the underworld. Oh, before that, he had beheaded her and tossed her head on a pile with her soldiers' heads. Now he retrieves her head and stabs the eyes. The Tigris and Euphrates flow forth.

Existence began in war and through war it was perpetuated. In the Assyrian worldview, the state was also the cosmos, the realm of holy order. Outside was chaos, unformed, unholy. This view was common to ancient belief systems in Mesopotamia and elsewhere, and persists in certain theologies today, perhaps most saliently in the Islamic idea of the Dar al-Islam and Dar al-Harb, the House of Peace and the House of War. The 'clear affinity between Assyrian expansionism and jihad,' writes the Assyriologist Mario Liverani, finds 'a direct line of transmission via the Old Testament.' Unlike in Islam, Judaism, and Christianity, however, the Assyrians believed the work of creation hadn't stopped with the gods. They didn't suffer from the nostalgia for a better, purer past that would become so central to holy war. Theirs was a *creatio continua*, and it was the responsibility of the Assyrian king to carry on the work of creation, to perpetuate the order the gods had introduced at time's beginning.

He did this through combat. It was official expansion and sacred rite. It was the means by which he communicated with the divine, connecting reality to myth, present to past, god to man. Political imperatives found religious justification, and vice versa. To the Assyrians, in other words, all war was holy—all war that *they* waged, at least—and holiness was warlike, to a degree that is hard for us to fathom today, even with the presence of movements such as the Islamic State.

In fact, the Assyrians were probably no more bloody-minded than any other regime of their time or since. What they were, for some reason, was better at depicting their bloody-mindedness and more eager to broadcast it. This was reflected most indelibly not in their writings (literacy was still rare, even in the court) but in their art, and in particular in the famous Assyrian friezes, with which the kings empaneled the interior walls of their palaces and temples at Nineveh and other cities. These you have probably caught a glimpse of in a museum or a textbook, along with the more beautiful giant winged bulls and lions with human heads, the lamassus. If you have seen the friezes, they may still be lodged or suppressed somewhere in your store of unwelcome memories. They rank among the most considerable, and most unnerving, martial art in history, unnerving not least because they also count as religious art. There is scene after scene of battle and enslavement and mutilation, of brutality of the most depraved sort, and these scenes abut scenes of worship.

The style is as unrelenting as the content. There is no background, only foreground, carved in low relief into the panels of what is now known as Mosul marble, a quartz-heavy limestone, grave but numinous when it catches the light, which came from a quarry just outside the city. Time is telescoped, collapsed. Battle is joined, opponent killed, gods propitiated in an eternal present of violence and supplication. The images were meant as much for the consumption of the heavens as humans, and there is something more than maniacal, something ecstatic, in their repetitiveness and simultaneity. This is the chanting of the crazed prophet, the hypergraphia of the militant ascetic. It is, in one historian's words, 'the splendor of divine terror,' and even in our era of savage entertainments and jihadi execution videos, of millisecond edits and smash-cut iconography, Assyrian sculpture retains its power to shock. Go to the Nineveh galleries at the British Museum or the Louvre, and you may see tourists with faces aghast.

Splendid, too, is torture, which the Assyrian kings looked on as strategic propaganda and sacrificial ritual. Impaling, dismembering, disemboweling, flaying, beheading—the friezes celebrate them all. Especially beheading. The Assyrians were obsessed with it. If they didn't originate that fetish, certainly no one in history, not even the Islamic State, has done more to expand the recreational and decorative range of disattached heads. If the friezes are to be believed, Assyrian warriors spiked them, made rings of them, hung them from trees, gave them to eagles to fly around with dangling from their beaks and talons, played catch with them.

The head thing reached its climax with Ashurbanipal, not just the most intemperate of the great Assyrian conquerors but the last. When Ashurbanipal, who was terribly proud of the fact that he could read and write, received some insulting letters from the king of Elam, Teumann, he got very exercised. He prayed to Ishtar, whom he'd elevated to the acme of the pantheon, for success in battle. She was listening, apparently, and Ashurbanipal defeated Teumann. He cut off his head, it goes without saying, and presented it as an offering to the gods at the gates of Nineveh. Then he rode to Irbil. There he went from temple to temple, thanking each god, Teumann's head still in hand. He also destroyed the statues of Teumann's predecessors, the previous Elamite kings, because, in a time when art and reality were one, it was essential to do away with every representation of the enemy.

Ashurbanipal and his own predecessors appear to have made little distinction between offensive and defensive war. The sacred realm was defended through offense. Preemption was protection, a paradoxical idea that was common in premodern warfare and is central to contemporary jihadi thought, with its conviction that the world is out to destroy Islam and thus must be attacked first. And it was of course the animating idea of the second American invasion of Iraq. Nor did they appear to attach ethical questions to killing. This was their work, even if they did enjoy it, or felt they ought to depict themselves enjoying it. Indeed, Ashurbanipal may have thought he was positively paying Teumann a favor in beheading him, bringing him from chaos to order, making his rival as pious as himself, bringing him to the truth. 'There will be established no peace without combat,' the Assyrian epic poem the *Tukultī-Ninurta* puts it, and 'A good relationship does not come without fighting.' Herein is the real perversity of Assyrian art and the Assyrian outlook, what gets you in the celiac plexus like the rumble of an airstrike: that hardcore Ishtarian element, the chokehold of eros and thanatos, of killing and love. *I behead you for your salvation as much as my own. I behead you because I love you.*

The friezes were uncovered only in the nineteenth century, when European excavations at Nineveh began. Until then our notions of Nineveh derive mostly from the Hebrew Bible, where it comes off hardly better. In the books of the Old Testament, the city is a byword for war and worse. Not just peerlessly cruel, Nineveh is a cruel paradox of a place, a flower of iniquity and yet an instrument of righteousness. The Assyrian kings make the pharaohs look like a family of Tibetan wet nurses. The Babylonians, whose abuse of the Israelites is better known, are pretty bad, too, but it is the Assyrians who get the Hebrew prophets into a particularly flagellant froth. What the prophets feel in the face of Assyrian abuse is not so much anger as shame, or the white-hot anger that can only come of shame—the shame of men abandoned by their maker. The prophets' own god, the Hebrew god, relies on these Assyrian reprobates to punish his chosen for their insufficient worshipfulness. God tells Isaiah that Assyria is 'the rod of mine anger, and the staff in their hand is mine indignation.' Isaiah prophesies that the Hebrews will be 'trod down like the mire in the streets' by the Assyrians, and so, for many generations, they are. He also predicts God will destroy Nineveh but declines to fix a demolition date.

God, possibly tired of the Hebrews' caviling and pessimism, seems at times to almost admire the Assyrians, with their triumphalist view of history. It could be He also enjoys their insights into historical irony. He may notice the inventive ways in which the sculptors of the friezes collapse history, showing one man climbing a siege ladder while next to him, touching him, another falls to his death. Make war and love today, for tomorrow you die. The riotous Assyrians bring out the Ishtar even in Him, we learn in Isaiah: 'O my people that dwellest in Zion, be not afraid of the Assyrian: he shall smite thee with a rod, and shall lift up his staff against thee, after the manner of Egypt. For yet a very little while, and the indignation shall cease, and mine anger in their destruction.' It is at moments like these that we recall why the most durable definition of the word Israel is *He who struggles with his god.*

Isaiah could at least filter the paternal malice through his own sense of irony and his superior talent for versification. Not so hapless, sputtering Jonah. We remember what befalls that prophet when he refuses to go to Nineveh to preach. We tend to forget the rest of the story. Having been spit up after three days in the depths, bleached white with cetacean gastric juices, Jonah at last agrees to the mission. He expects the Assyrian king will make great sport of his head and appendages, but better that than spend another three days inside a leviathan, he reasons. To his surprise, however, the Assyrians convert. The king himself dons sackcloth and squats in ash. Jonah is unconvinced. He implores God to do as he promised and level Nineveh. God refuses. Not only that, He repents of his plans, so touched is He by the Assyrian change of heart. Jonah, despondent, asks to be killed instead. To which God: 'Should not I spare Nineveh, that great city, wherein are more than sixscore thousand persons that cannot discern between their right hand and their left hand; and also much cattle?'

That really is how the book of Jonah concludes, on a livestock query. It is one of only two books of prophecy in the Hebrew Bible to end with a question. The other is that of Nahum, who, as it happens, picks up the story of Nineveh from Jonah. Historians believe Nahum was from a village near Nineveh. It could be he was an Israelite living in exile there. By the time he saw the palaces and temples of Nineveh, the friezes on the walls would have stretched on for, literally, miles. The experience might have been something like this: Imagine you are a foreign visitor to Washington, D.C., and you are walking around the perimeter fence of the White House. Instead of seeing the White House, however, what you see are huge high-definition plasma-screen televisions showing videos of American soldiers killing and mutilating their enemies. You are made to walk around the fence ten times.

It was too much for poor Nahum. 'Woe to the bloody city! It is all full of lies and robbery,' he wails, a place where

> horseman lifteth up both the bright sword and the glittering spear: and there is a multitude of slain, and a great number of carcases; and there is none end of their corpses; they stumble upon their corpses: Because of the multitude, of the whoredoms of the wellfavoured harlot, the mistress of witchcrafts, that selleth nations through her whoredoms, and families through her witchcrafts. Behold, I am against thee, saith the lord of hosts; and I will discover thy skirts upon thy face, and I will shew the nations thy nakedness, and the kingdoms thy shame. And I will cast abominable filth upon thee, and make thee vile, and will set thee as a gazingstock. And it shall come to pass, that all they that look upon thee shall flee from thee, and say, Nineveh is laid waste. Who will bemoan her?

Nineveh was finally laid waste, Nahum records. Ashurbanipal's great library barely survived his death. The year agreed upon now is 612 B.C. As always happens, the Assyrians' gory convictions of divinity reached their outer layer just as the empire reached its physical limits. The Israelites found in this evidence that God, though he may tarry, always delivers on a comeuppance—what the historian Peter Machinist has called the Jewish 'retributive theory of history,' this idea that the future must needs graft justice upon the past. A confederation of Babylonian, Elamite, and Median armies and the encroaching Scythian hordes probably helped. So, too, in some ancient accounts, did a flash flood caused by rainstorms. It brought down Nineveh's supposedly indestructible walls, once so wide you could run three chariots side by side on their battlements.

Nahum describes the siege of Nineveh as a house-to-house melee that lasts three months. By the time the Greek historian Diodorus gets hold of the story that has become three years. He relates that the last Assyrian king, Sardanapalus, knowing what the invaders will do if they get hold of him—precisely what his predecessors did to theirs—makes a pyre of downtown Nineveh. Into the flames he throws his gold and silver. Then his wardrobe. Next go in his concubines. His eunuchs follow. The order of value is unclear. Finally the king dives in.

Few bemoan Nineveh's destruction, as Nahum prophesied, and soon enough few remember her. When Xenophon arrives at Nineveh, around 400 B.C., in the company of the Persian emperor Cyrus the Younger and his army, he can't even learn the city's name. It is mostly deserted and bears a morbid pall. Its riches have long ago been carted off, its friezes buried in rubble and dust, its metal sculptures melted down for coinage. Nevertheless, Cyrus wants it. He is stymied until another trick of nature comes to his aid. 'A cloud hid the face of the sun and blotted out the light thereof,' Xenophon writes, while 'Zeus terrified the inhabitants by thunder, and the city was taken.' From the Persians Nineveh is won, seventy years later, by Alexander the Great; the Hellenes eventually cede it to the Armenians; they to the Parthians; they to a different set of Persians; and they to the Byzantines, at the Battle of Nineveh of 627 A.D., where, according to chronicles, the Emperor Heraclius and the Persian general Razates face off on the front line. When a fog rolls in and blinds the famed Persian spearmen, Razates challenges Heraclius to mounted duel. He is decapitated before he can get a thrust off. Carrying on with local tradition, Heraclius fits Razates's head onto the tip of his lance, bung-like. Meanwhile, the Persian emperor is rounded up and made to starve in a dungeon for four days. On the fifth he is drained of life with a loving point-blank archery barrage.

When the followers of Muhammad sweep in from the south, a decade later, and wrest Mosul from the Sassanids, they find a place richly crossbred with Judaism, Christianity, and Magianism, the dominant Persian monotheism. Soon Nineveh is surpassed in importance by the fortress city across the river, *al-Mawşil*, as it is known in Arabic. It is a propitious spot. A gateway to the Anatolian plateau, it is midway among four seas, where the floodplains of lower Mesopotamia give way to the Taurus Mountains, in a temperate belt between the peaks and the dunes. Graced with endlessly fecund soil and two blooming seasons per year, it takes on the nickname *Um-el-Rabiein*, Mother of Two Springs. It is an entrepôt in the trading routes that connect Asia and Europe, and a junction of power and faith, home to Arabs, Kurds, Armenians, Turkmen, Shabaks, Mandeans, and Circassians, among others. Many of them choose to convert to Islam, but many do not, and they are not forced. Practitioners of all the Abrahamic religions (the Hebrew patriarch had, according to custom, been born in Iraq) and their persecuted compeers are welcome—Zoroastrians, Yazidis, Sufi mystics, Manicheans, every sort of heretic and schismatic evicted from the empires that flank the city. Unlike in some other quarters of rapidly expanding Islam, there is no prohibition on Christian buildings in Mosul, and churches and monasteries abound. So beloved does Mosul become of the Nestorians, in particular, who have been banned from the orthodox precincts of Byzantium, they add to the city's corpus of creation myths one of their own. A monk living in Nineveh stood before the Tigris and drew a cross, it is said. He spread his cloak over the water. The cloak became a bridge. His fellow monks crossed the river and on the far bank discovered a garden. Around that garden they built a church. Around that church formed Mosul. The patriarch of the Jalili family, Mosul's most powerful for centuries, is a Christian convert to Islam.

'However many countries there may be in the world there are none so rich in faiths' as Mosul, the English Arabophile, diplomat, and archaeologist Gertrude Bell, who came to settle in Iraq, will later write. 'Beliefs which have been driven out with obloquy by a new-found truth, the half-apprehended mysticism of the East, echoes of Western metaphysics and philosophy, illusive memories of paganism—all have been swept together into these hills, where creeds that were outlined in the childhood of the world are formulated still in terms as old as themselves.' Her contemporary the British colonial official Harry Luke will add, 'It is rare to find, as one ranges the great Mosul plain, two consecutive villages peopled by the same race, speaking the same tongue, worshipping the same God.'

To this day, even conservative Moslawis are vocally proud of the city's tradition of diversity. 'Mosul used to be like a miniature of Iraq, with all its different peoples,' Abu Omar told me. 'I am a Muslim, but my neighbors were Christian, and I never saw any harm from them.'

When the Abbasid dynasty wrests control of Mosul in the eighth century, a slaughter unlike anything since the one Nahum recorded takes place. Thousands are killed. The historian Tariq al-Mawsil was a boy at the time. He tells how his mother hid him in the garbage bin in their home. Four soldiers come in and demand all the family's possessions. She gives them over. Unsatisfied, a soldier drives his sword through her. Tariq's baby brother flails in distress in his crib until he falls into his dead mother's opened belly. He tosses in the blood and entrails until he, too, dies.

But the Abbasids, like the Assyrians, are creators as well as wreckers. Iraq becomes the intellectual and commercial center of Islam and thus of the world. Mosul province comes to comprehend the lands from Turkey in the north, to the outskirts of Aleppo in the west, to the Persian frontier in the east. With its bounteous granaries, Mosul city is fought over incessantly. Moslawis get by. They team up with the sympathetic usurpers and toss out the villainous ones. The good and bad alike die horribly. Ibn al-Athir, chronicler of the Crusades, is Moslawi, and from him we learn of local pawns of fate such as the fair and tragic lord Jokermish. After seizing the city, he wins Moslawis' respect. When Mosul comes under siege once more, 'They fought fiercely and killed many because of their love for Jokermish on account of his good rule over them,' Ibn al-Athir writes. Mosul is next set upon by his arch rival, the hated Jawuli, known for 'cutting of hands and noses and blinding eyes.' Jokermish, his hemiplegia flaring up, is carried into battle on a litter. He is captured, tossed in a pit, perishes, al-Athir reports with the compression of a historian for whom death has become mere punctuation. Jawuli sends the head of a Jokermish deputy as tribute to the cadi. The Moslawis oust him. Jawuli is 'seized, killed, and his possessions plundered.'

The last great sultan to serve the Abbasids, Saladin, takes Jerusalem from the Crusaders in 1187 and thus becomes the most admired ruler in the history of Iraq, perhaps in the history of Sunni Islam. Saddam's comparisons of himself to Saladin during the Iran-Iraq war will be an early public leakage of his until then mostly private lunacy. But the truth is that, in his day, Saladin is more admired by the Frankish knights than he is by his fellows. He rampages through the Mosul countryside, press-ganging Muslims into his personal jihad. At the gates of Mosul city, al-Athir tells us, maybe with a touch of civic pride, Saladin is caught short. Twice he prepares to attack and twice begs off. 'Saladin viewed and assessed it and what he saw amazed him and overawed both him and his companions, for he held a great and mighty city, its walls and outworks crowded with men and not a battlement without a fighting man posted there. . . . He realized he was unable to take it and that he would retire disappointed.'

Closer to Mosul's heart is Nur ad-Din Zangi, the Abbasid atabeg (a kind of governor) of Mosul. Sure, after taking the Crusader city of Edessa, near Mosul, Nur ad-Din turns one of its churches into a stable and tears down two others to plug the holes in the battlements. And, yes, it is also said that, after his men kill the Crusader prince Raymond of Poitiers, Nur ad-Din sends the Frenchman's head and arms to the caliph in Baghdad. But such are the times, and it is equally true that, at Edessa, Nur ad-Din thanks Christ for curing his gout and greets 'the Christians with joy, kissed the gospel, saluted the metropolitan, and asked after his health,' according to a contemporary chronicler (a Christian no less). Jews flee the Franks to live under Nur ad-Din's fairer-minded rule. He settles three hundred Jewish families in Edessa, showing the metropolitan the real meaning of grace. When an interloper backed by a rival sultan tries to capture Mosul, Nur ad-Din calmly reasserts control, 'seized many who had caused the revolt, impaled them, and had the sultan's son killed secretly.' This is more to the taste of Moslawis than Saladin's showboating. Nur ad-Din's parting gift to the city before his death, in 1174, according to al-Athir, is the Grand al-Nuri Mosque. Today, Nur ad-Din is a kind of patron saint to Mosul—and, sadly, to the Islamic State. Abu Musab al-Zarqawi, the founder of Al Qaeda in Iraq and the forefather of the Islamic State, will claim it was Nur ad-Din who inspires him to his great deeds. And it is at the Grand al-Nuri Mosque that ISIS's leader, Abu Bakr al-Baghdadi, will proclaim himself Caliph.

In the 1530s, Suleiman the Magnificent annexes Mesopotamia into the Ottoman Empire. Sunni doctrine is imposed. The Mosul Vilayet, as the Ottomans call the region, finds itself sitting on Islam's sectarian faultline. Iraq becomes a center of Shia learning and of Shia opposition to the Caliphate. But by now Mosul is a kind of autarchy. Squeezed for millennia between empires, between the Assyrians and their rivals, then between the Romans and the Parthians, then the Byzantines and Persians, then the Turks and Iranians, Moslawis have learned through hard experience to keep two sets of books. They are near enough capitals to remain urbane yet distant enough to stay independent. With its brimming crop fields, prolific tanneries and looms (it is in Mosul that muslin originates), and thick-skinned janissaries, Mosul is essential to Istanbul's war machine, and the sultans build it into a major garrison, leaving the warrior caste that will last into Abu Omar's day, but Moslawis keep the frontier mentality. They resist the sublimity of the Sublime Porte. Their province is the breadbasket of the country, feeding Baghdad, but they never entirely come under the larger metropolis's thumb. According to some older Moslawis I spoke with, Mosul is the one major Iraqi city never to have a statue of Saddam. Writes Bell, 'Mosul has always been against the government, whatever form it should happen to assume.'

One astute student of Mosul politics whom I know puts it differently. He calls Mosul 'the end of the river.' When I ask him how he means that, he says, darkly, 'Like Conrad meant it.'

Abu Omar had fallen out with all five of his siblings save one. He thought they looked down on him because he depended on them for money. He remained friendly only with an older brother who went by Abu Fahad.

When I first spoke with Abu Fahad (who asked me to use a pseudonym), he was still in Mosul. The Caliphate had disabled the cell towers and forbidden mobile phones. They beat and executed people caught with phones. They were convinced the city was crawling with informants, which of course it was. But the Iraqi troops wisely set up mobile towers as they took ground, facilitating not just their own communications but communication between Moslawis stuck in the city and the outside world. When I reached Abu Fahad on his phone, CTS was moving on his neighborhood, Qadisiya, to the west of Zahra. I could hear explosions in the background.

'We're surrounded!' he yelled into the phone. 'There are big airstrikes! A lot of airstrikes!'

The connection cut out.

He and his family escaped Mosul a few weeks after Abu Omar. When they arrived at the Khazer camp, they moved into Abu Omar's tent. After a few nights of tight quarters, Abu Omar told him it was too crowded. Why not get his own tent? There were plenty. Abu Fahad found this unbrotherly and departed in a lather. The brothers hadn't spoken since. They were both living as refugees, a few hundred meters from one another, both too proud to effect a reunion.

'He knows where to find me,' Abu Omar grumbled.

The authorities at the Khazer camp could not tell me what tent Abu Omar's brother was in, so I spent a day walking around trying to find him. The camp had grown like kudzu since I'd first visited. Acres of tents had been added, consuming the hillside. The small market had turned into a bazaar that straddled the perimeter fence. There were a barber and a chicken rotisserie and a cigarette shop. Refugees had been assured or had assured themselves that Mosul would be taken quickly, that they'd be home in a matter of weeks. But then they'd met the refugees who'd come from towns miles from Mosul, towns that had been liberated months ago, who were still here. They were learning from their radios and word of mouth that the battle was not going quickly at all. Now they saw they would have to spend the winter here. It was an ugly prospect. Outsiders forget that, despite its troubles, Iraq is a middle-income country. Mosul was a mostly middle-class and wealthy city. Its inhabitants were unused to the deprivation they experienced under the Islamic State, but at least there they weren't entirely dispossessed. In the camp, they were.

As soon as he stepped from his tent, having heard an American was looking for him, I knew I'd found Abu Fahad. He had the same high forehead and penetrating eyes as Abu Omar. His weren't laughing, however. They were still and knowing and the wretchedness of his position told in them. After departing Abu Omar's tent, he'd found his own in a sector where many of his neighbors from Qadisiya had ended up.

'When I see them, you know, I just want to hug them and ask them how everything's going. We try to be there for each other. Everyone wants to go back, get out of this disgrace. We'd rather live in the middle of a fight, airstrikes and mortars. We want a rest from this degradation. This is no place for humans.' Though, he went on, he suspected Mosul wouldn't be much better once the jihadis and military were done with it. 'You'll find this killing that, that killing this, and so on. There will be many Daesh sleeper cells after the battle. This situation will never be sorted out. It will stay the way it is and get worse. Revenge upon revenge. What we really want from

America is to take us all there, bring us to Alaska or Chicago, us Moslawis. You can keep Mosul for yourselves. You can do whatever you want to do with Mosul, just take us to America. Let's trade cities.'

Trimmer and better-groomed than Abu Omar, Abu Fahad was also cleverer. He had been an army medic, treating the wounded of the Iran-Iraq and Gulf wars at a military hospital in Mosul. When it was converted to a public hospital, he served as chief nurse. He owned a pharmacy on the side. Living in a refugee camp was a vastly more stinging indignity to him than to his laid-off security-guard brother. Abu Fahad's son, Hamudi, was sixteen. He was three years younger than his cousin Omar, but more mature. His daughter, Maha, was the same age as Aya, but where Aya could barely bring herself to speak in my presence, Maha wanted to discuss everything: history, politics, religion, movies, especially movies. The Caliphate forbade movies, excepting their own propaganda and execution videos. In the camp 'we've set a record for watching movies, Hamudi and I,' Maha told me. Once again she could commune across the continents with her beloved Ryan Reynolds. In addition to him, she admired Hillary Clinton. Unlike my friends in the army, she knew Trump to be a hateful buffoon and was pleased to say as much. And Abu Fahad allowed her to say it—allowed her to discuss what she liked, in fact. This was rare.

From American movies Hamudi had learned about Hawaii, which he knew to be paradise on earth. He wanted to move there. Abu Fahad would take Alaska, Chicago, or really anywhere I could find him an American wife.

'He wants a tall one, with blonde hair and green eyes,' Maha said.

'I want four wives,' Abu Fahad said.

'He wants to live by sharia!' she said.

For her part, Maha would settle for Irbil, where several aunts, uncles, and cousins lived. But, she hastened to tell me—in this too she was a rarity—if Mosul was livable, she wanted to go back there. It was home. Despite everything, she loved it. She also loved to cook, and was good at it. In a cheap pot on the tiny gas burner the camp authorities had provided, she made us chicken and rice. I told her if she got back to Mosul, she should open a restaurant. I'd back her. She joked that there would be plenty of available spaces.

'Anyway, America is not that nice,' she said. 'There are lots of strong storms there. It's scary.'

I told her that was fine because Ryan Reynolds was in fact Canadian. In this she seemed to find confirmation of the soundness of her infatuation with him.

'Wishing is not enough,' Abu Fahad said. 'Either take me there or don't ask me these questions. I don't want to live in a dream.'

When I asked what life had been like in Mosul in the weeks before they escaped, Abu Fahad showed me a video on his phone. He'd shot it just before the Iraqi troops invaded Qadisiya. The jihadis had imposed an all-day curfew and the family hadn't left the house in days. In the video, Maha and Hamudi sit at a table in the kitchen over lunch. They are talking and laughing. Abu Fahad turns the camera towards himself to reveal a bushy beard, as required by the religious police. He stands and walks to the window and trains the camera on a lump in the street. He zooms in. The lump is a body, face down on the pavement. It belonged to a local mentally disabled boy who'd defied the curfew, probably unwittingly. A sniper had shot him. The corpse had been there for days.

In 2006, Abu Fahad told me, his wife was shot at a checkpoint manned by Kurdish and American soldiers. His children were in the car. As Maha and Hamudi listened, Abu Fahad described to me the crash of the bullets coming through the windshield, his harried pressing on the brake pedal. He was dragged from the vehicle and beaten unconscious by soldiers. Coming to, he found his wife's body beneath a blanket. His eldest daughter, who had watched her mother's head explode, he found in the backseat of the car, trying to eat shards of window glass.

'She went insane,' Abu Fahad said.

By this point Maha was crying. Hamudi stared fixedly at the ground.

'Let's change the subject, please,' Abu Fahad said.

I asked him to tell me how it was the Islamic State had taken power in Mosul with such ease. It couldn't have just been that the military and police were scared of the jihadis. There must have been more to the story. Yes, there was, he said. Before he went on, though, he wanted me to know something.

'We were one of the families who welcomed Daesh,' he said. He said it looking me in the eye, without a hint of abashment.

After the American invasion in 2003, Mosul was comparatively safe. There was some looting, but nothing like in Baghdad or other large cities. Mosul was unique in that it was presided over by an American general who was a cut above his colleagues. David Petraeus made himself as beloved of Moslawis as he was of his troops in the 101st Airborne. His soldiers didn't mind that he turned them into a kind of municipal workforce with guns, and nor did Moslawis. The 101st renovated the city, which had been moribund even before the invasion, neglected by Saddam in his last years in power. Petraeus funded construction, education, and medical projects, and the goodwill he generated kept an insurgency from forming right away. Going around Mosul, I met university professors whose departments Petraeus supplied with computers, power company engineers who recalled how good electricity service was during his tenure. Abu Omar still remembers the name of the American captain from the 101st who brought a doctor to his house when his eldest daughter was sick. When Abu Omar asked how much the doctor would charge, the captain handed him a stack of dinars.

Mosul became a model of how to conduct an occupation. But Petraeus was, inevitably, promoted, and just as inevitably a local insurgency formed. How could it not? Mosul was perhaps Iraq's most soldierly city, with the military academy and a base, and the country had, after all, been invaded and occupied. The insurgency originated with men like Abu Omar, veterans who had lost their pensions, and many their jobs, when the Coalition Provisional Authority disbanded the Iraqi military. They were joined by purged Baathists. There was no shortage of such disaffected men to recruit. FREs, the Americans called them: former regime elements. To their cause rallied anyone else outraged enough to take up arms against the occupiers. They were soon joined by jihadis, at first just Iraqis, then foreigners too. Mosul is only seventy miles from the Syrian and Turkish borders, and they slipped in easily. In 2004, insurgents set upon Mosul's police stations, forcing out the thousands-strong Mosul police force, a foreshadow of what would occur a decade later on a much larger scale. The boundaries between ideology and criminality became semantic. Even the most committed insurgents need funding, and the various underground groups colluded and competed over revenue from the smuggling routes into Syria and Turkey, some of which dated to the Ottomans, and over control of local extortion rackets. A U.S. Army general who later took command of Mosul told me it 'was a *Star Wars* bar scene of enemies. Americans were looking at it as us versus them, but in many cases it was them versus each other, a continuation of things that history and culture had produced in that area for three or four centuries. . . . At one point we counted eighteen different enemies that we were facing, and Al Qaeda was not the biggest, though it was certainly the most deadly.'

Eventually al Qaeda became the most deadly *and* the biggest. But

Al Qaeda in the Land of the Two Rivers, as the organization's Iraqi branch was officially known, was not al Qaeda as Osama bin Laden and its early leaders had envisioned it. The Iraqi branch was led by Abu Musab al-Zarqawi, a man late to the mosque. A Palestinian raised in the refugee camps in Jordan, his criminal career had begun at age twelve. When Osama bin Laden came across Zarqawi in Afghanistan later, in the 1980s, during the Soviet war, the billionaire's son and poet was not impressed with the reformed street thug and pimp. But since then Zarqawi had gained a reputation as a fearless workhorse for jihad and as a natural tactician, staging attacks in Jordan, no mean feat, and running training camps in Afghanistan and Kurdistan.

In February 2003, with the American invasion of Iraq a foregone conclusion, Secretary of State Colin Powell devoted a substantial portion of his speech at the United Nations to Zarqawi, in an effort to show a connection between al Qaeda and Saddam Hussein. At the time, Zarqawi was respected among his cohort but otherwise obscure. He was probably as surprised by this star-making cameo as bin Laden was, if more delighted. Powell, for his part, suspected Zarqawi had had no more to do with September 11 than Saddam had. He would later tell an interviewer 'it was not clear to me what the connection really was' and called Zarqawi 'a passing reference.' Nevertheless, he turned Zarqawi's messianic fantasies into reality. And, in another lucky stroke for the fortune-favored Zarqawi, who called it providence, America's war in Iraq coincided with the mainstreaming of the Internet, a machine which exceeded even cable news in its power to amplify the irrelevant. Zarqawi, who had once worked at a video store, was an early adopter. In 2004, in Fallujah, he beheaded the American contractor Nicholas Berg and uploaded the execution video. Jihad went online.

Bin Laden, fancying himself an inspiration to all Muslims, had many misgivings about Zarqawi, among them Zarqawi's hatred for

Shia Islam. Zarqawi, with the psychotic's flair for needless repetition, had called Shiites a 'sect of treachery throughout history and throughout the ages.' He justified killing them by reminding his followers that it was Shiites who'd helped the Mongols to sack the Abbasid Empire in the twelfth century. Now here they were, betraying Iraq again, except this time it wasn't Genghis Khan's army but the Americans. Really, though, Zarqawi was perfectly content to kill anyone, Iraqi or foreigner, infidel or Muslim, Shiite or Sunni. Bin Laden also resented Zarqawi's insistence that he and not just clerics had the power to declare Muslims, Shiite or Sunni, apostates. Still, holding his nose, the Sheikh, as bin Laden preferred to be called, handed over Mesopotamia to the Sheikh of Slaughterers, as Zarqawi liked to be called, and in so doing made real Powell's tale, ensured not just his own obsolescence but the advent of a new era of jihadism. Bin Laden unwittingly ushered in what would become the Islamic State, a thing which not even he, with his dream of global war, quaint by comparison though it seems now, could have anticipated, any more than Powell could have. A pair of false prophets, the fallen general and the disavowed heir conjured a perfect avatar of American fear. 'It was one of the great ironies of the age,' the journalist Joby Warrick writes in his book about Zarqawi, *Black Flags*. 'In deciding to use the unsung Zarqawi as an excuse for launching a new front in the war against terrorism, the White House had managed to launch the career of one of the century's great terrorists.'

Launched, then killed. Even American-made chaos-monsters are not exempt from the American celebrity cycle. Zarqawi died in 2006, after an F-16 dropped a 500-pound bomb on a house in Diyala province in which he was staying. His hagiography was swift. Zarqawi became the central martyr of the millennial-jihadi generation. At al-Nuaimi mosque, Omar told me, the imam went on and on about Zarqawi. 'He would always talk about Zarqawi,' Omar said. 'He would say, "May his soul rest in peace, he was a great guy," and I don't know what else.'

Before his death, Zarqawi had talked about establishing an Islamic polity of some sort in Iraq, and, interestingly, it was only in the uncertain months afterwards, when his surviving followers were on the run, driven from their bases in Anbar by the Sunni Awakening and the Surge, desperate for morale, that they began referring to themselves as the Islamic State in Iraq. They may have been trying to defy the news of their demise with a big new awning, or looking to bury their reputation for criminality beneath one for piety, or both. Whatever their motivations, they made laughable claims. They announced they were building up a new confessional federation, assembling prayerful ministries and such. It was piffle, viral marketing, but it took. Patiently, gradually, outside of the concern of Baghdad and the comprehension of Washington, a real organization known as the Islamic State in Iraq took shape. In 2007, its members briefly seized Baqubah, the capital of Diyala, southeast of Nineveh. Driven out of there, they pushed north. Mosul had long been a hub of foreign fighters, smuggled weapons, and other rough custom. By the following year, at least half of all attacks in Iraq were taking place in Nineveh, most in Mosul. A Pentagon spokesman said that for ISI 'to win, they have to take Baghdad. To survive, they have to hold on to Mosul.'

Maha, Abu Fahad's daughter, told me of that time, 'There was always fighting going on around our house, the sound of gun shots, bombs all day long. We got to the point where if we didn't hear these sounds for a day, we get bored. We got so used to them. I mean we've gone through a lot. I am fifteen, true, but I feel like I've lived a hundred years.'

Some of ISI's recruits believed in the cause. Others were looking for a competitive salary. ISI could pay more than most jobs, more even than the government. By the late 2000s, it was taking in nearly a million dollars a month in Nineveh, its largest profit center in Iraq, according to a RAND Corporation report. Most of that came from gas and oil rackets, protection rackets, smuggling, and embezzlement from public works and private business. ISI's meticulous internal records, a good many of which have been salvaged, make for a fascinating study in concerted recreancy. The organization had a sophisticated administrative structure, accountants, compensation tiers, a perks system that included housing and per-capita family allowances. Every member had a profile, with his skills listed and rated, along with his goals. As the attacks on Mosul's officials, police, and soldiers increased, and as suicide bombings became the weapon of choice, a check mark in the DESIRES MARTYRDOM field in a member's paperwork was particularly attractive. ISI's leaders prided themselves on their egalitarian inclinations, and not just in the matters of whom they killed and sent to their death. In the Nineveh chapter of ISI, the largest line item in most yearly budgets was salaries, on which was spent four times as much as the next-largest, military operations. Payoffs to tribal and clan leaders were, I've heard, significant, but less formally accounted for.

By 2011, when American troops withdrew from Iraq, ISI, only five years earlier a mere notion, was dancing what it sang. A family of Mosul court clerks I met described how the jihadis infiltrated the criminal justice system, winning over lawyers and judges through religious appeals, intimidation, and bribery. They created their own alternative sharia court system in which maiming and death were punishments. Eventually all levels of the government were coopted. Some Moslawi officials profited by the collusion, but many, maybe most, cooperated to survive. Even if you had the courage to report to the police or the governor's office that you were being threatened by ISI into, say, handing over the details of a government contract, there was no way to know whether the administrator or cop you went to wasn't himself compromised. ISI became a shadow government.

An official I got to know, the director of the Nineveh provincial planning department, received threats and offers from the jihadis for years. He described it as living 'between two fires.' So what did you do? I asked. Resigned himself to death, he said. 'If it was regarded that I should die on this day, then ok, I die. It's the life. This is the life.' An analyst of Mosul politics told me 'If you're in the provincial government in Nineveh, you're like a mayor in Sicily at the height of the Mafia's power. They tell you that they want to get part of a contract for building a road. You know full well that they're going to skim eighty percent. You have two choices. You and your family can get killed, or you can go along with it.'

The insurgents came to an epiphany: the worse they made life in Mosul, the more the security forces would persecute ordinary Moslawis. Those ordinary people would blame not the insurgency, which they couldn't see, but the government, which they could. They would come to hate the government and would look for an alternative authority. That alternative would be ISI. Moslawis old and radical enough to have belonged to the Iraq Communist Party in its heyday recognized the strategy. The Bolsheviks had called it 'heightening the contradictions.'

To aid this strategy, ISI could not have asked for a better accomplice than the Iraqi government. The 2005 elections in Iraq brought to power the Islamic Dawah Party, a stridently Shia party that had formed in the 1950s and been banished from Iraq by Saddam in the '70s. The next year, with American assistance, Nouri al-Maliki, a Dawah operative who'd lived in exile for most of his adult life, including seven years in Iran, became prime minister. He proved a disappointment, then a disaster. In defiance of the new constitution, he consolidated power, appointing himself, at various times, defense minister, interior minister, and national security minister. When he was returned to office, in 2010, not even his Iraqi supporters nor his last few backers in Washington could claim to take the election seriously. It was commonly understood by Iraqis—and by no means only Sunnis—that Washington had rigged the election for Maliki. It was also taken for granted that Maliki was doing the bidding of Iran. This was too narrow an explanation of his policies but there was a good deal of truth in it.

The Arab Spring began the next year, as the Americans pulled out of Iraq. Maliki was despotic but not blind. He was aware he was as hated by many Iraqis as Mubarak was by Egyptians, or Qadafi by Libyans. So he denatured the Iraqi military and police, attempting to create a palace guard and head off a coup. He replaced competent commanders with amateur loyalists, stocked the ranks with Shia militiamen. Only a few units, such as CTS, maintained their independence. At the same time, he went after Sunni leaders, sometimes claiming they were colluding with the insurgency. Officials in Nineveh and every other Sunni-majority province were arrested and forced out of office or into exile. Sunni-majority cities like Mosul Maliki neglected or abused. Government services disappeared. The security forces went after Sunni men en masse, harassing them, jailing them, torturing, murdering. At checkpoints Abu Omar and Abu Fahad and their families were, as a matter of course, insulted, called terrorists, Baathists. Every Sunni family they knew in Mosul had the same experience. This went on for years. For Moslawis, the government became morally indistinguishable from the insurgency, and then worse than the insurgency—just as the insurgents had known it would.

When I ask Iraqis who initially supported the Islamic State, like Abu Fahad, about their thinking at the time, or about how it was the jihadis could have taken so much of Iraq so quickly, Maliki isn't just one of the first reasons they cite—his name is almost always the first word out of their mouths. It would be impossible to overstate the extent to which Maliki, who was replaced in 2015, was and is despised, the extent to which Iraqis believed he primed their country to be turned into the Caliphate. For many Iraqis I know, his regime had the devilish contours of an Assyria or Babylon in the Old Testament. For them, there is only one culprit who bears more responsibility—America.

In 2010, a reclusive militant named Abu Bakr al-Baghdadi took over ISI. His given name was Ibrahim Ali al-Badri al-Samarrai. As it suggests, he was from Samarra, another city devastated in the American occupation. There, in 2006, Zarqawi's people had bombed the golden-domed al-Askari shrine, one of the holiest sites in Shia Islam. The incident is often credited with igniting the civil war that followed. Baghdadi appears to have studied Islamic law at Saddam Hussein Islamic University in Baghdad, where he presumably picked up the toponym of his nom de guerre. He fought in Fallujah under Zarqawi and was arrested there. He was imprisoned at Camp Bucca, an American-run detention facility so infamous for radicalizing inmates it was known as Al Qaeda School. After being released, he rose through the ISI ranks. After taking command, he pushed his way into the Syrian civil war and renamed his group the Islamic State in Iraq and al-Sham. (Al-Sham was a medieval Islamic province in what is now Syria.) ISIS became an army as well as a movement and Baghdadi showed a flair for promotional torture-killings—of soldiers, civilians, rival jihadis. When the al Qaeda home office reprimanded him, in 2013, he broke off, taking much of ISIS with him. He allied with ex-Iraqi military and other revanchists. On January 1 of the following year their columns rolled across the Syrian border into Ramadi, the capital of Iraq's Anbar province. Next they took Fallujah. Saddam's hometown of Tikrit followed. By the late spring of 2014, ISIS controlled much of northwestern Iraq. In many places, soldiers and police fled before the jihadis even arrived. Baghdadi had positions within heavy artillery range of Baghdad. The capital girded for invasion. It was hit with a wave of suicide bombings.

Instead of moving on Baghdad, however, Baghdadi turned his attention north, to Mosul. When he activated his sleeper cells there, in the first days of June, and dispatched his columns toward the city, it was his for the taking. Whether through anguish or pragmatism, or both, many Moslawis—people like Abu Omar and Abu Fahad— had come to see Baghdadi, vicious as he was, as the only alternative to Maliki. To reject the Iraqi government was, in a sense, to accept the Islamic State by default. It didn't hurt that Baghdadi's followers seemed invincible. Several hundred of them expelled several thousand Iraqi forces from Mosul in about seventy-two hours. They barely needed to fire their rifles. The optics of the arrival were triumphant, redemptive. The jihadis' tanks and APCs, seized from American-supplied bases, made for a perfect travesty of the triumphal American parade into Iraq eleven years before. The avatar of American fear appeared on every news channel in the world. Abu Fahad remembered it vividly. June 9.

'I was at a car shop, looking to sell and buy cars. That was my hobby. I saw Iraqi army Humvees passing by the street shouting, "Go back to your homes! There's a curfew! Stay inside your homes!" I rushed to my car and started driving back home. There were so many cars on the road, I didn't reach my house for three hours. We had no idea what was happening. It was very sudden. Later in the evening we heard the soldiers knocking on doors and begging for clothing so they could disguise themselves. Some people helped, some didn't. Most didn't. We saw them taking off their uniforms, right in the street, dropping their weapons, abandoning their Humvees, fleeing Mosul.'

The government disappeared. It was as though every Moslawi like Abu Fahad who'd ever cursed officialdom, wished it gone from his life, had been granted their wish overnight. In its place, suddenly, were men in long beards and cropped pants, wearing Rhodesian chest rigs, smiling and greeting Abu Fahad and his neighbors politely, wishing them peace, apologizing for the damage done on their way in and promising to clean it up soon.

'I am telling you, it was so normal in the beginning. They entered as if they were tourists. They weren't even shooting. People just went on living as before, going out and everything. They took over the city so smoothly. By Friday morning at 10 a.m., they were driving around Mosul as though they'd always been there.' He went on, 'They didn't come in talking about religion. They were connected with al Qaeda, we knew that, of course, but they were very nice and treated people very well. They even allowed you to smoke on the street at first. We stopped going to work for about a week, and then went back. They weren't punishing anyone. They would say, "We're the Islamic State and we're here to liberate you from the infidels."'

'They came in as revolutionaries,' Abu Omar had told me, his chest swelling and his forehead lifting with vicarious pride as he said it.

'There were no more checkpoints,' Omar had added. 'No traffic jams, no arrests of young people, no beatings. There was freedom.'

In Mosul, the jihadis knew, they had to take a sophisticated approach, making different appeals to the city's different social strata. To poor Moslawis they promised to expel the city's corrupt plutocrats. To Moslawi plutocrats they promised renewed prominence. They held town hall–style meetings in which Moslawis were encouraged to talk about their ideas about Islam and their hopes for the future. For kids, they held games and Koranic memorization contests. They passed out well-produced literature on the streets. That the organization had relied on corruption to come to power could for the moment be ignored. For now the Caliphate represented a political revolution, a class and generational revolt, at least as much as—maybe more than—an Islamic one. In its concept of Islam, Baghdadi's organization is commonly called Salafi. Salafism is a kind of retrograde Sunni revivalism, sometimes quietist, sometimes violent, that holds that Islam and its territories should return to the practices of the Salaf, the roughly century-long period of Islam's first generations, the time of 'pious predecessors' and 'rightly-guided caliphs.' The American invasion of Iraq was the spark for contemporary Salafism. The sectarian civil war that followed was its first great crucible. But, as one Moslawi researcher put it to me, 'Religious ideology might have been the last point of identification with the Islamic State for many Moslawis.'

One day I accompanied a general, Riyadh Jalal Tawfiq, commander of the 9th and 16th, the only two regular army divisions out of roughly twenty that had proved even remotely capable of fighting the Islamic State over the previous two years, to meet a group of sheikhs and elders. They were from the Shammar tribe, an ancient tribe whose domain stretches across the Levant and Arab Peninsula. The Caliphate could not have taken so much of Iraq without the help of sheikhs, who often wield the real power, sometimes the only power, in places like Nineveh. Many sheikhs opposed the jihadis, some had fought against them, but many backed them, too, just as many had backed al Qaeda. While some may have done so because they agreed with Baghdadi's vision, it's a safe bet that the guiding impulse was pragmatism. The tribes had seen Iraq cycle through so many regimes over the centuries, Muslim rulers, Ottomans, the British, kings, prime ministers, and presidents, Saddam and the Americans and Maliki; they had learned to work with whoever was in power. Like other tribes, the Shammaris were divided over the Islamic State. Some of its families had fought, others abetted.

General Riyadh and every other high-ranking commander at work in Mosul had to take many meetings with sheikhs. Beneath all of the meetings flowed the same undercurrent of awkwardness and hypocrisy. The conversations had their ritual: the general would try to make the sheikh comfortable, emphasizing the Islamic State's foreignness, its criminality, its lunacy; he would assure the sheikh he knew his tribe had opposed the jihadis, had every scorn for these fanatics. The sheikh in turn would agree adamantly; would call the jihadis thieves, drug addicts, morons, dogs, sons of dogs; would recount his own brave stand against the bastards. Together general and sheikh would run through the litany of the Islamic State's non-Iraqi possible origins; it was a Saudi plot, a Turkish plot, a Jewish plot, a homosexual plot. If none but Sunnis were present, Iran would come in for calumny. Shaking his head solemnly, the general would express regret at how the military treated Moslawis before. He would assure the sheikh he'd been opposed to this behavior all the while, had never liked Maliki. The sheikh would agree, cautiously, never mentioning outright the dark-brew hatred for the government and the army that he had felt, that the general knew perfectly well he probably still felt. To keep peace now, the two men would agree, the government needed the sheikhs and the sheikhs the government, otherwise only the devil knew what all internecine bloodletting would result once Mosul was liberated. There was little point in confession or apology. Those were implied, as was the fact that, given slightly different circumstances, this odd couple might be trying to knife each other.

'People have started really cooperating with us,' General Riyadh told the Shammari sheikh and elders. 'Moslawis are helping us identify Daesh. The other day, someone led us to eighteen members. Six or seven weren't important. But the others were important. One was a judge. Another was a real a son of a bitch. Until now, we haven't caught a single jihadi who's sane. They're the most messed up people, you can't imagine. No one with a level head has joined them. No one raised properly.'

The sheikh, his face a mask of civility, began 'Here, there is no Shia, no Sunni, no sectarianism—'

But before he could go on, one of the elders, his brother, broke in.

'Honestly, Mosul was a messed-up city to begin with,' he said. 'Daesh only made it worse.'

Another man added, 'With all due respect to all the original sheikhs, sadly some of our own people went with Daesh.'

The sheikh, trying to resume command of the conversation, said, 'You know, Mosul is famous for its privacy in everything. Now, each one of us is talking about his own family, his private matters. I will tell you, we are three hundred men in my family and not one of us joined the jihadis. Not one of us took that disgusting path. In other families, when someone joined them, the others would copy him. Before you knew it, you had twenty-five guys in one family with Daesh. They weren't doing anything, just sitting in their shops. But they were preparing to fight. But no one from our family. I swear on the Koran.'

His brother spoke up again.

'Daesh, they infiltrated every level of society. Engineers, police, soldiers. That's how they persuaded so many to join. So if someone wanted to just live, to have a normal life, you had to join them. Those people who joined, they mixed solid with liquid. Everything got mixed up. Nowadays, you can't differentiate between old and young, sick and healthy. Your bile is now my bile. Everyone was mixed up in it. Most people didn't have the fortitude to say no to them.'

'The truth is, they revealed people's real faces,' said the other man. 'Don't forget, they came from every background. They were the factory workers, they were the professors, even artists. They had knowledge about everything. They knew how to do anything. They used all of their methods inside Mosul.'

Abu Bakr al-Baghdadi understood that the Islamic State's advent must feel to Moslawis welcome, and, more, foreordained. It must not smack of foreign conspiracy nor of happenstance. He grasped the metaphysics of jihadism better than the garish Zarqawi had, better even than bin Laden. Whatever it had begun as in Afghanistan in the 1980s, al Qaeda central had long since evolved into an elitist cabal of mostly highborn Arab men. Its leaders seemed to spend their time now reproaching the next generation of leaders, men like Zarqawi and Baghdadi. Baghdadi understood that to stay relevant, jihadism must enter the age of digital populism. And to do that, the movement's tone must change, from exclusive to inclusive. His must appear to be an ecumenical theocracy. The Islamic State would be open to all, not just the elect, to men and women, Arab, European, African, Asian, American, born Muslims and converts, people merely considering converting. Only the barest knowledge of the Koran was required, and no knowledge of Arabic, nor of history. On the contrary, the less knowledge of history the better. History until the Caliphate was a lie. You were encouraged to celebrate not just your piety but your individuality, to go online and tell your personal story of awakening and redemption. More than the propaganda coming out of the al-Hayat Media Center, more than the snuff films, it was these stories that brought to the Islamic State new citizens.

Baghdadi understood like few of his vocation that, as William Taber puts it in *The War of the Flea*, the seminal study of insurgency that has become a seminal handbook for insurgents, 'Guerillas are of the people, or they cannot survive, cannot even come into being. Terrorism, while it arouses the popular will to revolt, is at the same time a manifestation of that will.' Though Baghdadi also knew the value of finding more like Zarqawi. He saw the populist power in the spectacle of terrible acts, the truth in Taber's further observation that 'in a revolutionary situation the criminal, the psychopath, may become as good a revolutionary as the idealist.' Or, as Mussolini had put it, 'revolutions must be considered the revenge of madness on good sense.'

On July 4, 2014, Baghdadi climbed the minbar at the Grand al-Nuri Mosque in Mosul, on the western bank of the Tigris, to proclaim the existence of the Caliphate and himself its Caliph. Whether he chose this day to pique Americans he did not say, but it must have been on his mind. More significantly for Iraqis, on the same day Maliki announced he would seek a third term. Like the branding guru he in a way was, Baghdadi declared, first, that his organization was henceforth to be known as the Islamic State, and not the Islamic State in Iraq, nor as the Islamic State in Iraq and al-Sham, nor as ISIS, the acronym with misleading Egyptian overtones that had taken hold in the English-speaking world, nor as ISIL, the variation that replaces al-Sham with Levant, and especially not as Daesh, an acronym for al-Dawla al-Islamiya fi al-Iraq wa al-Sham, which Baghdadi considers derogatory, apparently because it is too close to the Arabic word *daes*, meaning one who is intemperate.

He went on:

> The time has come for those generations that were drowning
> in oceans of disgrace, being nursed in the milk of humilia-
> tion, and being ruled by the vilest of all people, after their long
> slumber in the darkness of neglect—the time has come for them
> to rise. The time has come for the community of Muhammad
> to wake up from its sleep, remove the garments of dishonor,
> and shake off the dust of humiliation and disgrace, for the era
> of lamenting and moaning has gone, and the dawn of honor

has emerged anew. The sun of jihad has risen. The glad tidings of good are shining. Triumph looms on the horizon. The signs of victory have appeared. Here the flag of the Islamic State, the flag of monotheism, rises and flutters. Its shade covers land from Aleppo to Diyala. Beneath it, the walls of the false leaders have been demolished, their flags have fallen, and their borders have been destroyed.... The Sunnis are masters and are esteemed, the heretics are humiliated. The ... legality of all emirates, groups, states, and organizations, becomes null by the expansion of the Caliph's authority and the arrival of its troops into their areas.... So rush Oh Muslims and gather around your Caliph, so that you may return as you once were for ages, kings of the earth and knights of war.... And by Allah, if you disbelieve in democracy, secularism, nationalism, as well as all the other garbage and ideas from the west, and rush to your religion and creed, then by Allah, you will own the earth, and the east and the west will submit to you. This is the promise of Allah to you.

As religious-militia-leader keynote addresses went, this one wasn't overlong, made up mostly of buoyant phrases such as those above and a number of points of housekeeping. Baghdadi went over the implementation of court and school systems, the new Islamic State currency, his intended tax reforms, and offered a series of scholarly justifications for the Caliphate's creation. Thanks to his monotonic voice, his listeners may have missed an important line that came about ten minutes in: 'It is not permissible for anyone who believes in Allah,' Baghdadi said, 'to sleep without considering as his leader whoever conquers them by the sword until he becomes Caliph and is called the leader of the faithful, whether this leader is righteous or sinful.'

Whether this leader is righteous or sinful. Now that he was Caliph, in other words, he would do as he liked. *L'état, c'est moi.* Power is its own argument.

With his incredibly swift advance through Syria and Iraq, Baghdadi had proved an estimable military commander. With the preachment at al-Nuri, he showed himself to be something else again—a demagogue of the first water. It was Baghdadi's first recorded appearance as far as anyone outside the Islamic State could find. Very little was known about him, much less than was known about Zarqawi when Powell made him famous. Listening to the speech, you had to ask not just Who is this guy? but What has this guy been reading? It couldn't just be the Koran, as he would have us believe. His grasp of revolutionary optics was too good, his retributive theory of history too keen, his grievances and irredentism too perfectly rehearsed. He was calling on revolutionary and reactionary traditions in Islam, harking back to the seventh century and to the Abbasids, invoking what the historian of jihad David Cook has called militant Islam's 'collective historical consciousness of a necessity to be superior,' its conviction that the rightful course of history was derailed when Islam put down the sword—but he was evoking much more as well. You heard melodic lines coming in from revolutionary France, from Russian anarchism, from fascist Italy. You caught notes of Saint-Just, Sergey Nechayev, F. T. Marinetti—Marinetti, who had arrived at his Manifesto of Futurism, in 1909, in an Istanbul mosque, of all places. On a hoary old prayer mat, beneath a new electric bulb, ramming past against future, the Italian poet and WWI artillerist 'crushed our ancestral lethargy' and made to 'glorify war—the only hygiene of the world.' Baghdadi, with his jowly jaw and haughty black-eyed scowl, even looked like Marinetti. Enshrouded in black robes and his black-and-gray beard he was otherwise featureless, inscrutable, a digital apparition.

If Baghdadi knew his Taber, and I'd have a hard time believing he hadn't at least skimmed *The War of the Flea*, he disregarded another crucial tenet. The guerilla, writes Taber, 'finds his strength in his freedom from territorial commitments.' I.e., he doesn't start by seizing cities. If the Islamic State's own information, and credible outside sources, are to be believed, between the time of Baghdadi's speech and the fall of 2016 hundreds, perhaps thousands, of men and women from dozens of countries moved to the Caliphate, many to Mosul. But even taking into account all of these people, Baghdadi knew perfectly well he didn't have anything like enough bodies to counter the ten thousand Iraqi forces going into Mosul, to say nothing of the roughly ninety thousand militiamen, Kurdish peshmerga forces, and police massed outside the city; nor to contend with the Australian F-18s, British Typhoons and Tornados, American F-16s, A-10s, F-22s, and B-52s, helicopters and drones flying above it; nor with the batteries of HIMARs and Paladins and Caesars hurtling 155-mm shells from the firebases surrounding it; nor with the squads of international commandos infiltrating it. Baghdadi never announced how many fighters he had in Mosul—outside estimates ranged from several thousand to ten thousand in the whole of Nineveh—but however many they were, they weren't enough.

Surely Baghdadi had known that once he committed to holding territory, and particularly once he held Mosul, his movement and his army would have to become a government? Surely he knew that, whatever disbelief in democracy and secularism he urged in his speech, he would now have to answer to his citizens' democratic complaints and secular demands—that life in the Caliphate wouldn't be all sermons and swordfights? Yes, we know he knew this. We have the Islamic State court records and Islamic State birth certificates and Islamic State school textbooks and letterhead and money to prove he knew it. So, then, cognizant as he was, shrewd as he was, must Baghdadi not also have known that, in attempting to hold a city of Mosul's size, he was forfeiting the tactical advantages of jihad—mobility, surprise, groundlessness—that he was, in his belligerent nostalgia, not rolling the clock all the way back to the Salaf, but only back to the twentieth century, that he was returning post-9/11 combat to conventional warmaking, to a matter of men and machines and materiel, making of Mosul a set-piece battle and giving America what it had been pining after for nearly two decades—the opportunity to confront jihadis straight up, to finally apply the Powell Doctrine, the doctrine of overwhelming force, to the War on Terror? And knowing this, knowing there was no way to hold Mosul, no way to win, must Baghdadi not also have known, even as soon as he took Mosul and proclaimed himself Caliph, that this stunning coup, this achievement his forebears in jihad had only dreamed of, that it also guaranteed his failure—that the apex of his jihad was also its end? Or was that the point?

Maybe that was the point. Baghdadi's theological message to Moslawis was vaguer than his political message. He did not mention his beliefs about the end of the world in his speech, but it was understood that, among the traits handed down to the Islamic State from Zarqawi was a stout apocalypticism. In his dispatches from the Fallujah frontlines in 2004, where he'd commanded Baghdadi, Zarqawi had compared the battle to the seminal wars of Islam's first century and referred to American forces as the new 'Byzantines.' This was a *malahim*, he insisted, an apocalyptic showdown. 'We believe in the portents of the Day of Judgment. We believe in the narration of the Prophet,' Zarqawi would go on to write, the next year, in *Our Creed and Methodology*, the Islamic State's equivalent of the Declaration of Independence—or, maybe more aptly, given the internal bloodletting in the jihadist movement that followed, the Declaration of the Rights of Man and of the Citizen. An ambitious autodidact, Zarqawi appears to have educated himself in Islam's apocalyptic literature, the passages of the Koran and the Hadiths (the sayings of Muhammad and his followers) and commentaries on them that discuss the cataclysms that will precede the Day of Judgment. By the time of his death, Zarqawi had become endlessly resourceful at reading everything as a portent of the end. And, finally, it wasn't just his pornographic violence, nor his insistence on declaring apostasy, nor the fact that the American price on his head came to equal the Sheikh's, that turned bin Laden off him; it was his raving about the Day of Judgment and his crucial role in it. Bin Laden had made his own name formulating a story of Islam's renewal and triumph, promising deliverance to Muslims, *all* Muslims. He wasn't going to have this sadistic parvenu playing the Robespierre to his Danton, hijacking the plot and cutting history short. Bin Laden outlived Zarqawi—there are many who believe bin Laden saw to this—but he lost the argument. Thanks to the American war in Iraq, and then to Zarqawi, contemporary jihadism was shot through with apocalypticism, and the Islamic State was no exception. Indeed, under Baghdadi, the group became messengers of the millennium.

Like other Moslawis who at first welcomed the Islamic State, Abu Fahad tried not to dwell on these questions in late June of 2014. He had seen the new billboards around Mosul, the welcoming ones that read *The Islamic State: A Caliphate in Accordance with the Prophetic Method*, and he knew what that meant. The prophecy foretold the end. But maybe Baghdadi was thinking beyond insurgency, imagining the Caliphate could evolve into a permanent feature of the regional political landscape, like Hezbollah or Hamas. Maybe Baghdadi believed that, like the Taliban, his group could recede and resurge. If Baghdadi was a pragmatist, like any good military commander, Abu Fahad figured, then Mosul stood a chance. But if the Caliph was as thoroughgoing a millenarian as Zarqawi had been—if Baghdadi sought 'to live in this world only for the purposes of bringing about its speedy and total destruction,' as Nechayev had advised the anarchists—then Mosul was in for a very ugly time of it, Abu Fahad knew. All he could do was direct his hope toward one of the first scenarios. Abu Fahad wasn't a zealot. He wasn't even particularly devout. He hated Maliki, but he didn't hate Shiites as such. He had Shia friends. But he had watched his country invaded, occupied, turned upon itself; his city degraded from a 'paradise,' as he described the Mosul of his youth, to a hell; his wife killed; himself and his family and friends humiliated by soldiers of the army he'd once nursed to health; his children driven mad, denigrated, denied futures. To a man like that, sane as he is, talk of a millenarian utopia, of any utopia, of any improvement of life beyond the malediction it has become, holds promise.

'They told us "We will not stop until we reach Rome!"' Abu Fahad told me, quoting the Islamic State rallying cry, taken from the medieval caliphs. 'I thought, let's start with Baghdad, then we can talk about Rome.'

And at first, he went on, Baghdadi's people were as good as their word. Not only did they not ruin Mosul in conquering it, as some Moslawis had feared they would, but they improved it. They opened new markets, fixed sewers, lowered rents, collected donations for the poor. They hired an army of trash collectors to clean up the streets. They built new roads. An engineer at the state power company who kept his job under the Caliphate, as so many municipal employees did, told me the Islamic State began installing electricity meters in houses to cut down on waste and graft. It didn't work, but it was a good idea. Abu Fahad was asked to stay on in his job at the hospital and readily agreed.

The Caliphate promulgated a new city constitution. Its sixteen clauses encouraged Moslawis to live peaceably, promised justice for all, and forbade the ownership of weapons. For months the religious police didn't bother men about smoking or growing out their beards or changing their dress. Women were asked to wear longer, looser abayas, but were not made to cover themselves entirely.

'In the beginning, we felt safer with Daesh,' Abu Fahad said. 'There was *more* peace, not less.'

The jihadis renamed their seized territories. The portion of Nineveh they controlled they changed to Wilayat Ninawa, in the Ottoman tradition. They kept Qadisiya, Abu Fahad's neighborhood, named as it was for the location of one of the decisive battles of early Islam, where, in 636 A.D., the Prophet Muhammad's followers first vanquished the Persians. The name of Abu Omar's neighborhood, Zahra, they weren't as keen on. They redubbed it Zarqawi, in honor of their martyred progenitor.

As I prepared to leave Abu Fahad's tent, the subject of his brother came up. Besides the tent imbroglio, there was another reason behind their falling-out. According to Abu Omar, Abu Fahad's son, Loy, had not just welcomed the Islamic State like his father. He had joined it and fought for it. Without mentioning this, I asked Abu Fahad about his son—whether he was still in Mosul, if he was staying safe. He said he was and, after some time, conceded that Loy had been very enthusiastic about the Caliphate, more than anyone else in the family.

'He was very religious,' Abu Fahad said. Loy had been driven to extreme devotion by his mother's death. 'And to tell you the truth, he did support their ideology. But he didn't support their actions.'

He clearly sensed I'd heard more.

'If you've been told anything else about Loy, don't believe it,' he said.

3

During the battles for Ramadi and Fallujah, those cities emptied out, their residents leaving for camps or fleeing to safety in other parts of the country or world. The Mosul operation was vastly more complicated because so many Moslawis didn't leave, at least not immediately. Some stayed because the Caliphate was executing people who tried to escape the city, some because they refused to abandon infirm family members or leave their houses to be looted, some because they'd worked with the Caliphate in some capacity—many, many more Moslawis had done this than will ever admit to it—and worried they'd be killed or imprisoned. But most stayed because they were asked to. In the days before the Mosul operation commenced, the military dropped leaflets from helicopters onto the streets, requesting residents not flee. They would be protected, residents were assured. The Iraqi security forces had changed. They were no longer in the business of abusing their fellow citizens. Moslawis would be safe.

The generals decided on this tack in part because three million Iraqis had already been displaced by the war against the Islamic State by the time it reached Mosul, and the country could not absorb another mass exodus. But the generals were also placing a wager: that they could use the civilian population to their advantage. Their intelligence suggested that, after two-and-a-half years of deprivations and depravations, Moslawis' anger at the Islamic State was as hot as it had been at the government before the city's fall. If the security forces behaved, Moslawis could be a source of assistance, intelligence, good publicity. And at first the wager paid out. The troops saw protecting Moslawis as no less important than killing jihadis. They treated civilian wounds, helped them salvage their homes, bury their dead, gave them food and cigarettes, played with their kids. The Moslawis in turn opened their homes to the soldiers, cooked for them, warned them of booby traps and weapons caches, helped them identify collaborators.

In the battle's first months, the soldiers were greeted as saviors, with tears and kisses, hugs and hosannas. The jihadis had been greeted by many Moslawis as saviors, too, it is true, and a lot of the people now kissing and helping the soldiers would, three years earlier, have run them out of town, but the effusion was no less sincere for that, I am convinced. There was a real mutual understanding, Moslawis having lived under the Caliphate for so long, the troops having fought it for almost as long. Some soldiers were frustrated with the slow pace of the siege and blamed the bothersome residents, or saw all Moslawis as insurgents—but most soldiers I got to know, like Karim and Ali and Rasul, genuinely felt for Moslawis, admired their resilience and stoicism. This though most of the soldiers were Shia, from Baghdad and points south, while most Moslawis were northern Sunni Arabs. You could call it a suspension of disbelief. The deeper function, I sensed, was a certain native preference for forgiveness.

The interactions between the civilians and troops could be heartening, or disturbing, or funny, or heartbreaking, sometimes all of those things. They were always interesting.

One day, I witnessed this scene:

By December, the troops had fought their way to a neighborhood called Adan, about halfway between Zahra and the Tigris. CTS troops were conducting a food distribution at an intersection, where hundreds of Moslawis had gathered. As usual, there were not enough ration boxes, and the crowd shouted and raced among the trucks, vying for what was left. Soldiers fired into the air to try to keep order.

At the command post, in a commandeered house, they bundled into the courtyard a middle-aged man in a greasy blazer, tracksuit pants, and sandals. He had been caught driving a car. In the military-controlled sectors, Moslawis were not allowed to drive vehicles other than donkey carts. The man was softly protesting his innocence to a lieutenant.

'I wasn't—'

'Don't raise your voice with me!' the lieutenant barked. 'What are you doing? You're saying you weren't helping Daesh?'

'No, I wasn't helping them. I was only using the car.'

'You were using the car to help them.'

'I, well, that is—'

'So what, you were just playing with the car?'

'I swear to God—'

'Leave God out of it. If God had any luck, he wouldn't have given you your brain. Who do you think you're fooling? What were you doing with the car?'

'I helped a family.'

The lieutenant snorted contemptuously. The man improved his posture and, clearing his throat, attempted to change his tone to one of solemn formality.

'My dear sir,' he commenced, 'please allow me to—'

But the lieutenant was now on his phone. The man looked to one of the soldiers and said, 'You see, it was only me and my brother . . .' as he was led inside.

A woman entered the courtyard with her teenage son and young daughter. The lieutenant greeted her warmly and familiarly as she confidently pulled off her chador. The lieutenant led her and her children through the house into a back room. He pulled back a heavy curtain to reveal floor-to-ceiling windows and a glass door leading onto a narrow deck and a high dividing wall. This family lived in the house on the wall's other side. They had left when the fighting in Adan had begun, a few days earlier, and now they couldn't return to their house because the street on which it sat was the front line. But they could get to it through the command post. Each day, the lieutenant helped them check on their home.

Her son, who appeared to be about thirteen, bounded up onto the wall and from there leapt onto a metal awning on the second floor of their house. The daughter, perhaps seven, held her mother's hand and they both followed the boy with their eyes.

'Go in through the window,' his mother called.

'I know, mom,' he called back.

'They broke it anyway,' she added to the lieutenant.

'It's ok, just check,' he said, 'see what's there.'

'Our neighbor's place was hit by a mortar,' she said.

Her son yelled something.

'Open the door to the kitchen!' she yelled back, and, to the lieutenant, 'You think I'm scared, but I'm only afraid of God.'

He smiled.

The son emerged, threw a scarf to his mother, and leapt down.

'God bless your family,' the lieutenant said as he led them back out.

While most soldiers I knew did go to great lengths to protect civilians, the favor was not extended to suspected jihadis. If you spent time in Mosul, you eventually saw prisoners beaten, tortured, and, with enough time, murdered. A journalist friend was with a band of federal police. He awoke in the middle of the night to gargled screams. He sat up to see a prisoner with wires attached to his appendages. The police were sending electricity into the man. A group of soldiers I spent a night with showed my colleague a video of them decapitating a prisoner with a small, blunt knife. A major I met had trained as an attorney. When the war was over he wanted to practice human rights law. He had a policy of summarily executing captives he believed to be jihadis. When I asked how he squared this with his professional aims, he explained the Islamic State had forfeited its human rights. 'It's true we have human rights here and that sometimes terrorists get trials, but Daesh doesn't deserve anything like that. They kill innocents at every opportunity.' I offered no rejoinder to the major. He was killed by an IED not long after.

Most of the interactions I saw between soldiers and suspected jihadis were more ambiguous. One day I watched this:

I was sharing a hookah with a sergeant when a middle-aged man approached. His teenage son dragged his feet alongside him. The man wanted to turn over his son, he explained to the sergeant, because he had taken a job as a street cleaner with the Islamic State. The job had lasted ten days, a year earlier. The sergeant, whose name was Salam, wasn't overly interested. Nor was the son, Idris, whose expression suggested this was only the latest in a years-long litany of paternal complaint. Salam, the left side of whose head was mottled by a burn scar, asked the father why he was only turning in Idris now.

'Because yesterday the minister announced that those who worked for Daesh but did not bloody their hands will be forgiven,' the father said. 'I swear, he has not done anything bad. If he had, I wouldn't have turned him in. I would have helped him escape.'

Salam asked Idris if what his father said was true. Idris said it was. He'd been a student but dropped out when the Islamic State took over his school, he explained, and went to work at his uncle's tea shop. The religious police shut it down because of the hookahs, he added, looking at Salam's hookah.

'Did you take the job because you needed the money?' Salam asked.

'Yes,' Idris said. 'I needed money to buy a motorcycle.'

I laughed, then stopped laughing when I saw no one else was laughing. I was the only one among us who found this funny, apparently.

'He's a young man,' the father said. Salam nodded. A young man, a motorcycle—fair enough. But, his father went on, he didn't want Idris riding a motorcycle, and while he liked that his son was motivated to get a job, he didn't want him working for the Caliphate. Salam nodded. On top of everything else, the father continued, Idris had informed his boss in the Islamic State of his father's contempt for the group.

'He told them I didn't like them,' the father said. 'That's why they jailed me and beat me.'

A small audience of locals and soldiers had gathered by this point, each newcomer being filled in on the family drama, and they murmured disapprovingly when they heard this. However, when Idris and his father agreed that, whatever else their faults, the Islamic State had taken sanitation very seriously, the audience murmured in agreement.

'Don't lie to me,' Salam said to Idris. 'Did you join Daesh because you fought with your father?'

Idris shrugged.

'Yeah.'

'This is what happened in Mosul—every kid who fought with his dad joined Daesh,' Salam said. 'Well, if he didn't do anything bad, he can just go.'

Another soldier intervened. He was short and athletically built, with a necklace and teeth that competed for space in his mouth. He had the air of one those lesser players on the high school football team who makes up for his lack of field time with arbitrarily cruel tackles of his teammates during practice.

'So you were only a garbage man?' he said to Idris. 'You could have at least been a fighter.'

He stepped behind Idris and belligerently caressed his neck with one hand. With the other he dangled over Idris's shoulder an adjustable wrench. It was too small to be overtly menacing, but he turned it in his palm and retracted and clamped the jaw in such a way to suggest it held torturous possibilities Idris could only imagine. The boy's eyes went wide.

'Ibrahim, have you become an investigator?' Salam said.

'How do we know if his file is clean?' Ibrahim said. 'What if later we find there's more to it?'

'If we take in everyone who's worked with Daesh at some point,' Salam said, 'we'll have to take in all Mosul.'

Idris's father, by now clearly regretting his decision to turn Idris over, repeated that he was certain his son had done nothing wrong. But it was too late. Idris was brought into a requisitioned house and patted down. In a back bedroom, his ankles and wrists were tied with cloth and he was pressed onto the floor. Ibrahim came in and sat on the bed across from him.

'Look at you. Just look at you. You were even working with them. We'll just wait for the intelligence officer and then we'll see.'

The intelligence officer arrived with Idris's father in tow.

'So you're saying your son hasn't done anything and that you're turning him in just for being a garbage man? This makes no sense,' the officer said. And to Idris: 'Let me give you some advice. Just be honest with us. Tell us everything. If you don't tell us the whole story now, and we find other sources who tell us more, you know what will happen? You'll just be killed and tossed in the street with the rest of Daesh.'

Over the course of the afternoon, locals filed in to have a look at the captive. Idris looked up at them blankly, they down at him unimpressed. Ibrahim and a younger, gentler soldier walked in and out of the bedroom, addressing Idris with threats and placations. They appeared to want to enact a good-cop-bad-cop routine, a vaudevillian one. The gentle soldier brought Idris a foam container of rice and tomato sauce, and untied his wrists. Idris said he wasn't hungry.

'Animal!' Ibrahim yelled at him. 'If he tells you eat, you eat! Drink, you drink! If one of us tells you that you have to throw yourself into a fire, you'll do it.'

'Listen, we're not telling you to throw yourself in a fire,' the gentle soldier said. 'We're just telling you to eat.'

'This animal here, we tell him to eat, and he won't. Son of a donkey! Animal! Son of a sheep!'

Another soldier came in and said to Idris, 'Imagine if you get married one day and have kids, and your son goes and does something like you've done. How would you feel?'

Idris ate. After lunch, Ibrahim took a nap on the bed across from him as Idris looked on. When he awoke, Idris said he wanted to pray.

'Of course, now you want to pray! If I were you, and had decided to join Daesh, I would have at least worked in a supermarket, something that would have fed me. Not a garbage man. They're garbage, and you were their garbage man. Garbage and garbage! How did you come up with that? What's the matter, your head isn't clear? Let me clear it for you.'

Ibrahim slapped Idris.

'Is it clear now?'

'I swear I've done nothing,' Idris whimpered.

'Don't worry,' the gentle soldier said. 'It will be all right.'

Every CTS position I saw in Mosul was as insecure as the one in Zahra. No checkpoints, no regular sentries, sometimes not even a perimeter. Locals wandered in and out. The soldiers were usually obliging. Near the triage station in Gogjali, on a slope overlooking east Mosul, was a nascent neighborhood, a scattering of freestanding structures, half-finished homes, cinderblock foundations. Some were inhabited by their owners or refugees, others abandoned. One of the latter, a modest one-story house that once aspired to two stories, had held enemy fighters or served as a stopping place for them as they tried to escape the city. On the cement floor of the small courtyard was a discarded Rhodesian ammunition chest rig and by that, in a sink, a pile of hair of what had once been a beard. Occasionally you came upon just such perfect tableaux.

CTS had moved in. To my untrained eye, this at first appeared to be just another command post in a requisitioned home like the one in Zahra. Someone better versed than myself in the instruments of high-tech warfare would have understood the significance of the large aerials on the roof and on the APC idling in front. What I noticed was that, on the ground floor, the soldiers who sat on the overstuffed wall-to-wall sofa set smoking and drinking tea and studying their phones, as they would have done in any command post, were also shooting covetous glances at the stairwell, on which they were not permitted. It wasn't until I ascended the stairs that I saw why this was: on what would have been the second level, and was now instead a kind of terrace, was the coalition's forward air command. From here the air war on Mosul was being directed.

It was a sparse and alarmingly vulnerable affair. To the south, the terrace was blocked from view by a wall, the only wall. The rest was surrounded by a waist-high parapet, meaning it was exposed on three sides. From a decent vantage to the north or west or east, you could have monitored it, or shot at it, or shelled it. There didn't appear to be such a vantage, but then there didn't appear to be much of anything, so filled was the air with smoke and dust. That the place was never blown up by the jihadis seems a miracle.

On any given day there were several Iraqi generals on the terrace and officers from at least three different national militaries. The operation revolved around an Iraqi colonel, the Joint Terminal Attack Controller. He was the nexus among the CTS field commanders, the Iraqi high command and the coalition, and, happily for everyone, he was one of the best-liked officers in CTS, a favorite of foreigners, particularly of the Americans. He spoke perfect American English and perfect American military jargon in a perfect American accent that he had either picked up on a stateside base or won through a Higgins-esque gift for mimicry. He discussed *helos* and *mike-mikes* with total confidence. A pair of two-way radios and a quartet of smartphones passed in endless cycle through his hands. Sometimes he handed a phone to one of the pair of air controllers who sat at a folding table facing onto the city. The two men wore CTS uniforms, but that was a ruse. Fine of feature and haughty of glance, they could have been spotted as European, and specifically Gallic, from one of the Reaper drones flying twenty-thousand feet above us. They spoke rapid-fire French to one another and slow English and Arabic to the others. They monitored a tablet computer that displayed camera feeds from the UAVs and typed on a laptop whose screen was tiled with chat windows. It was through these that strike requests were relayed and discussed. Over the radios came British, Australian, and American accents from various coalition offices and aircraft.

When things were busy, everyone doing their job and appreciating the others doing their jobs, the strike requests coming in, being passed up the chain, being granted, the bombs coming in, rumbling the city, the terrace was a nervy, comradely spectacle, and it gave you a glimpse of the grandeur, if I can use that word, of this war, of war. There was no better outcrop from which to bear witness to the sheer mystical velocity of twenty-first-century mechanized-digitized combat. Words were spoken, words were written, and then missiles hurtled from the sky. Words into bombs. Speech into death. The jihadis may have believed they were carrying out God's will, but the men on this terrace could summon it.

I would find out later that the strike request exchanges were taking place on a WhatsApp channel. Armies, air forces, an infinity of munitions, and it was all being orchestrated via a free chat application you download to your phone in five seconds. I didn't know whether to be amazed or appalled. I was amazed *and* appalled. It was farcical. It was ingenious. It was perhaps the single densest example of a technological current in the war I could only think to call occult. And once you started noticing them, the occult techno-wrinkles were everywhere. There was that magical GPS mapping application the troops had on their phones, like a self-aware cellular sand table. There were the videos of engagements, uploaded and transferred instantaneously, so that fighters on one front could get their *lolz* or shed their tears watching fighters on another. There were the privately recorded videos of executions and torture, countless of them, shared round the theater on WhatsApp and Signal and Telegram, uploaded by jihadis and soldiers alike, dwarfing in number and sometimes in horror the official videos the al-Hayat Media Center put out. Everyone knew someone who'd been killed on the Internet. There were the pictures on Facebook—soldiers with prisoners, soldiers with rubble, soldiers with body parts, soldiers with corpses, soldiers with Americans, soldiers with their mothers. Anything would do. One infantryman showed me a picture of him in Baiji, standing in front of his Humvee before the flattened cityscape holding a giant blue teddy bear. Another showed me a picture of his three-year-old son at home handling a pistol. ('I want him to learn to fight.') Aside from everything else happening on it, Facebook was hosting a kind of underground war economy. I met a Yazidi woman who was captured by the jihadis and brought to Syria. She escaped with the help of a people-smuggler her husband found on the site, where you could also buy and sell looted archeological artifacts. You could sit for hours at a checkpoint or in a command post with the troops as they scrolled through one app after another, browsing this cyber-hem of the war, and I often did. But anyone in the world who wanted to tune into this fight could, without filters. Never had a war been so uncensored.

The technology could get to be too much. I knew an intelligence officer whose impossible job it was to stand in the waves of Moslawis as they fled from embattled neighborhoods, asking their names. He was like a lone pier pole in a typhoon. When someone took pity on him and stopped, he would check their name against a database of suspected jihadis which he held before him on an iPad. One day I saw him and asked how many names the database had grown to.

'Thirty-eight thousand,' he said.

'How many matches have you had?'

'Four.'

Then there was simple talking on the phone. In its modest way, this was the most astounding technological achievement of all. The Islamic State forbade phones and disabled the cell towers and televisions in Mosul. In liberated neighborhoods you'd see green circles with lines through them spray-painted on the privacy walls on corners. These were signs from the jihadi engineers that meant the satellite dishes on that block had been confiscated or disabled. But this was 2016, for god's sake. God himself couldn't have gotten rid of all the cellphones in Mosul if he'd wanted to. Moslawis found ways to keep their phones and to talk on them, lying down below parapets in the dead of night, whispering, crouching in closets, climbing into bushes in gardens. It was impossible to truly enslave anyone in a country where 3G was standard.

The jihadis took pictures, too. A disturbingly high percentage of them included house cats. They loved cats because the Prophet Muhammad is said to have loved cats. I defy you to find a stranger image than a bearded man in a headscarf holding aloft an assault rifle in one hand, pointing to the heavens with the index finger of the other, while beside him, staring into the lens, is a cat.

I would love to know the mental acrobatics the camera-shy Baghdadi went through to sanction all this. He knew the Internet and social media were essential to his success, and yet he was too sanctimonious and too old (born in 1971, we think) to be entirely comfortable with it. What was *that* pitch meeting like? *You see, my Caliph, what we'd like to do is live as though it's the seventh century, as you suggest, except for the apps. We keep our apps. The Salaf, but with Google and stuff.*

In the 1960's, Jerry Rubin said that to be a revolutionary you needed a color television. The Islamic State updated this: to be a jihadi you needed a smartphone. You impose future upon past, collapse time, by gorging on an eternal digital present. War has always been defined by and best described with paradox and irony, and this is as true of holy war as any other kind of war. The central paradox of modernday jihad? Its idea of time. The jihadi would roll the clock back by kicking it forward. 'Salafism,' writes the scholar of jihad Shiraz Maher, is 'a philosophy that believes in progression through regression.' Is the jihadi a radical or a reactionary? An irredentist or a futurist? Both, he would say, not seeing the contradiction. He is an historical ironist with no sense of irony.

Sometimes the men on the terrace left off talking and typing to gaze onto the smoldering city. What did they feel, if anything, I wondered. Accomplishment? Vindication? Awe? Mortification? They couldn't see the death they caused, not really. You almost never saw someone die in an airstrike. Usually they destroyed buildings. If the missile hit a jihadi vehicle or mortar team in the open, the drone cameras might pick up a body or body part. But that was rare. You saw the plume, maybe a large piece of frag spiraling slowly in the air. With the air so thick, though, mostly you just heard and felt the impacts.

Naturally, Washington claimed that the accuracy of this air war was second to none. So-called deliberate strikes on Islamic State positions and assets, the result of surveillance and intelligence work-ups, were so vetted, so pinpoint, American military officials assured journalists, that the number of accidental civilian casualties would prove vanishingly low. Even the dynamic strikes, the spontaneous responses to the strike requests being called in by field commanders, had to be approved by a chain of generals and lawyers that stretched from Mosul to Baghdad to Florida. If you were on the U.S. Central Command email list, you received from MacDill Air Force Base, in Tampa, a daily email, subject heading *Strike Release*, that listed the previous day's targets in Iraq and Syria. Sometimes there were several, sometimes several dozen, but no matter how many there were, Centcom implied, with a lack of any information to the contrary, every strike was a resounding success. Every missile hit its target and only that, destroying x piece of jihadi equipment or x piece of jihadi-held infrastructure, killing x number of jihadis. At the bottom of every email was this explainer: 'A strike, as defined in the Coalition release, refers to one or more kinetic engagements that occur in roughly the same geographic location to produce a single, sometimes cumulative effect in that location.' And this disclaimer: 'These strikes were conducted as part of Operation Inherent Resolve, the operation to destroy ISIS in Iraq and Syria. The destruction of ISIS targets in Iraq and Syria also further limits the group's ability to project terror and conduct external operations throughout the region and the rest of the world.'

But standing on that terrace, if you were being honest with yourself, you had to smell horseshit. The missiles were coming in constantly and they were being directed by a bunch of guys using WhatsApp in an abandoned building. How accurate could they really be?

In the early days of the battle, the Iraqi generals were what I called welcoming but what any military professional in a less companionable country would, rightly, call wildly indiscreet. They allowed me and other journalists to hang out on the air command terrace all day. The French-speaking pair regarded us with indifference. The only people who clearly wanted us to leave—certainly the most advisable attitude—were the Americans, but they deferred to their Iraqi counterparts. Every morning a Special Forces contingent pulled up to the air command in a fleet of jaunty new Joint Light Tactical Vehicles. It was never clear who they were, whether SEALs, Green Berets, Army Delta, or something else. They wore no unit insignia nor rank indicators and no one was going to ask. They looked exactly as you had come to expect such men to look since those officially unofficial photos of bearded commandos on horseback had trickled into American newsrooms from the Hindu Kush in late 2001: mid-to-late thirties, rangy, nimble, watchful, reproachful, bearded, bearded with beards that seemed to grow as much from their modified MP5 and SR-25 rifles as their faces, beards with their own air of predation. They didn't acknowledge you aside from an expressionless glance, maybe a quarter-inch nod if they understood you to be American. The one time I exchanged words with one, I offered him a coffee. The better roadside groceries on Highway 2 stocked cold sweetened Turkish coffee, the cans barrel-shaped and heavy, and I always carried at least a half dozen in my backpack, along with at least two packs of cigarettes, to smoke myself and to offer to Iraqi soldiers as an icebreaker.

'Coffee?' I said, holding up a can to a square-jawed, blue-eyed, golden-bearded man on the terrace.

'No, thanks,' he said, politely and in such a way that we could share in the groveling irrelevance of the gesture and his contempt for me.

In Iraq, the Mosul offensive had at least two names. The first was Operation Fatah. The word means victory or conquest in Arabic, and refers specifically to the conquests of the first century of Islam. The Iraqi media tended to prefer Operation Nineveh We Are Coming, or, sometimes, Operation We Are Coming Nineveh. Both versions made the offensive sound like a number from *Godspell*, but at least you felt pangs of solidarity when you saw NINEVEH WE ARE COMING superimposed in chyron in the upper corner of Iraqi television newscasts. The same could not be said for the name used by the Americans, who insisted on calling it Operation Inherent Resolve. Another of the Pentagon's witless fumblings for meaning, this. Leaving aside the contradiction—either something is the product of resolution or it is inherent, it is not both—inherent as opposed to what, you had to ask. Extrinsic? Provisional? Was there some lesser theater of this war being treated to Operation Incidental Appointment? 'Inherent Resolve' had a faintly begrudging air, too, I always thought, as though Washington were saying to Baghdad 'We'll help you, because we are exceptionally principled people, not because we don't blame you for your mess.'

You didn't need to see actual Americans to be reminded of the American era in Iraq. Reminders were everywhere. Sometimes they were encouraging or amusing.

Combat in east Mosul stretched into the new year. By the middle of January 2017, the Iraqi troops were in shooting distance of the Tigris. On the 13th, they captured Mosul University. The immense campus, which had once accommodated thirty thousand students, spread down a slope toward the river. After seizing the university two-and-a-half years earlier, the Islamic State had closed the social science, earth science, humanities, literature, and art departments, everything but the medical and engineering schools. A young man I met who had been pursuing a history degree once asked a jihadi why. What was the point of forbidding the study of even Islamic history?

'We have a new history,' the jihadi told him. 'We have the *right* history.'

It was rumored the chemical engineering department had been kept open so chemical weapons could be manufactured. Whether or not this was true, the coalition felt it necessary to bomb the university painstakingly. After Iraqi troops secured the campus, journalists rushed there, hoping to find who knows what, beakers of green bubbling liquid, maybe. What they found instead was hill after hill of rubble. It was by far the most devastated quarter of east Mosul. This didn't intimidate the students and professors who were clamoring to return to class. Within days they were back on the campus.

Among the charred remains of the academic buildings, you could see evidence of that brief period of Moslawi-American bonhomie in 2003. There were American-donated computers and books and furniture. Professors spoke to me fondly of David Petraeus, who had made building up the university a priority. Now both the Nineveh provincial government, working in exile from Irbil, and Baghdad claimed they had no money to help mend the campus, so the students and professors had begun taking matters into their own hands, fixing and cleaning, bringing supplies and tools from home. I met a group as they gathered in the vestibule of the languages and literature building, where the jihadis had set alight a pile of desks and bookshelves. The building was equipped with a sprinkler system and the flames had been quickly extinguished. Students were now pushing brooms across the slate floor toward the entranceway, sweeping out begrimed water and wood shards. One leaned his broom against the wall and approached me. Would I like to see the building? he asked. Indeed I would. We walked the halls. He pointed into empty classrooms, telling what courses had been taught in them. I nodded and made loud noises of approval. We looked in at the language lab, where two professors were repairing a window frame.

'I don't see the reason we're not back here studying,' the student, whose name was Karam, told me. 'There's everything. There's chairs.'

He was an English literature major, and, outside of the occasional minor syntactical error, spoke marvelous English, with a grasp of obscure idiom and a talent for both immodesty and self-effacement.

'This used to be my classroom. I sat at the front, of course.'

'Teacher's pet?' I asked.

'Not really. Because I'm smart, not because I love teachers. I love to study. Our studies were interesting. I wasn't the best student in high school because we had physics and mathematics and stuff. I don't like those stuffs. English is really my passion. Shall we go on?'

As we ascended a flight of stairs, a courtly presence materialized at my side.

'My favorite professor,' Karam said.

'I teach English poetry,' the professor said. 'Renaissance. Wyatt, Surrey, Raleigh. Wyatt was the first one to bring Italian poetry into English, you know. Then he was the first to define the sonnet.' None of which interested the jihadis, of course. 'They said that poetry is forbidden. *Haram*, they called it.'

Unlike many of his colleagues, who found work in other parts of the country, the professor had stayed in Mosul under the Caliphate. He'd taken the time to translate into Arabic a dictionary of literary symbols and to read a lot of Donne. 'I like how he expressed his feelings through ideas.' He'd reread Macbeth, too, because it felt relevant. 'But especially the poem that is appropriate for our situation, *The Waste Land*. In the Islamic State, thought stopped. Only survival mattered. We only move. We can just move. Eat and sleep. Mind stops.'

Macbeth also meant a lot to Karam, a theater buff with a gothic bent. He'd been working on a paper about Marlowe's *Doctor Faustus* when the department was closed. He was fascinated, he told me, by 'the deal that the doctor made. The idea is interesting. To see how he suffered. How he gave himself to the devil, for a purpose, and then he lost everything. He wasn't happy.' The resonance with jihadism was enough that neither of us had to remark on it.

We walked into the English library. Miraculously, the jihadis hadn't touched it. I read out titles, seeing what caught Karam's fancy. *Lord of the Flies*. Didn't know it. *Portrait of the Artist as a Young Man*. Maybe he'd read it. *Jane Eyre*. Boring. *Joseph Andrews*—

'—So boring,' Karam said, which was how he felt about most of the alleged classics he'd been made to read. 'We read *Wuthering Heights* as first-years. It's really boring too. Truly, I think that. And most other students think that as well.' While waiting for the university to reopen, he'd read thirty novels, some for future coursework, some for pleasure. The highlight, the book from which he'd learned the most about human nature and the dark depths of the soul, he said, was Stephen King's *Pet Cemetery*. Certain resonances with jihadism occurred to me and perhaps to Karam as well. He and a classmate were trying to convince their professors to introduce more current fare into the curriculum. 'If we studied something really modern like *The Da Vinci Code*—that would be really cool.'

Some Islamist movements have found their first flowering on university campuses. Such was the case with the Taliban, for instance. This doesn't appear to have happened at Mosul University. Karam could think of only one student in his department who'd joined the Islamic State. Of this his classmates learned only after the boy had died. The loss wasn't widely mourned. He had been a blowhard and not much of a scholar.

'He used to be high all the time, actually,' Karam said. 'He got killed at the end of 2014. When he got killed, we're not supposed to be happy about people's deaths, but we were.' He and the late jihadi had had one friend in common, an aspiring anarcho-nihilist. Now *he* had been a good student, Karam said. Very sharp. I pointed out the Islamic State was nihilist in its way. Karam considered this. 'Maybe, maybe. The nihilist boy, he was really sad when his friend the jihadi was killed.'

Usually the reminders of the American era were not encouraging nor amusing. One day I was with General Riyadh, who, as the operations in the east wound down, had been tapped to oversee that side of the city once it was pacified. He was looking for a headquarters, and was driving around town inspecting abandoned mansions for the purpose. The house we walked into now was on a hillside near the university. There were no obvious signs that jihadis had lived in it, but it had been looted and picked over and the contents of the drawers of the desks and bureaus that had once inhabited the rooms, of which there were, in the local custom, far too many, too small and oddly shaped, had been turned out into piles on the floors. While the general and his retinue looked around, I knelt over a pile in a hallway.

In it were the personal papers of the man who appeared to have owned the house in the early years of the occupation. He was an engineer by trade and had done well by the Americans. There were contracts and certificates for payment, issued by the 101st Aviation Brigade for the reconstruction of an airfield totaling several hundred thousand dollars. Below these was an Arabic newspaper called *Other Direction: An Independent Weekly Political Journal.* The issue date was August 12, 2006. An amateurish photomontage on the cover showed a crying woman and child with American soldiers layered in, appearing to converge on them. The story concerned the case of Steven Green, a Kentuckian private in the 101st who was accused of killing an Iraqi family, not in Mosul but Mahmudiya, a village south of Baghdad. After the murders, Green had allegedly raped the one survivor, a fourteen-year-old girl, then killed her, too. She'd become known as The Virgin of Mahmudiya.

Green's case had made headlines in the States, though nothing like in Iraq. It would come out during the trial that Green had been a severely abused child, beaten mercilessly by his brother, referred to by his mother as 'demon spawn.' Like many enlistees who joined the Army in the mid-2000s, when it was so desperate for volunteers to go to Iraq, Green had been granted a 'moral waiver' for his stints in jail. He was a reader, an autodidact who found the books to justify his hatred. A senior officer was surprised to see Rousseau in his bunk bookshelf. Green had theories. 'This is almost like a race war, a cultural war,' he told friends, as the journalist Jim Frederick recounts in *Black Hearts*, his book about the Mahmudiya case. 'And anyone who is not going to go fight in it is a coward. They can say it's about this or that, but it's really about religion. It's about not even which culture is going to rule the Middle East, but which culture is going to rule the West.' A lieutenant who tried to befriend him recalled that Green eventually came to believe that everything, even the West, ought to be consumed in this global war, that 'pretty much everybody beside himself was bad. Democrats were bad. Republicans were bad. JFK was an idiot. Abraham Lincoln was a dumb ass. Everybody outside of his town in Texas was an idiot. But then, all the people inside his town were idiots too. 'If we just killed everybody in Iraq,' Green would say, 'we could go home.' An editorial in *Other Direction* concluded, 'The only way to wash away the American shame is to give [Green] the death penalty.' Green wasn't given the death penalty but the editorialist's wish was granted after a fashion. Five years after being convicted, Green hanged himself in his prison cell.

Other stories in the paper described a massacre in Najaf and the fighting between Hezbollah and Israel. A headline asked, 'Who is Responsible for the Collapse of the Mideast?' It was a rhetorical question, of course. Another editorial, entitled 'Thanks America, But . . . ', read:

> Every nice gesture deserves a thank you. After the Americans occupied Iraq in April 2003, with the reason of finding weapons of mass destruction, they said they wanted to do away with dictatorship and create democracy. This deserves a thank you. But what is the truth? I hear some politicians thanking America, and I'd like to say thank you in my own way. So thank you America, you freed Iraq, which used to be one country. And now you want to divide it, as a favor to the Jews.

I found another newspaper in the pile. It contained a full-page cartoon showing George W. Bush as a sweating Uncle Sam with the body and ears of a kangaroo. He was holding a rifle and had pipelines for feet. They dripped oil into a puddle beside a skull. On the kangaroo Bush's pouch was branded the Star of David and inside it were crowded a man holding a clutch of boom microphones and a placard reading *Abu Dollar*; a sheikh with another placard reading *Persistence and Shame*; and an old woman, her breasts hanging over the fringe of the pouch, who may or may not have been Golda Meir, and whose own placard read *American British Jews in Kangaroo*. It was a suggestive if perplexing scene.

Toward the bottom of the pile I found the engineer's passport. The monochrome photograph showed a man of noble visage. Below his abbreviated, steeply sloped forehead were a thick, painterly brow, narrow eyes, turgid cheeks, a resolutely level mouth, and an adamant, slightly cleft chin. He wore a checkered blazer and an open-collar Oxford. When I picked up the passport, from the pages fell the left half of a torn color snapshot. The photo appeared to have been taken at the birthday of a little boy, maybe the engineer's son. A woman in a floral robe kneels beside the boy. The boy kneels forward, over a cake. They are smiling.

Of the Iraqi generals I got to know, I liked General Riyadh the best. He understood Mosul politics as well as anyone in the Iraqi military. He had been the army commander in Nineveh in the late 2000s, when ISI regrouped there, and had fought the jihadis ably and bravely. Known to be among the most honest of generals, he was liked by the Americans, whose expertise he valued and with whom he worked closely. It was calamitous but not surprising, then, when Maliki replaced Riyadh in Nineveh with a loyalist, a general who will go down in Iraqi history as the man who abandoned Mosul to the Islamic State. Maliki's successor, Haider al-Abadi, reinstalled

Riyadh in Nineveh, in 2016, making him the commander of all regular army ground forces.

That's not why I liked him. I liked him because, in any context other than a war, he would have been unbearable. Physically, he was the sort who used to be called a *fireplug*, and in his case the description would have been doubly apt because he had not just the shape but the temperament and tenor of an active hydrant. He couldn't have been more than 5'4", and was nearly as wide as he was high, with closely cropped white hair on the sides of his head, none on the top, and a paintbrush mustache that was white too but that he dyed shoe-polish black.

By the last week of January, the enemy's final enclave on the east side was in a neighborhood in the northeastern corner called Arabi. I rode there in Riyadh's convoy. We moved on a highway at the foot of a hillside. On the hilltop was an incredible sight: a church's cupola had been knocked off the structure and onto the ground, presumably by an airstrike, but somehow the cupola had remained in one piece, its vault open to the sky. It was as though the building had been the victim of some sarcastic divine fillip. Looking at it, you thought for half a second, 'Maybe God is backing the jihadis?'

Fleeing families walked the highway in the opposite direction. This incensed Riyadh. Didn't these people know he was in the process of emancipating them? He instructed his driver to stop and waved down a father.

'Why are you leaving?' the general demanded.

'Everyone else left,' the father said.

'Everyone! Where are you all going?'

'Hedbah.'

'Well just stay there, I suppose.'

The convoy entered Arabi, a wealthy district of sizable, freestanding homes. On a sidewalk, in three piles, was what remained of an

Islamic State fighter. The most recognizable section consisted of his head, shoulders, and arms, his right hand clenched, as though around a detonator or trigger. His lower body was not nearby. Riyadh's Humvee arrived at an intersection where soldiers of the 16th Division had gathered to celebrate. Arabi had just now been taken, or such was the news passing through the crowd. No one had told the general this, and hostile gunfire was still audible in nearby streets, but when Riyadh stepped from his Humvee, the men cheered. Hearing these encouraging sounds, residents emerged from their homes. A grandmother and her middle-aged son opened a gate on the corner. An adjutant of Riyadh's approached them.

'May the general pray in your home?' he asked.

Riyadh's entourage filed into the courtyard and removed their shoes. At Riyadh's side was an air force general who was playing the part with every ounce of his being. Though not at that moment in a cockpit, he nevertheless wore a flight suit, leather bomber jacket, and mirrored aviator sunglasses. As he came into the yard, he leaned down to the grandmother and said in a mock-menacing voice, 'We're with the religious police.' Then he smiled to indicate he was joking. She didn't smile back, either because she didn't understand the joke or didn't find it funny. Unoffended, he laughed and stepped inside.

While Riyadh prayed in a back room, kneeling next to a space heater, a colonel fell into conversation with the son.

'Where was Daesh's closest base?' the colonel asked.

'It was in a nearby house. But I didn't even know they were there until the house was bombed. I didn't know about any of these things. I just went to work and came home. I only went to the mosque about five times while Daesh was here. The old imam was very good, but he left when they came.'

'You didn't hear any of the sermons from their imam?'

'Our house is close to the mosque, so I could sometimes overhear. They talked about killing. They cursed the Americans.'

'When they were preaching,' his mother said, 'I would pray in here. Pray that they wouldn't go to heaven. Pray they'd be killed.'

'Was there a base in the mosque?' the colonel asked.

'I swear, I didn't see anything,' the son repeated. He just went to work and came home. There was nothing else to do. He did have one interaction with the religious police, though, he admitted. He was stopped by a patrolman on the street. His pants were too long, the patrolman informed him. They would have to be hemmed above the ankle in the 'Afghan' style. The patrolman offered two options: either he went to a tailor or the patrolman would hem the pants for him on the spot. Hizbah patrolmen carried scissors specially for this purpose. The man chose the tailor. Having nothing better to do, the patrolman accompanied him and looked on as the tailor hemmed the pants.

When the fighting in Arabi began, the son got worried Daesh would come into their home and find him in normal-length pants again, so he put the short pants back on. They were still on him now. The colonel looked down.

'They don't even look like pants anymore,' the colonel said. 'What is this, a skirt?'

The colonel and generals laughed easily, the son nervously.

'I'm so happy God killed Daesh,' his mother said.

Riyadh finished praying and he and his men left. They were continuing up the street when gunfire broke out nearby. Bullets chirped overhead. He stopped to wait. As he did, a group of four dejected-looking soldiers trudged slowly by.

'Where are you going?' the general asked.

Without looking at the general, a soldier grunted dismissively.

'What's the matter?' the general demanded.

'We're tired and we're hungry,' the soldier snapped.

Riyadh's thick neck went scarlet and his eyes spherical. He marched his small feet to the curb and got within inches of the man's face.

'Don't you know who we are!? Don't you know who I am!?' he bellowed. He tapped his starred epaulet. 'These are the same in every military in the world! I'm the general of all ground forces!'

He ordered someone to fetch a ration box. As they unpacked the crackers and sardines, dejection turned to shame on the soldiers' faces. They tried to be conciliatory but Riyadh cut them off, instructing them, 'Eat and leave.' He continued up the street, now crowded with rejoicing locals. They embraced him, kissed him, pulled out their phones to take pictures with him. A man approached with his young son whose cheeks were painted with Iraqi flags. A woman, her cheeks wet with tears, kissed Riyadh's cheeks.

'God bless you, God protect you,' she told him. 'We're so tired. But now we can eat comfortably.'

'We will raise the Iraqi flag now,' her teenage son said.

'We had no respite from Daesh,' she said. 'They gave us no rest.'

'It's ok now,' the colonel told her. 'Just report anything abnormal you see.'

The woman, beaming, giddy, had to go on.

'When I first saw the soldiers, I started kissing them. Kissed all of them! I can't contain my happiness. I kissed them!'

'She even kissed their feet,' her son said. 'I can't blame her.'

A man approached in a state of great agitation and launched unbidden into a breathless tale of suspense. A few days earlier, he explained, a jihadi had come to his house and tried to kick him out. When he refused, the jihadi did not hit him, but did depart in a fit of pique. Later he saw the same jihadi jumping around on the roofs of the surrounding houses with a grenade launcher. Spooked, the man moved into a friend's house. He was still living there.

'It's killing me to know there's a man with a grenade launcher hiding in my house,' he said. 'It's been three days. I know he's still there. I just want to feel safe in my own home.'

Riyadh sent a soldier with the man to check his house.

At the end of the street the general encountered three men who appeared to be in their early twenties, one of whom was bearded. This was a rarity. With the exception of the very old, Moslawi men made a point of shaving when they were confident the Islamic State had left their neighborhood. It was a way of presenting themselves to the troops as nonjihadis and, also, I sometimes sensed, of psychologically expelling the Caliphate.

'You should shave that beard,' Riyadh told him, before asking how he could steer his convoy on to the north. The young men gave him directions. The entourage walked back to their Humvees. The convoy slowly drove out of Arabi and back onto the highway. A group of officers walked alongside. We'd been moving only a few minutes when a shell came in with a high whistle and a *thwack* no louder than a very loud firework. Almost perfectly aimed, it landed next to the hood of the Humvee in front of mine, the general's Humvee, amid the group on foot. A quick hail of fragment, a gust of smoke. In moments the air had cleared. The general and his Humvee were unharmed, but cut down on the ground before me, quicker than would have seemed possible, were four perfectly dead men.

Immediately it was obvious what had happened: someone in Arabi had seen the general, followed his movements, and notified a mortar team. The general might even have spoken with the artillerist. Maybe it was the young bearded man. Or the man with the child with painted cheeks. Maybe Riyadh had been kissed by his would-be killer. There was no way to know.

Riyadh jumped from his Humvee to help. Another shell thudded into the hillside. The injured were picked up. One stayed on his knees, vomiting. Two ambulances sped in and loaded on three corpses. The last corpse was laid on the hood of the general's Humvee. The convoy followed the ambulances back up the highway, past Arabi, past the fleeing families, to a commandeered home.

There the corpses were already in body bags when I arrived, one on a gurney on the sidewalk by the gate, the rest on stretchers on the slate floor of the courtyard. Weeping soldiers bent over them. A large, gruff captain collected the dead men's wallets, phones, and IDs, wrapped them into bundles with medical tape, and wrote their names on the tape. Riyadh stood on the far side of the courtyard alone.

'Bring a flag!' a kneeling man wailed.

He and the captain got in an argument about whether to drape an Iraqi flag over a body now or to wait until the morgue.

'Someone get a flag!' the man yelled again.

A flag was brought.

'Put it around the edges,' Riyadh instructed from across the yard. But the folding was not done to his liking. He marched to the corpse, knelt down, and carefully tucked the corners of the flag into the space between the body bag and the stretcher.

'Fuck these Mosul people!' the soldier wailed.

II

NINEVEH WE ARE COMING

The tale spoke clearly: whatever brotherhood human beings may be capable of has grown out of fratricide, whatever political organization men may have achieved has its origin in crime.

—HANNAH ARENDT

raq and its neighbors are lazily spoken of as congenital grudge holders, countries that refuse to get past the past. But Iraqis, I find, have a genius for putting things behind them. They excel at expedient commemoration. By the time of the rise of the Islamic State, they had got the metabolizing of misfortune down to near simultaneity. What choice did they have?

A student of Iraqi politics said this to me: 'If you're living in Nineveh, you've switched masks many times in the last fourteen years. To us it's quite unthinkable to join a terrorist group knowing that you won't always be in it. It won't necessarily follow you. You'll get forgiven. In Iraqi culture, you can kill people, you can kill people's siblings, and you can be forgiven. It doesn't always work, but there's an expectation you'll have a good chance. You can't take vengeance for everything bad someone's ever done to you in Iraq. If you did, every Iraqi would be dead.'

Though the Caliphate lasted barely more than three years in Iraq, the period produced more memorials than anyone cares to count. Even before the battle for Mosul, public shrines to war martyrs were everywhere, from the climes of the Zagros to the fishing villages of the Gulf, the Iranian border to the Arabian desert. Placards and signboards and billboards and photograph collages and bouquets of plastic flowers and candles, sticking and hanging and piled and leaning at roadsides and checkpoints and intersections, at mosques and restaurants, at highway crossings, on bridges, on overpasses, on hillsides and riverbanks, nailed and pasted and taped onto walls and lampposts and windows and guardrails.

I arrived in Baghdad in July of 2016 in the midst of a bombing spree. A car bomb had just killed three hundred people in Karrada, a mainly Shia commercial district. The torn building façades on the market street were covered over with black netting, like a vast crepe, from which hung poster-size photos of the victims, if not three hundred then very nearly that many. I drove to Dululiya, a town on the Tigris near Tikrit, where two years earlier the residents had banded together to keep the Islamic State out, a rare thing in those days when the jihadis seemed unstoppable, especially in Sunni towns. At the entrance to Dululiya was a new cemetery for the citizen-soldiers who died in the Battle of the Four Million Rounds, as the fight for the town came to be known. (Who conducted the tally of bullets, no one is sure.) A low, red-painted cinderblock wall surrounded several dozen graves, each grave topped with a placard-sized photo of the deceased. The cemetery is on the roadside, directly next a checkpoint, so that, driving into the town, you must look at the faces, you have no choice. I continued north, to Mount Sinjar, where thousands of Yazidi men were slain and their wives and daughters and sisters forced into sex slavery, and where Kurdish peshmerga troops fought to protect them and Kurdistan. A highway hillside had been terraced and the terraces planted with what appeared from the distance to be boxy saplings. As I approached, they turned into wood-encased television sets. Only when I was in front of them did I realize these were plaster reliquaries, their exteriors painted brown, white inside, each containing the framed photo of a slain peshmerga.

The only sector of Iraq's economy that wasn't devastated by the Caliphate was printers, who were kept alive with death. After a bombing or a firefight, pictures of the deceased were sent electronically or hand-delivered to a print shop, where the images were enlarged and decorated, icons and symbols superimposed around the victims' faces. Flowers, guns, flags, birds, Korans. If the dead person was Shia, the shrine of the Imam Hussein in Karbala or of the Caliph Ali in Najaf might float near their face; if Sunni, the Dome of the Rock in Jerusalem; if a Kurd, the silhouette of the Zagros. The memento mori came in all sizes. They ranged from wallet snapshots to, in the case of the so-called Speicher Massacre, one of the largest plots of land in Iraq.

In the second week of June 2014, after seizing Mosul, jihadis encircled a group of Iraqi Air Force cadets as they tried to escape the Tikrit Air Academy, which was still known by its American name, Camp Speicher. They were brought to what had once been Saddam's palace compound in Tikrit, a city about halfway between Baghdad and Mosul on the Tigris. On a riverbank escarpment, they were executed one by one, most by way of bullets to the back of the head. Some were kicked into the water, others tossed into mass graves. The graves were so large they were picked up by satellite cameras.

Though it was unapparent at the time, the Speicher Massacre would prove the first major reverse for the Islamic State. The killings disgusted many moderate Sunnis who had until then identified with the jihadis' mission—for it wasn't just to fed-up Iraqi Sunnis that the group's message appealed. Support was expressed by Sunnis in many countries, and not just by extremists, but by people like Abu Omar and Abu Fahad, people you and I would consider sane and sympathetic. It appealed to Sunnis who looked at the wider Sunni stage—the selfish monarchies of the Gulf; the brutal, secularist military of Egypt, which had deposed and imprisoned the legitimately elected Muslim Brotherhood; the imperious Turks; Iran-dominated Lebanon—and saw a void of valid leadership. To the many Sunnis who felt that Iran had taken control since the American invasion of Iraq and worried that this development would be their ruin—and it is difficult to find a Sunni person in Iraq, or beyond, who doesn't hold this fear to some extent—the Islamic State's revolution felt, in ways, like a long-awaited answer to the Iranian revolution; 2014 was, in a sense, the Sunni 1979. Anyway, they held out hope that it might turn out that way. But, seeing the Speicher videos, sympathizers who had explained away the Islamic State's carnage as rumor, or propaganda, or the unfortunate results of a just war, could no longer fool themselves. Over fifteen hundred unarmed cadets, the great majority of them Shia, were executed. The Islamic State, whatever else it might be, was a death cult, it was now all too obvious.

It was also the Speicher Massacre that convinced Iran it had to get involved in the war against the Islamic State, and the Iraqi government could not afford to turn down the help even if it wanted to. In early 2015, a combination of Iraqi forces and Iran's al-Quds Force, a branch of the Republican Guard that answers directly to the Ayatollah, attacked jihadi-held Tikrit. In April of that year they won the city back. For Iraqis who couldn't brook the Islamic State but also worried Baghdad was doing the bidding of Tehran, al-Quds's presence was confirmation of their suspicions, but even they had to admit that the victory in Tikrit was a desperately needed bit of good news. It was the first major city to be recovered from the Caliphate. For the next ten months, the war seesawed, with the Islamic State losing and recovering ground, the Iraqi forces fighting ably one day and ineptly the next. Then, in early 2016, the troops took Ramadi, the first city the jihadis had seized, two years before. This would prove the hinge of the war.

The governate of Anbar, of which Ramadi is the capital, is proverbially rebellious. Iraq's biggest province—for square mileage it surpasses Greece—Anbar is considered by geographers less Levant and more Arabian Peninsula; its flat expanse of steppe and desert, in Iraq's western extremity, shares more borderland with Saudi Arabia, Syria, and Jordan than it does with the neighboring Iraqi provinces, though its two biggest cities, Ramadi and Fallujah, are near Baghdad. Governed largely by tribal tradition and sheikhs, Iraq's poorest and least-educated region, Anbar is also the Sunni heartland, and by the time of the rise of the Islamic State it had long been the nerve center of Sunni opposition to the government—both political and criminal opposition. To say anti-Maliki sentiment ran high in Ramadi would be like saying anti-Obama sentiment ran high in survivalist compounds in Wyoming.

After the American invasion in 2003, when Abu Musab al-Zarqawi was considering where to base Al Qaeda in Iraq, Anbar was the obvious choice, and it wasn't long before his men controlled Ramadi. Foreign fighters flocked to the city, hoping to kill Americans. In his book *A Chance in Hell*, the journalist Jim Michaels recounts an interrogation by Americans of a Ramadi insurgent. 'You own (the) street for one hour a day,' the man told his questioners. 'We own it for the other twenty-three.' Ramadi's fortunes rose and fell through the Sunni Awakening and the Surge, but mostly fell, until, by late 2012, its residents were at their rope's end with the Maliki government. They began protesting. The demonstrations spread across Anbar and to other parts of Iraq. By the next year, thousands were taking to the streets every Friday. The marches clogged highways. Permanent protest camps went up. Maliki cracked down. The camps were fired upon, even shelled. Protesters were jailed, beaten, killed. In Anbar, the movement turned into a 'tribal revolution' backed by local politicians and Sunni sheikhs. Quietly, it was also infiltrated by the Islamic State, which by that point controlled most of the border region in neighboring Syria.

For reasons that are still not clearly understood by anyone outside Maliki and his confidantes, he pulled security forces out of Anbar. Many Iraqis will tell you that Maliki was knowingly leaving Sunni Iraq to the ravages of the Islamic State, and that his plan only backfired when the jihadis incurred into Shia areas. They will add that it was Maliki who later ordered troops to abandon Mosul. Whatever the prime minister's thoughts might have been, Baghdadi saw the opportunity, and, on January 1 of 2014, jihadi columns crossed the border from Syria and rolled into Ramadi. Soon they held about half the city. The soldiers and police made a poor showing, many of them fleeing or hiding, but this was the first city in Iraq the jihadis had invaded, and the mortal dread of them hadn't yet fully set in. Otherwise Ramadi would have fallen entirely. As it was, those security forces brave enough to fight managed to hold on to Ramadi's other half. A stalemate ensued, punctuated by an intermittent war of attrition. Ramadi lived half Islamic State, half Iraqi state. Neighborhoods were taken, lost, taken again. These were the 'dark days of the war,' as one military analyst put it to me.

After eighteen months of this, Ramadi was finally liberated in February of 2016. So badly was the city damaged, though, that residents weren't allowed back en masse until the following summer, when I went there, moving in the wake of the Iraqi troops as they advanced northwards toward Mosul. To Ramadians, 'liberated' seemed a very rosy term. Whole districts were not just uninhabitable but unrecognizable.

Short of everything, including traffic cones, the soldiers and police now occupying the city had demarcated the lanes of their makeshift checkpoints with 88-mm shell casings. Into the casing's hollows they'd stuck bouquets of pink plastic flowers. Barricades of car parts, paving stones, and rubbish still blocked roads. Lines of blindfolded captives—whether suspected insurgents or just Sunni men, it was impossible to know—were marched to police stations. Troops were clearing bombs, but the work wasn't nearly done. The privacy walls of the cleared buildings bore spray-painted check-marks, the uncleared x's. On a curb on the central thoroughfare, what the Americans had called Route Michigan when they were stationed here, sinister hardware was stacked neatly—rows of pres-sure plates, casings, detonators. In the residential streets of what had been the Islamic State–held neighborhoods, where the final fire-fights for the city took place, everywhere you looked there was the bulge in the dust of a tripwire or a jerry can with calcified chemicals around its mouth. In some homes the machine-gun emplacements and sniper nests were still intact, bulwarks of cooking-gas canisters and upturned credenzas and on-end mattresses crammed between doorjambs. The rooms were so chewed with gunfire they looked like caves, not rooms. It was impossible to imagine people returning to these places.

Yet, they were. I watched as a taxi pulled up to a block-long moun-tain of rubble and parked. It was unclear why; there was no one hail-ing a taxi—there was no one anywhere. The driver, an old man in a faded gray dishdasha, got out and disappeared into the wreckage. Within the wreckage, it turned out, was his home. Its second level had been sheared off in an airstrike, as though by a giant lathe, but the first was standing, tentatively. Where his front gate had been, the taxi driver had hung a blue plastic tarp. He lifted it and beckoned me through. He had returned four days earlier, he explained, expecting to find nothing. But half his house was still there. The problem was it couldn't be reached. So he had rented a bulldozer and cleared the path that was now his front walkway.

'We think there are bodies in there,' he said, pointing to the ten-foot-high mound of splintered furniture and cinderblock where his front yard had once been. From the mound's peak protruded the front wheel of a motorcycle. 'We can smell them.' He kneeled, put his nose to a hole in the low wall that was keeping the mound at bay, inhaled quizzically, and invited me to join him. 'Smell that?'

Nearby, a man was carting charred rubble from his home in a wheelbarrow. He had been the first to return to this street, he told me, and had searched the houses next to his for bombs. He'd found one and painted a warning on the privacy wall: THIS HOUSE HAS BOMBS. In his own house, he had defused a bomb. It was on the curb now. He kicked it.

'Don't kick that!' another man yelled at him. 'It could explode!'

'I already took off the cables.'

'It doesn't matter, don't touch it!'

A woman came to her door. She recalled that, soon after the Islamic State arrived, there was a knock at this same door, now battered but still on its hinges. She opened it to find two young jihadis. Politely, they explained their unit would soon attack an army position nearby. They recommended she absent herself. The whole thing would take no more than two days, they assured her. She thanked them and packed. Two-and-a-half years later, she'd come home. Like the walls of most of the houses, hers had holes big enough to hop through— the egresses of the elaborate system of passageways and tunnels the Islamic State had built throughout Ramadi, as in every city it took. Through these they could move without being scrutinized by air surveillance. They had departed with some of her furniture, but she felt lucky comparatively, she said, pointing across the street, to a row of pancaked houses and, in front of them, a truck-length crater in the pavement. The crater was filled with crude oil. There, a tanker had been detonated. To create a smokescreen to obstruct the airstrikes—and, you sensed, just to continue the wreckage—the jihadis had set ablaze as much of this neighborhood as they could.

A furniture dealer named Abdula showed me into his home. He and his family had just moved back, too. He thanked God that, unlike the houses of his neighbors, leveled or picked clean, his was untouched aside from the bullet and shrapnel holes on the façade. The looting was more galling in its way than the destruction, Abdula said. One neighbor had come home to find not a stick.

'He returned and all he saw was the walls.'

Abdula's home was in what had been a government-controlled neighborhood, but only barely: his street was a kind of demilitarized zone. When, in 2014, it had become clear that both the Caliphate and the government would stand their ground, the jihadis tied a laundry line to a nearby home, crossed the street, tied the other end of the line to the home opposite—as Abdula recounted this, he lifted a hand above his head and, with a smoking cigarette, described a line in the air—and then draped blankets over it. This was the divider between Iraqi Ramadi and Caliphate Ramadi.

At times the stalemate was oddly peaceable, he recalled. He had clients in Islamic State districts and he was permitted by both the real police and the religious police to go back and forth. Some differences he noticed were overt. Over there, for instance, the court building now bore a sign reading 'Military Court of the Islamic State.' Homes and businesses which the Islamic State had taken over bore spray-painted signs reading 'Property of the Islamic State Endowment.' The black-and-white Islamic State standard, with the words No God but God in roughhewn Arabic, was everywhere, of course, stenciled on walls, hoisted on flags, hand-lettered on vehicles. Other differences were more subtle. On shop awnings and billboard advertisements, the faces of models had been cut away, or the man's face remained while the woman's was painted over in black.

We drove to Abdula's furniture shop. The upper stories of the building had been collapsed by an airstrike. He climbed over loose cinderblock and shattered glass and the remains of his metal awning and through an empty window frame. The display area had been plundered. Through a jihadi-made hole in the wall he climbed into the adjoining commercial space, which had been used for bombmaking, it appeared. On the unfinished cement floor were sacks of coarse gray powder, empty cigarette packets and two neat piles of human excrement. Another hole led into Abdula's dusky rear showroom. Its overstuffed living room sets and fussy armoires sat untouched and quilted in dust.

'My father opened this store in the 1960s,' Abdula told me. 'It was the best furniture store in Ramadi.'

He walked down the street to say hello to a pair of brothers who owned a photography shop. Somehow, it was unscathed. Abdula looked admiringly at the intact, newly cleaned windowpanes. Inside, he studied two photographs, hung side by side, that the brothers had taken years ago. They showed the same stretch of downtown Ramadi with a before-and-after effect. The photo on the left, taken in 1998, contained a lively scene of shoppers and cars.

'It was the sanctions era, but things weren't bad,' a brother said, referring to the period, after the Gulf War, when Iraq was smothered by international restrictions on trade.

In the photo on the right, the same buildings were mostly destroyed, the shops were shuttered, and there was no one on the street. I assumed it had been taken in the last few months.

'That was taken in 2007,' the other brother said. Pointing to the left of the frame, he added 'Over there was the American base.'

This shop and Abdula's had survived the American occupation.

The city had been rebuilt. Ramadi would survive the Islamic State, too, and people would need pictures of their dead loved ones, and new furniture.

'God willing,' Abdula said.

'God willing,' the brothers said.

After the victory in Ramadi, the Iraqi troops made their way north and west along the Tigris and the Euphrates. In a pair of nasty fights, they took Hit, then Baiji. Next fell the key refinery city of Qayara, where the sight of civilians making their way to safety would bring Ali, the otherwise jaded infantryman I would meet at the triage station in Gogjali, to tears. Qayara survived all right, Hit could be salvaged. Baiji, however, looked to have been inhaled off the earth by some vengeful deity. I drove through it one afternoon and didn't register there had been a city there.

'How far are we from Baiji?' I asked my translator.

'That *was* Baiji,' he said.

In the last week of May 2016, CTS moved on Fallujah. A bitter, months-long battle was predicted. The city was a byword for jihad. The twin battles of Fallujah, in 2004, were the hardest-fought of the American occupation, today studied by Marine cadets on the sand tables of Quantico no less than in scrawlings in the sand in insurgent training camps. In Fallujah Zarqawi first saw beyond Islamist sedition, to Islamic statism, and to Armageddon.

But in just over a month, CTS prevailed. They were commanded in Fallujah by General Abdulwahab al-Saadi. It was Abdulwahab who, four months later, I would watch turn his back on the sniper in the minaret in Tahrir. This was characteristic of the general, whom I met in Fallujah after victory was declared there. He was the first Iraqi general I'd ever interviewed and I could hardly believe my luck. 'Central casting' doesn't begin to get at it. He was tall, taciturn, exquisitely aloof, handsome in that universal military way—rectangular of skull, lantern of jaw, with a permanently folded brow and a perfectly graying curly flattop, as though a portraitist was overseeing his aging. Shelby Foote once described a Civil War general's expression in photographs as looking as though 'he were dictating terms for the camera's surrender.' That was Abdulwahab's face every hour of the day except for when he slept, and then, too, for all I knew.

'Seventy to eighty percent of the population of Fallujah stayed there when Daesh took over,' he told me, adhering to the military custom of quantifying everything in terms of percentages the means of whose calculation remains a mystery. The difference in his case was he offered the percentages with a shrug that made it clear that I, and vastly more importantly *he*, could take or leave them. Thus the percentages became fact. We were sitting in the opulent office in a ministry building in which he'd installed himself. 'That is many more people than in other parts of Anbar,' he went on. 'There was a lot of sympathy for Daesh here. Some stayed because they were too poor to leave, but many stayed because they believed Daesh's arguments.' Fallujah is known as the City of Mosques. In reality, it probably has no more mosques than any other Iraqi city, but the nickname did point up an infamous zeal-ousness among Fallujans that the general clearly found distaste-ful. 'If Fallujah has a hundred thousand residents,' he said, with a rumor of a smirk, 'ninety thousand of them claim to be clerics.' Only ten to fifteen percent of the jihadis in Fallujah had been for-eigners, he estimated. The rest were Iraqi. And young. 'Most of them were teenagers, between thirteen and sixteen. The problem of radicalization doesn't start with Daesh. It starts in school. In the U.S., you don't have schools for radicalization. Here, we do.'

I asked how it was the Islamic State had managed to hold the city for so long, given its proximity to Baghdad and the Iraqi military's long experience here. His brow lifted microscopically.

'By force,' he said.

Thirty-four years of fighting had left Abdulwahab with a kind of sweeping ontological spite. He had been drafted in 1983 and was assigned to the special forces. Like Abu Omar, he fought in Iran and Kuwait. His faithful service didn't keep Saddam from having his brother, also a veteran and officer, murdered. After 2003, Abdulwahab, who was not a Baathist, had no problem entering the American-led Iraqi military. He did battle with the ex-Baathist militias, the Shia militias, Sunni jihadis, al Qaeda, taking all comers, all over the country.

As a matter of course, Iraqi troops exposed themselves unnecessarily to danger, not wearing protective gear, refusing to take cover, leaving their positions unsecured, as though in an effort to show the Islamic State, and one another, that they too could handle martyrdom. Abdulwahab was the most incautious of them all, without question the most heedless field commander I saw in Iraq where his own safety was concerned, but not because he welcomed death. He simply had no time for it. Death wouldn't dare. The other CTS generals went to the front only occasionally, their visits usually timed to coincide with those of television camera crews. Abdulwahab went every day. He was interested in every bit of the war, and liked checking on his men, who revered him. He wanted to be as close to the fighting for as long as possible, only leaving when he got bored. I often went with him. He always exited his Humvee as soon as he could, walking into streets where doors were still being knocked down, loose ordnance still being blown up. When a shell exploded nearby he'd frown disobligingly and shrug one shoulder. Seeing me get low, he'd laugh. These were the only times I saw him laugh. And

I never saw him wear more than a leather jacket for protection. I don't doubt he would have enjoyed shooting a militant, but he'd shot so many in his day, and that would have involved having to pick up a weapon, aiming it, making sure the guy was dead—too much bother. He didn't carry so much as a pistol. All of CTS wore black uniforms, but in Abdulwahab's case it seemed to mean something. It felt like a rebuke to the Caliphate's childish obsession with black, a recovery of the color from their ostentatiously morbid aesthetic. In this war, black is mine, Abdulwahab seemed to be telling the enemy, and you may borrow it only when your corpse goes necrotic.

I saw Abdulwahab apprehensive only once. The scene:

A man waved down the general's convoy. Typically for him, Abdulwahab told his driver to stop for the man. The general opened his Humvee door and asked what was wrong.

'Please come, there's a bomb in my home,' said the man.

In his front yard, the man, a diminutive jeweler who by the looks of him had a nervous temperament before the Islamic State arrived, recounted that he'd fled a week ago as the soldiers approached this neighborhood. He'd come back home that morning with his brother, who was now in the yard with us. He'd found his house intact. But he believed jihadis had been living in it, a suspicion he arrived at thanks to three pieces of evidence, all found in his daughter's room: (1) Two plates of rice that he was pretty sure hadn't been there when they'd left, (2) A helmet which he was all but sure did not belong to his daughter, and (3) An undetonated suicide belt which he knew certainly wasn't hers. He explained to Abdulwahab's men how to get to his daughter's room and they walked inside. Abdulwahab moved as though to follow, then stopped. The first fold in his brow asked 'Do I want to get blown up today?' The second fold said 'No, I suppose I'd rather not get blown up today.'

He stayed outside. The jeweler kept talking.

'Daesh pretended they didn't like gold, but in fact they stole every-one's gold. They would take the most beautiful and heaviest pieces. They kept them or sold them. I know because they sold pieces at my shop.'

A soldier emerged from the house carrying the suicide belt out-stretched as you would a dead snake. The device was wrapped in red electrical tape. He crossed the street to an empty lot piled with rub-ble and refuse. He carefully climbed up onto a pile, steadying him-self with his free hand, laid the belt on the crest of the pile, climbed down, and hurried back across the street. The soldiers raised their rifles and began shooting at the belt.

'I'm going to pray now,' the jeweler said, backing behind his gate.

But they couldn't get the thing to explode. After a few more shots, the soldier who'd placed the belt on the pile ran back across the street, found a shard of wood among the refuse, climbed back up the pile, and stuck the wood piece upright beside the belt in an effort to warn any foragers passing by that if they were considering rooting around in the refuse here, they ought to be aware of the unexploded suicide belt.

'Do you need anything else?' Abdulwahab asked the jeweler.

'Just a picture,' the jeweler said.

Abdulwahab stood next to jeweler as his brother attempted to take a photo on his phone.

'It won't work,' the brother said, playing with the phone.

Without waiting for a resolution, the general shrugged and stepped from the yard and into his Humvee.

Abdulwahab had employed four thousand troops to dislodge the Caliphate from Fallujah, he told me, and 2,200 jihadis had been killed. This seemed high, considering I was hearing similar figures for the entire population of jihadis in Mosul, which is many times the size of Fallujah, but I didn't question him. The fighting in Fallujah was house-to-house, but not chaotic, he explained, taking place according to a meticulous plan set along nine axes across the city. It was by far the best executed operation of the war, proof that CTS, if not the rest of the Iraqi military, had what it took to seize Mosul.

'How long did it take you to take Fallujah?' I asked.

'Thirty-four days,' the general said.

'That's fast,' I said.

He frowned.

'America took Iraq in twenty days,' he said. 'Iraq took Kuwait in one day.'

We drove into Fallujah. On the highway access, light poles were jackknifed over themselves. The concrete slabs of what had once been the off-ramp lay on the charred remains of an exploded tanker. From the ramp you drove over what had been a six-foot-deep trench, now filled in. Expertly made, it was dug at a perpendicular angle to the roadway and stretched around the city's southeastern perimeter. Beyond it was a sand wall. The jihadis had constructed five such lines of defense to prepare for the final battle. On Baghdad Road, the main thoroughfare, palm trees whose palms had been blown or burned off threw long, cylindrical shadows across downed power lines that splayed, like shorn hair, across the cratered pavement. In the bazaar, metal shutters had been rocked from the clothing stalls by explosions. The dishdashas and knit white prayer caps now lay in mounds in the arcade. Outside the bazaar, a hand-painted sign explained that women were to appear in public only fully covered, in dark clothing that did not suggest their bodily form, and only in the company of their husbands or male relatives. 'These are the principles of the Prophet,' it read. This last point was driven home by a pair of wires hanging from a beam, where violators were strung up to be whipped and then left in the sun as shoppers looked on.

In the brutal heat, CTS was handing Fallujah over to the federal police and Shia militias. Exhausted soldiers now stood around in shorts and T-shirts in the yards of the houses they had commandeered, salvaging old generators and hooking them up to deep freezers so that they could chill the palettes of water that local well-wishers (led, as it happened, by a Shia cleric) brought in pickup caravans. The soldiers had wedged bouquets of pink plastic flowers into the bullet holes in the windscreens of their Humvees. Beneath an overpass, one squad had armed itself with paint rollers and buckets of red paint with which it was painting over a fifteen-foot-high Islamic State standard. In the middle of a boulevard, next to their Humvee, the men had assembled a living room set, three ornate sitting chairs, a rug, and a standing fan. On one side of this impromptu patio was a destroyed mosque, on the other a sweets shop whose windows and walls had been blown out but whose vinyl awning, decorated with immense photos of enticing foods, had somehow remained intact. The sweating men were confronted with big, sweating scoops of ice cream and lush bananas and mangoes. They were forced to look at this as they ate their rice and tomato sauce. The main plaza was by the two bridges from which Zarqawi's men had hanged Nicholas Berg's headless body and the burnt corpses of other American contractors; the latter was dubbed 'Brooklyn Bridge' by the Marines in 2004. In the plaza, the soldiers replaced the Islamic State flag with an Iraqi one, but they did not repaint the flagpole, still striped in black and white.

When, two years earlier, the jihadis had seized Fallujah, they had made directly for the city's impressive central hospital. They converted the building to a headquarters, a choice which bore certain obvious practical advantages. The doctors could treat their wounded fighters. It was the most modern facility in Fallujah, with computers, an industrial kitchen, the best generators around, and was next to the central mosque, the lovely teal-domed al-Khulafa. Less obvious to Fallujans at first was the hospital's symbolic value. It extended the Caliphate's psychological power beyond the battlefield and the prayer rug. *We control you in health and in sickness, in life and in death.* Though the battlefield was never far from their minds: the hospital was also the best defensive position in the city.

I accompanied a group of policemen as they inspected the building. They walked by a wheel-less ambulance, its windscreen crushed; stepped over a row of morgue trays; passed a grass plot with a small, new grave in one corner. A man put his hand down to his waist to indicate the height of the body buried in it. During the fighting, he explained, it was too dangerous for locals to take their dead children from the hospital to the cemetery, so they buried them on the hospital grounds, wherever they could find dirt. In the emergency ward, framing and ceiling tiles hung down like jungle understory. Gurneys and wheelchairs idled as though waiting for their occupants to return. In the lightless pharmacy stockroom in which the Islamic State fighters had bunked, there lay, amid blankets and shoes and a teapot, a discarded Rhodesian chest rig. A policeman shined his mobile phone on it and saw written in Arabic, in faded blue felt-tip, *The Uzbeki.*

'Another foreigner,' he said.

As he walked around the hospital, the policeman placed keepsakes in a plastic shopping bag and read official memoranda, on Caliphate letterhead, scotch-taped to the walls. The phrases hinted at desperate last days in power. One memo:

> To all brothers and section chiefs, may God bless them: All brothers should bring back their families immediately to the Fallujah sector within twenty days from the date of this notice. Whoever violates it will not be allowed any time off.

For the past week, the policeman and his unit had been watching over the hospital. Their only orders were to stay put. They slept on the floor of the gatehouse and in the ambulance lane had set up a PKC machine gun on a tripod, which they gathered around and regarded with a certain proprietary delight. He went outside and joined them, and looked through his booty: enemy shell casings and a black nylon utility belt. He explained that he'd known the hospital well even before taking up this post. He was from nearby. All four of his children had been born here. He'd lived through the two American sieges of Fallujah and had been a policeman during the height of Zarqawi's power. But, he said, 'None of that was as bad as this.'

When the jihadis came to Fallujah, in the spring of 2014, those police who had the money to fled. Those who didn't hid. And those who couldn't hide gave themselves up. They were forced to stand up in mosques and public squares, in front of crowds, and recite the *tawba*, a script of regret and repentance for having worked for the infidel government. He fled to Karbala with a hundred other families, basically his entire neighborhood. He returned as the battle was ending, finding his city in flames for the third time in a just over a decade.

'Why do you keep coming back?' he was asked.

'Fallujah is our home. Anyway, it's not as bad as Ramadi.'

This was true.

He picked up from the ground what seemed to be a wig. He held it aloft, revealing a strap meant to go around the back of the head. It was a costume beard, presumably worn by an Islamic State fighter with insufficient facial fertility or too few years to grow a proper jihadi beard. Though they'd seen the thing many times, the other policeman laughed.

Many of the jihadi corpses turning up in Fallujah were, it appeared, the victims not of combat but of their own comrades. As

CTS closed in and the shame of the impending and inevitable defeat increased, the Caliphate leaders saw spies and shirkers everywhere. I went with another group that included an intelligence officer to the mansion of a well-known local building contractor that the jihadis had converted into a prison. The intelligence officer said he believed most of the prisoners had been disgraced jihadis, arrested for betrayal or cowardice or some other infraction. The sitting rooms and bedrooms had been turned into cells, sheets of steel welded over their doorways and windows. In an ornate atrium, beneath a sky-lighted dome decorated in brightly painted relief wood carvings, was a guard's chair, its seat still well-indented from a bony backside. Next to it were three sacks of shriveled dates, a lot of date pits, and several short strands of knotted rope, coiled in such a way as to suggest they'd until recently been wrist or ankle cuffs.

From the mansion we continued on through wreckage-strewn streets to the Fallujah Women's Teachers Institute, which had served as a court and execution chamber. In the main corridor, the scent of dead flesh hung heavy in the air. There was a cluster of overturned cabinets. The files of the young women who'd once studied here, their photographs stapled to the corners of blue folders, fanned across the floor. We came to a courtyard and in unison everyone put their hands to their noses. A policeman pushed aside a chalkboard that lay in the dirt. The sunlight illuminated a human fibula. The bone jutted from what, upon closer inspection, proved to be a shallow cavern beneath the paving stones. We stepped closer. The hole was full of corpses. They were in such a state of decay—no longer bodies, not yet skeletons—it was impossible to tell how many were inside. Maybe ten, maybe twenty. In a hallway we found another mass grave beneath the floor. It had been covered over with a carpet and sofa.

'Probably also jihadis,' the intelligence officer told me.

Upstairs, in an arts-and-crafts classroom, students' pieces were still pinned up: a brushy beach scene, a dancer with a dress of plastic spoons. Scraped into the wall between them, as though in some half-censure, half-imitation of the artwork, was a man's name: Abu Assam al-Ansari. The warden, apparently. We found his office. In addition to an ineptitude for burial, Ansari appeared to have had artistic ambitions of his own. On his desk was a Styrofoam cup on which he'd drawn his name and the Islamic State standard, as though he'd been designing some heraldic chalice. On a bureau was a wood carving of a map of Iraq, something a ten-year-old might make in a shop class, with blackened grooves demarcating the territory the Islamic State had taken. And in pride of place, on the wall before the desk, hung a canvas of Arabic calligraphy. Possibly Ansari had made it to buoy his spirits as he waited for the battle of Fallujah. In an unsteady scrawl of green and red glitter paint was written, 'The Islamic State of Iraq and Syria Remains and Expands.'

With his rifle muzzle, a policeman knocked the canvas to the floor.

Later, at the police station, the men looked through Caliphate documents they'd collected at the teachers' college and prison. They read a circular that addressed the issue of recidivism:

> It has come to our attention that many policemen and soldiers who claimed to repent are unrepentant, have in fact returned to being apostates and have conspired against Sunnis or supported those who worship fire and admire the Crusaders or Shiites. Thus the Islamic State has decided to establish the following rules for repentance and to keep penitents in Fallujah in order to secure the religion, honor, and wellbeing of Sunnis: Unrepentant policemen are not to sit in groups with penitent policemen. Former policemen are to notify the Islamic State of any change of address. . . .

They perused records of divorce cases. It seemed many women had taken the opportunity of the Islamic State's rule to part from their husbands. There was testimony from the case of a wife who'd gone to the Caliphate court declaring 'I demand to file a claim against my husband Adnan because he is sterile. He married me less than three months ago and had no sex with me except in the first week and then he said he was sick and could not take the pills he was taking before. He left a month ago and did not give me any money.' In a response, Adnan submitted that 'the family of my wife prevented her from approaching me. I had sex with her the first day of our marriage and did not feel any sickness. The same on the second day. But now I am sick and am taking pills I got from Abu Suhaib. It is religious medicine. My wife wants to come back to me.' Relying on a Koranic citation, the judge ruled in the wife's favor.

The policemen laughed as they read. They laughed because they were reminded, once again, of the sad, desiccated sexual component of the Islamic State, which reeked not just of pornography but of impotence. In these records was yet more proof that spiritual priapism left little blood for actual erections. It was a running joke that the real reason foreign fighters come to Iraq was because the women in their home countries wouldn't go near them. They had to rely on the sex slaves provisioned by the Caliphate's unspeakably wicked Department of War Spoils. The Islamic State's name in Arabic lends itself to a wordplay; with a few changed characters, it becomes The Fuck State. Going around liberated areas, you'd see the group's logo crossed out and *Fuck The Fuck State* or *There Is No More The Fuck State* written over it.

They laughed, too, because of what the case of Adnan and his wife said about life in the Islamic State. It said the same thing the striped flagpole in Fallujah's plaza and the warden Ansari's crafts said. Namely, that life in the Islamic State was boring. The predictable and irreducible fact of a terroristic theocracy, the fact the jihadis never mentioned in their promotional materials, was boredom, mind-emptying, rage-inducing, afterlife-inviting boredom. Between the bouts of violence and prayer and painting things black, there was absolutely nothing to do.

2

Reverence for General Abdulwahab didn't stop at his troops. On his rounds on the front lines, the general met and spoke with ordinary Iraqis who braved fire to rush into the street to hug and kiss him. He was the one field commander everyone knew not just by name but by face, a celebrity. Fighting on the east side of Mosul hadn't finished yet when talk began of his being appointed military governor of the city once the battle was over. Billboards showing Abdulwahab carrying a child went up at intersections. 'Mosul's savior,' they read.

For Moslawis, the general was a kind of reincarnation of another local hero. In 1743, the Persian conqueror Nader Shah, fresh from savaging the Mughals, set his sites on Mosul. A civil defense force was assembled by a Moslawi tribal leader known as Haj Husayn. The story goes that Husayn trained every man, woman, and child to shoot a bow and arrow. The battle against Shah would be a fight of right against wrong, a jihad, Husayn told them, a word that didn't dissuade Christian and Jewish Moslawis from pitching in. For eight days and nights, the vicious Shah—the Alexander of the East, as he was known—bombarded the city. When Mosul was enflamed, Moslawis organized fire brigades. They said mass prayers. They held out. Finally Haj Husayn dispatched his holiest warriors, the Fedayeen, to meet the Persian general, a reputed giant, on the battlefield. Husayn asked them to wear their armor but they said 'We are martyrs! We will wear nothing but our coffins!' They repulsed Shah. The resistance to the Persian siege became a kind of founding myth of modern Mosul. It was the story that parents told their children and grandparents their grandchildren during the war with Iran, during the American war, the civil war and, now, the war to expel the Islamic State. Now some Moslawis called Abdulwahab a latter-day Haj Husayn.

The general had come to Abu Omar's street in Zahra. Abu Omar was still wearing a long beard. 'When Abdulwahab al-Saadi saw me, he said "Let's shave that beard for you," ' Abu Omar told me. 'So he brought the razor and shaved it for me. They also brought cigarettes for me to smoke. I showed the general all of the Islamic State houses around mine.' How much of this was true I couldn't say, but it was more evidence of the general's popularity.

When I visited Abu Omar at the Khazer camp, he was always eager for news from the front lines, though he usually knew more than I did. He kept in touch with friends still in the city by phone, kept a radio on all day, and though it was winter now, and the camp was frigid at night, he sold a space heater to buy a television. It was the first time he'd been able to watch the news in a year. But he'd bought the television more for Omar, Aya, and Amina than for himself, he said. There was nothing else for them to do in the camp. There was a school, but he forbid Aya and Amina going to classes. When I asked why, he lowered his voice, not low enough that his children couldn't hear, and said 'You know, the boys here have been deprived for more than two and a half years. They haven't seen any women in that time without face covers on.

I worry they might take pictures of my girls and publish them on the Internet.'

As for Omar, school would be wasted on him, his father said. Abu Omar couldn't get through a conversation without demeaning his son. I was impressed at how unbothered Omar seemed by this abuse. He appeared to have reconciled himself to the fact that his father was an occasional bastard. He was always profoundly respectful and serene in my presence. This was remarkable for a nineteen-year-old anywhere, never mind one who'd been through what Omar had been through and was living in a refugee camp. It made me suspect he wasn't nearly so dim as his father claimed. At first, before Abu Omar and I had established a trust, it would have been disrespectful to address his son directly, rather than through his father. But after several visits, we were comfortable enough with one another that, one afternoon, I did.

'So, Omar—' I began.

'Don't ask Omar anything!' Abu Omar said with a laugh. 'Ask me.'

'Why can't I ask Omar?'

'He doesn't know. He doesn't know anything. He was always home when the Islamic State was in Mosul. He wasn't socializing with people outside. He was always home. He was isolated, isolated.'

Omar quietly regarded his father.

'I think he knows something,' I said.

'No, it won't benefit you to talk to him.'

I was surprised when Omar spoke up.

'It's ok,' he said. 'If I know something, I'll tell you.'

'No, he doesn't know anything,' his father insisted. 'He's not like me.'

'Omar seems smart to me,' I said. 'I think he knows what he's talking about.'

'I know Omar is smart'—this was the first time I'd ever hear Abu

Omar compliment his son—'but he doesn't know how to express his knowledge.'

'That's not true,' I said. 'When he's allowed to speak he's quite clear.'

'It's ok. Anything I know, I'll tell him,' Omar repeated.

I brought up Abu Bakr, the preacher at al-Nuaimi mosque whose sermons Omar so enjoyed. Almost every Moslawi I'd interviewed had claimed that once their local mosques were taken over by the Caliphate's imams, they'd stopped attending. Many were lying, I knew. But Omar had never attempted to hide the truth from me.

'Did you know him personally?' I asked.

'Yes, I knew him,' Omar said. 'I mean, I knew him by appearance from the mosque, from when he was preaching.'

'What did Abu Bakr say in his sermons?' I asked.

'I don't want to tell you,' Omar said. 'I swear to God I don't want to. He was talking about Jews and Christians.'

Abu Omar cut in again, but this time, surprisingly, to encourage Omar to go on.

'There is democracy here, son, you can speak.'

Omar smiled sheepishly.

'He was saying Americans are pigs,' he said.

'It's true of some of us,' I said.

'He was saying bad things about Arabs too!' Abu Omar said. 'He was insulting Saudis and Iranians, talking shit about everyone. Daesh considered everyone an infidel.'

'He was saying many things,' Omar said, 'but I don't want to mention the words he was using. You might get angry with me.'

I assured him I wouldn't.

'But you are our guest here. Father, tell him he is our guest here and I should respect him.'

I assured him again.

'Ok, well. He was saying Americans are filthier than pigs, and that the Iraqi soldiers worship America like a god. He said that Americans—no, he wasn't calling them Americans, he was calling them *Jews*—he said the Jews want to destroy Islam.'

'That's true,' Abu Omar cut in. 'The real founders of the Islamic State are America and Israel.'

'Abu Bakr was saying that?' I asked.

'No, *I'm* saying it,' Abu Omar said. 'I'm telling you.'

I asked him to explain.

'I once saw an American analyst quoted in a post on the Internet. He said the Americans could liberate Mosul in twenty-four hours if they really wanted to. The Iraqi army had been trying for six months, no for a year, two years, and hadn't been able to. And after that we saw someone saying that the Shia militia had surrounded the Islamic State and was about to attack—but the American airstrikes acciden- tally threw weapons and support to the Islamic State. This didn't happen once, but many times. Do you really think America, with all its technology and strategy, with all its strength, that it couldn't defeat the Islamic State in a day if it wished?'

I told him I thought the Islamic State was a very clever insurgency and that any military would struggle against it.

'Not the American military!' he said. 'How was it the Islamic State was even able to enter Iraq? How was it they were able to expand as they did? An American satellite can reveal what's inside your stomach. They couldn't see this? When the Americans withdrew from Iraq, they said, "As soon as we leave, the country will return to chaos." And look what's happened.'

'And Israel?' I asked

'Ah ha! Now let's talk about Israel. Israel is America's spoiled child. America and Israel are causing all of this, together, so that the Arabs won't unite against Israel and win Palestine's war. Mus- lims are united, but Saddam was Israel's agent and America's agent.

So when he turned around and attacked Israel, the Americans turned against him.'

I nodded while trying to keep my eyebrows level.

'Tell me,' he went on. 'Who do you think is leading this operation, the Americans or the Iraqis?'

I told him that the Iraqis were certainly doing the fighting, but obviously with ample help from American forces.

He laughed.

'This is only what they want to show you! America gave the order to attack, the exact date and moment, and it was done. You're a journalist. You should know this without my having to tell you,' he said. 'This has all been planned for twenty years. What's happening now was all planned twenty years ago. America planned it.'

'But wasn't it obvious Mosul would have to be invaded from the day the Islamic State took it?' I asked.

'What are you talking about—Sykes-Picot was signed a hundred years ago!' he said, referring to the 1916 agreement between the British and French governments to divide up the Levant when the Ottoman Empire ended during the First World War.

Getting over the sudden collapse in time, I said 'But that was the British and the French, not the Americans.'

'Yes, when it was originally signed. Turkey was also responsible for the Islamic State's invasion. Where did the Islamic State come into Iraq from? From Turkey! They went from Turkey into Syria and Iraq. People say that in the Turkish parliament today, there is still a chair held for the Mosul Vilayet, for Nineveh.' He turned to the translator. 'Tell him I've read about all this. I read a lot of books. Tell him my eyes have become tired from reading so much.'

No doubt Abu Omar had read a lot, but in wartime, truth is inseparable from rumor, and in Iraq, history is always cut with conspiracy.

The problem is, the more you learn about the history of Iraq, the more plausible the conspiracies become.

For residents of the Near East—and in Iraq, for Moslawis especially—the fall of the Ottoman Empire was the single most defining event of modern history before the rise of national independence movements. For the first time in four centuries, there was no caliph overseeing Sunni Islam. Levantines, so long accustomed to foreign rule under the sultan, now found themselves in limbo and in the midst of a conflict whose armies—French, British, Germans—they hadn't seen since the Crusades. In 1917, the British conquered Basra, then Baghad. The next year they ignored the armistice and took Mosul.

Suddenly, the problem that had vexed the European imperialist powers for so long—the 'Eastern Question,' as they termed that hemispheric impediment to colonial expansion and Western Christianity that was the Sublime Porte—was no more. Hoping to 'awaken the fanaticism of Islam,' the Kaiser had convinced Sultan Mehmed V to declare jihad, luring him to his doom; now it was the turn of the victorious Allies to export their own age-old animus to the slicing up of the Turkish dominion, not unlike what the Assyrian Empire's fractious opponents had done two-and-a-half millennia before when Nineveh fell. The British looked mainly forward while the French, with their perverse cocktail of *l'esprit de la révolution* and nostalgia for *l'ancien régime*, a paradox familiar to the jihadi, eyed the past. The shame of the loss of the Frankish Crusader kingdoms to Saladin and Nur ad-Din had never entirely passed from the national memory. When General Henri Gouraud, hero of the Marne, arrived at the former's tomb, in 1920, he reportedly couldn't help gloating. 'Saladin, we're back!' Gouraud is said to have exclaimed. According to one account he even kicked the tomb.

European interest in Iraq, as Mesopotamia had begun to be called (the etymology, unclear, may originate in the Persian *eragh*, meaning lowland or riverland), had many engines: pragmatism, greed, oil, but, also, belief, nostalgia, shame. Before WWI, British foreign policy had been divided between those who'd wanted to bolster the Turks, insulation that they were between Russia and the British Raj in India, and those who were for putting an end to the long Turkish hold on the Holy Lands and stopping the massacres of Greek, Armenian, and Assyrian Christians. In the latter camp were British politicians who had been more enchanted by the stories of Isaiah and Jonah at church than those of Xenophon and Diodorus at Eton, and chief among these was the new prime minister, David Lloyd George. An advocate of the fledgling Zionist Organization, he felt God had chosen Britain as his tool to restore the Jews to their homeland. 'Palestine, if recaptured,' George said, 'must be one and indivisible in order to renew its greatness as a living entity.' That a Zionist-controlled Palestine could also serve as a 'buffer Jewish state,' as some diplomats put it, to protect the Suez Canal, didn't displease him.

George's main obstacle was his main partner, France, just as the central concern of his French counterpart, Prime Minister Georges Clemenceau, was countering growing British power in the Levant. On both men's minds was the prospect—the inevitability—of the next great war, a war which, with every other European empire gone, they assumed they would be fighting against each other. So, secretly, the two countries drew up a plan to divide the Ottoman lands, with what is today Iraq, Jordan, and Palestine, roughly, going to Britain, and Syria and Lebanon to France. The lead British negotiator was Mark Sykes, a well-intentioned dilettante and sometime anti-Semite who had been brought over to the Zionist cause by men smarter than himself. Sykes was, latterly, also an advocate of Arab self-determination, and in those days, it's amazing to think, the two causes were not inimical. (Chaim Weizmann, the leader of the Zionist Organization in London and future president of Israel, had early warm relations with Faisal I, the future king of Iraq.) Sykes had got his appointment not on the strength of his Arabic—he spoke none— but thanks to his name and his travel writing, the best-known volume of which was *The Caliph's Last Heritage*. Ostensibly a paean to the Near East, the book is in fact, as you discover when you actually read it, as few of his boosters in Downing Street probably bothered to do, something else. It could be Sykes's rancor toward the region originated in his first trip there, as a child, when he'd had to watch as his mother seduced (or was seduced by) their tour guide. *The Caliph's Last Heritage* is in fact a crass batter of sentimentality and violent contempt. The author seems to feel an acute shame revisiting these places. Sykes reserves his worst for Mosul, that 'foul nest of corruption, vice and disorder' whose inhabitants embodied every facile Eastern stereotype—'eloquent, cunning, excitable and cowardly . . . Ready to riot and slay for the sake of fanaticism as long as they are in no danger.'

Sykes's French counterpart in the negotiations, François Georges-Picot, was no more interested in Arab independence than he was in Jewish autonomy and had his own familial shame to live down. He was the son of the imperialist party official who'd nearly driven France to war with Britain in the Sudan. Picot *fils* was himself a member of Le Comité de l'Asie française, whose position, as set forth in one memorandum, was: 'We should have to do no more in the Levant than reap the harvest of seven centuries of French endeavors.' When, at the Paris Peace Conference in 1919, a colleague of Picot's asserted that French rights in the region dated back to the Crusades, Sykes's colleague T. E. Lawrence reminded the man that the Crusades had not, in the end, been much of a success for Europe.

The Sykes-Picot Agreement at first gave Mosul to France. But a new issue arose when oil was discovered beneath Mosul. Or, rather, noticed; Iraqis had been using petroleum for millennia, putting asphalt in their palace walls, calking dhow hulls with bitumen. The leading British prophet of warfare, Winston Churchill, was ahead of his time in recognizing the martial importance of the stuff. Churchill had not cared much for school nor church, and, to his shame, had never learned Greek or Latin, never mind Arabic or Hebrew, but he had been in the pro-Turkish camp before the war, thanks in part to a personality trait mostly absent from the posthumous hagiographical haze—a serious respect for and fascination with Islam. Churchill liked to call Britain 'the greatest Mohammedan power in the world,' meaning that the British Empire included, by some measures, more Muslim subjects than any other, even the Ottoman Empire, and he liked to argue that his countrymen had a moral obligation to these people.

In his book *The River War*, Churchill reported on events in Sudan, where a charismatic Sudanese jihadi, Mohammed Ahmed, led an uprising against the British in the late 1890s. Churchill showed a remarkable sympathy for Ahmed, or the Mahdi as he was known to his followers, the Islamic term for a messiah, writing that he

> gave the tribes the enthusiasm they lacked. The war broke out. It is customary to lay to the charge of Mohammed Ahmed all the blood that was spilled. To my mind it seems that he may divide the responsibility with the unjust rulers who oppressed the land, with the incapable commanders who muddled away the lives of their men, with the vacillating Ministers who aggravated the misfortunes. But, whatever is set to the Mahdi's account, it should not be forgotten that he put life and soul into the hearts of his countrymen, and freed his native land of

foreigners. The poor miserable natives, eating only a handful of grain, toiling half-naked and without hope, found a new, if terrible magnificence added to life. Within their humble breasts the spirit of the Mahdi roused the fires of patriotism and religion. Life became filled with thrilling, exhilarating terrors. They existed in a new and wonderful world of imagination. While they lived there were great things to be done; and when they died, whether it were slaying the Egyptians or charging the British squares, a Paradise which they could understand awaited them. There are many Christians who reverence the faith of Islam and yet regard the Mahdi merely as a commonplace religious impostor whom force of circumstances elevated to notoriety. In a certain sense, this may be true. But I know not how a genuine may be distinguished from a spurious Prophet, except by the measure of his success.

The River War, whose candor might have ruined Churchill's name but instead helped make it, goes on to question Field Marshal Herbert Kitchener for his suppression of the uprising, where his behavior called to mind the Assyrian king Ashurbanipal. A national hero and war secretary during WWI, Kitchener reportedly dismembered the Mahdi's corpse and defaced his tomb. Churchill did not mention in the book, but did to friends, that he even suspected Kitchener had returned to England with the Mahdi's head. Churchill admired the Sudanese holy warriors, just as he had the Afghan warriors, and as he would come to admire the Iraqi warriors. He was even known to relax in Arab robes at home. (As late as 2014, the English newspaper the *Independent*, having found a joking letter from Churchill's sister-in-law on the subject, ran the breathless headline 'Sir Winston Churchill's family begged him not to convert to Islam, letter reveals.') But he knew a great deal more about naval warfare than he did about Islam, and as Lord of the Admiralty he had had the foresight to convert the British fleet from coal to petroleum before the war. Now he counseled that oil, not religion, should be the central issue in Iraq. When, before the Paris conference, Lloyd George sat down with Clemenceau to decide the fate of Iraq, the Frenchman lamented that 'the art of arranging how men are to live is even more complex than that of massacring them.' He asked Lloyd George what amendments to Sykes-Picot he desired. Lloyd George is said to have replied, 'I want Mosul.'

Clemenceau, having cottoned to the scheme, made his price for the place French partnership in the Iraq Petroleum Company. Meanwhile the Turks were threatening to reoccupy Mosul and the British caught wind that Washington might be plotting with them. The 'Eastern Question' became the 'Mosul Question.' In one of its first tests, the new League of Nations tried to negotiate the fate of Mosul. Once again Moslawis found themselves squeezed between empires. America was eventually made a partner in the IPC, though that didn't prevent its spies from exploring the option of backing the Iraqi nationalist rebels who'd begun sabotaging British encampments. Today we can take some small solace from the fact that the carving up of Iraq did worry some of the more prescient Americans in the region. One missionary said to Gertrude Bell, 'You are flying in the face of four millennia of history if you try to draw a line around Iraq and call it a political entity.'

The most important line turned out not to be a border but a pipeline, and it ran not around Iraq but out of it, from Mosul west and south through Jordan, ending in the Palestinian port city of Haifa. *Time* magazine was saying less than it might have but more than it knew when it called the pipeline the 'carotid artery of the British Empire.' The duct cut into the sacred heart of the world, blending oil and religion, a compound whose combustibility few then guessed.

Certainly to protect Britain's stake in Palestine, and perhaps partly to fulfill some sacred duty, Lloyd George's foreign secretary, Arthur Balfour, promised a portion of Palestine to the Zionist movement. And still today, for Levantines, it is a toss-up which betrayal was more catastrophic: Sykes-Picot or the Balfour Declaration. Just as Balfour inevitably comes up in any discussion about history with any Palestinian, no matter their politics or level of education or age, so Sykes-Picot comes up with any Iraqi. It is the beginning and end of every conversation about Iraq's existential predicaments. Or it used to be the end. Now the end is America.

The colleagues of Sykes who knew more about Iraq than he or any other diplomat, T. E. Lawrence and Gertrude Bell—she is often credited with 'creating' Iraq, though usually by Britons, not Iraqis—came to advocate Arab independence. When they saw the British government intended to ignore them and practice indirect rule by propping up pliant martinets across the region, both left their posts in despondency. Bell killed herself in her bedroom in Baghdad. Some believe Lawrence's death, too, was suicide. Their ends were read by their Arab friends, rightly, as bad omens. Though the pair had not been without their own imperial blind spots about Iraq. Like Sykes, like so many foreign visitors, Bell had been undone by Mosul, where, she wrote, 'hatred and the lust of slaughter weigh like inherited evils, transmitted (who can say?) through all the varying generations of conquerors since first the savage might of the Assyrian empire set its stamp on the land.' She went on, 'The organization of discord is carried to a high pitch of perfection in Mosul. The town is full of bravos who live by outrage, and live well. Whenever the unruly magnates wish to create a disturbance, they pass a word and a gratuity to these ruffians.' She concluded, 'Nowhere will the Arab national movement, if it reaches blossoming point, find a more congenial soil, and nowhere will it be watered by fuller streams of lawless vanity.'

Evidently this attitude made Bell's fellow archaeologists, many of them little more than relic hunters, feel better about looting Mosul of its ancient heritage. Excavations had begun at Nineveh in the previous century, and you could walk down the banks of the Tigris and see whole chunks of the Assyrian palaces and temples tied to rafts, floating downriver toward the Gulf, where they were loaded on ships for the journey to London, Paris, and Berlin. They were an immediate sensation in Europe, the clearest evidence yet that the origins of European civilization lay not in Athens and Rome, but, as historians were beginning to understand, farther back and farther east. At the Great Exhibition in London, you could see Sennacherib's and Ashurbanipal's palace rooms reconstructed beneath the glass arcades of the Crystal Palace. Time collapsed as Nineveh, a city until then only known as a place name in the Bible, suddenly physically existed. You were walking through it while on a stroll through Hyde Park. And what a stroll! A Nahum-like stroll by the friezes depicting war and torture and enslavement. What did the Europeans think of their origins now, looking at those vicious sculptures? Rudyard Kipling, for one, took the hint. 'Lo, all our pomp of yesterday is of one with Nineveh and Tyre!' he wrote on the occasion of Queen Victoria's Diamond Jubilee. He lived to see the Crystal Palace become the home of the Imperial War Museum after WWI.

In Iraq, meanwhile, replacing the ancient carvings was a tide pool of weaponry left by the war. It was as though the purloined friezes came to life. The guns were taken up by Iraqi independence fighters. Having been stunned by the Assyrian art back at home, the commanders were now stunned by the fighters in Iraq and their stealthy 'Bedouin warfare'—what we would call guerilla tactics, or harassing fire. The independence movement unified veterans who not long before had been fighting against one another. It also unified Sunna and Shia. Clerics of both sects declared jihad against the

British 'infidel government.' When the rebels marched on Mosul, Churchill, now war secretary himself, apparently decided he could no longer afford to indulge in cross-cultural sympathies or to condemn instances of barbarity—so long as they were committed by his side, of course.

Looking for a cheap way to put down the revolt, he turned to the Royal Air Force, newly independent from the army. The RAF had recently proved its lethality by bombing into submission a Somali Islamist rebellion against British rule that had been inspired by the Mahdi's in Sudan. The airmen now promised Churchill they could subdue the Iraqi rebels for a fraction of the cost of ground troops. With Britain sunk in war debt, he assented. What followed is among the nastiest forgotten atrocities of the twentieth century: the RAF's operations in Iraq mark nothing less than the advent of aerial war on a civilian population. Fifteen years before Guernica, the British were bombing unarmed Iraqis. They bombed them first to quell the rebellion; then they bombed them to punish them for not paying taxes; then they bombed them for target practice. A pilot boasted that in forty-five minutes an Iraqi village 'can be practically wiped out and a third of its inhabitants killed or injured by four or five planes[.]'

Almost as bad as the cruelty of the lost episode was its sophism. This fresh savagery bore the name of goodwill. Much nicer to drop explosives on civilians from the air, went the argument, than to shoot them with bullets on the ground. Air Marshal Hugh Trenchard (nickname: 'Boom') told Parliament that 'the natives of a lot of these tribes love fighting for fighting's sake,' and thus that 'they have no objection to being killed.' A general noted the 'natural fellow feeling between these nomad Arabs and the Air Force. . . . Perhaps both feel that they are at times in conflict with the vast elemental forces of nature.' Aerial bombardment was said to exert a 'moral effect' on its victims. It was, some suggested, divine in its mercies.

Even T. E. Lawrence had postulated that in the Arab mind bombing was seen 'not (as) punishment, but a misfortune from heaven striking the community.' Another officer said, 'Bombing from the air is regarded almost as an act of God to which there is no effective reply but immediate submission.' Free of the carved Mosul marble slabs, Ishtar revived. The sentimental instinct and the killer instinct were merged. Terror was love.

Iraqi nationalists nonetheless ended up killing two thousand British troops, most of them Indian conscripts. Churchill advised, unsuccessfully, pulling out of Iraq entirely. In a letter that could have been written by Robert McNamara, maybe even Donald Rumsfeld on a very lucid day, Churchill conceded: 'Week after week and month after month for a long time to come we shall have a continuance of this miserable, wasteful, sporadic warfare.'

By that point history had outpaced him. Islam and anticolonialism, too, had merged. In Asia and Africa, declaring jihad became another way of declaring independence and vice versa. This was recognized by some Europeans. A Paris professor wrote, 'The revolutionary idea among us and the messianic idea among the Muslims share the same instinct, the same aspiration.' Movements arose in Sudan and Somalia, India, Egypt, Libya, Morocco, Algeria. Over the course of the twentieth century, nationalism, Pan-Arabism, and Islamism crossbred and eventually ignited a more esoteric independence movement—the ambition to create an Islamic state. The rise of a generation of despots in Muslim countries and events in Palestine focused and embittered this ambition. *The Neglected Duty*, a screed written by one of the assassins of Egyptian president Anwar Sadat in 1981, read: 'If the religious obligations of Islam cannot be carried out in their entirety without the support of an Islamic state, then the establishment of such a state is a religious obligation. . . . If such a state cannot be established without war, then this war is a Muslim religious obligation as well.' By 1995, Algeria's Armed Islamic Group, inspired by the success of the Taliban, could proclaim the entire country to be in a state of apostasy and set itself the task of redemption through the mass murder of civilians.

The Islamic State, in other words, is only the latest in a long series of attempts to create an Islamic state. The original attempt, of course—you'll excuse the sudden telescoping of time—was that of Muhammad and his followers. We find jihad-based polities being tried in West Africa in the eighteenth century, in Spain in the fifteenth, and, most notoriously, in Iran in the eleventh century with the Assassins, the Shia separatist group that believed the course of Islam had gone awry and that the way to set it to rights was to kill officials—as intimately as possible, with daggers. They were touchingly literal about Muhammad's insistence on never putting a fellow Muslim to the sword. They often ensured their own capture and martyrdom, and in as much were, perhaps, Islam's first suicide-murderers.

The Islamic State is not even the first such movement to dismember Iraq. Indeed, eighth-century Mesopotamia was home to Islam's first great revolutionary group. That group, the Kharijites as they were known, were famous 'for their vigils, excessive prostration in worship, fasting, recitation of the Koran, and fear of Hell,' as one historian writes. The Kharijites also treated women equally and refused to accord any more respect to the caliph than to ordinary Muslims, their creed being 'Authority belongs to God alone,' whose distance from No God but God is negligible, if there is any distance at all. It was an outlook that allowed them to justify assassinating Caliph Ali, the murder in which Islam's central sectarian schism, between Sunna and Shia, originates. Not coincidentally, it was also in Iraq that the first Shia rebellions against Sunni domination of the religion began, just as it would be in Iraq (and not Iran), eleven hundred years later, that the Ayatollah Khomeini began his revolution.

The Kharijites reached the apex of their jihad when they occupied Mosul. Critics of the Islamic State, including other jihadis, have got in the habit of calling Baghdadi's followers modern-day Kharijites. The comparison is admissible save for one important difference, which is that the Kharijites were better and more self-aware writers. Wrote one Khawarij poet:

We care not, once our souls have passed away,
What you do to our bodies and severed members.
We hope for paradise when our skulls lie beneath the dust,
Like dried up colocynth.
I am a man whom my God will resurrect at his appointed time.

In 1937, a year after Iraq's first military coup and the largest Arab uprisings against Jewish immigration to Palestine to date, months after Germany reoccupies the Rhineland, days after Guernica is bombed, a boy is born to a man named Hussein in a village hard by Tikrit called al-Awja. It means 'crooked.' The boy comes from a tribe as old as the dirt and a family as poor as it and he sleeps on a dirt floor. He is kicked awake by his stepfather, Hassan the Liar, as he's known around town, for insisting on the honorific *hajj* though he's never been to Mecca. 'Get up, you son of a whore!' Hassan hisses at the boy, and tells him to go steal eggs from the neighbors.

The boy becomes one of the Sons of the Alleys. He works as a tout, a cigarette seller, a coffeehouse waiter, fending off the grabby pederasts; he sells watermelon on the Mosul-Baghdad trunk line, dreams about what's happening in those big cities. Corruption, irreligion, that's what's happening, says his uncle and mentor, a former soldier and ex-convict whose hatred of the British and British-backed king of Iraq, Faisal II, is such that he is known not by his given name,

Kairallah, but as *Sharallah*, the Violence of God. The Violence of God
counsels his nephew to instead admire the Nazis, with their populist militarism and their hatred of Jews. Iraq has allied with Hitler,
and this time, Sharallah believes, the Germans will not disappoint.
Under them, Sunni Arabs will unite and force out the infidel foreigners and apostate Shia.

The boy finds politics before religion. He takes part in the 1952
protests against Faisal II. His talents as an organizer and as a street
tough blossom simultaneously. He leads student protests, and, when
that fails, leads the student protesters in beating up shopkeepers
who refuse to close their stores in support of the protests. In 1958,
rebellion begins in Mosul and spreads out. Faisal is executed; the
king's uncle is dragged through the streets and dismembered, and
what remains of him is left hanging from a streetlamp in downtown
Baghdad for two days; the prime minister is run over with cars, then
buried, then disinterred, then chopped to pieces. Disappointed not
to be among the choppers, the boy, now a man, and an aspiring poet,
makes up for it the next year by murdering an ally of the new prime
minister, Abd al-Karim Qasim. He establishes his credentials with
the Fascist-inspired Baath. He attempts to kill Qasim, shooting his
motorcade. He flees to Egypt, where he is steeped in Nasserite Pan-
Arabism and where, perhaps, he begins a long relationship with the
C.I.A., despite his contempt for America. ('You cannot buy an Arab,'
the run-over-and-dismembered prime minister had quipped, 'but
you can rent one.') Another rebellion the following year, and this
time the bullets don't miss Qasim. Iraqi state television viewers are
reminded of this every night for a week, as the same footage is re-
aired again and again. It shows a mutinous Iraqi soldier picking up
and dropping Qasim's dead appendages. Finally the soldier grabs the
corpse by the hair, lifts his head, and spits in his face. The son of
Hussein, who watches this clip ecstatically, has begun calling him-

self Saddam, an invented name taken from the Persian verb meaning to crush or destroy. He is the one who destroys.

The Baath takes full control of Iraq in 1968. A fellow Tikriti is president but Saddam is the real power. After demonstrations in the Shia strongholds of Najaf and Karbala arranged by the Dawah party, Saddam begins executing Shia clerics and leaders. This is mostly ignored by his foreign boosters, however, because Iraq has otherwise become one of the most educated and, in its way, progressive nations in the region. Thousands of illiterate adults enroll in reading classes (they're made to, upon pain of imprisonment), and Saddam calls for equality for women. UNESCO gives him an award. He uses oil revenues to give generously to other countries, especially Palestine. He is the new Nasser, the unifier of Arabs.

In 1979 he takes power in a bloodless coup and, after a decade of peace and prosperity, attacks Iran. The Baath is, nominally, secular, and Saddam at first portrays the war as a struggle of Iraqi enlightenment versus Persian superstition, his modernity versus the Ayatollah's backwardness. But the worse the war gets, the further back into the past and into myth Saddam must reach. He calls himself the new Saladin. He calls the war the second battle of Qadisiya, the *Qadisiya Saddam*. He is right at least in this sense: the war reopens Islam's sectarian chasm. He imprisons thousands of Shia, alleged traitors, and exiles another two hundred thousand members of the sect to Iran. Eventually every Iraqi man under the age of fifty-two will be called up and more than two-thirds of the country's male population will serve. As many as a half million people—no one will ever know the real figure—will die in what is called the first great war of the third world.

No sooner has the shooting started then he is commissioning monuments to the war dead, as though willing them that way. In 1985, he announces plans for the first monument, calling it, four years before an armistice, the Victory Arch. It is composed of two arms emerging from the ground, their hands grasping two crossed swords. The bronze limbs are taken from plaster casts of Saddam's own arms. The swords are supposedly made from the metal of the weapons of fallen Iraqi soldiers. Around the bases of the monument, the height of the Arc de Triomphe, piles of helmets, supposedly those of fallen Iranians, are cast in cement. Around the country, murals are painted of Saddam in Ashurbanipal-like poses, riding in chariots, attacking enemies with bow and arrow and spear. In some, time collapses: an Assyrian-style Saddam charges forward with archaic weapons and assisted by a helicopter or a fighter jet or a Scud missile. In 1989, he marks the armistice by holding state burial ceremonies—for the Babylonian kings. Reconstructing ancient Babylon, he replaces the bricks with new ones inscribed thus: THE BABYLON OF NEBUCHADNEZZAR WAS REBUILT IN THE ERA OF LEADER PRESIDENT SADDAM HUSSEIN. He renames the province of Mosul as Nineveh.

Sunk in debt, he invades Kuwait. He makes a devotional matter of its rapine, referring to this war as 'The Call.' No one hears it. So he points out Kuwait was an invention of the imperialists after WWI. He is not invading but reunifying. 'O great Iraqi people, sons of our great people, valiant men of our courageous armed forces,' he proclaims on state television, 'Satan's follower Bush committed his treacherous crime, he and the criminal Zionism. The great duel, the mother of all battles, between victorious right and the evil that will certainly be defeated has begun, Allah willing.' The valiant men of his courageous armed forces break ranks and flee homewards. Those unlucky enough to take Highway 80, having been promised safe passage by the Americans, are incinerated in their thousands by American missiles.

The Mother of All Battles—it becomes the official Iraqi name for the First Gulf War, all six weeks of it. As an Iraqi referring to the war, you are, officially, required to call it that. All evidence to the contrary, Saddam tells Iraqis it was a victory. A victory, and a vindication, he insists, but at the same time a shameful victimization at the hands of the imperialists, he laments. The retributive theory of history redoubled. The struggle against America is Iraq's eternal struggle, he declares. Every year, you must commemorate The Mother of All Battles, the contest of 'truth against untruth.' He orders printed commemorative postage stamps. One stamp memorializes an accidental American bombing that kills over four hundred Iraqi civilians in an air raid shelter known as Amariya. Iraqi media calls it 'the worst criminal action by the U.S. in the twentieth century'—put forward 'as the Iraqi equivalent of Guernica or even Hiroshima,' as Jon Lee Anderson notes in *The Fall of Baghdad*. On the borders of the stamp, in vertical type, is written DISASTROUS U.S.A.&ALLIEDS ATTACK AGAINST AL AMIRIYA SHELTER, ON 13/2/1991. The art inside the borders shows a grief-stricken woman in a black abaya. She is set against a beatific yellow glow and holds outstretched to you a stiff infant. From the child's back hangs what at first appears to be a bed of chewing gum, then drapery. Finally you savvy this is supposed to be dripping blood. The picture resembles a crude pietà. Crude, but no cruder, it turns out, than the scene at the shelter, where the heat from the blast is so intense that, as one journalist writes, 'bodies fused together so that they formed entire blocks of flesh, a layer of human fat an inch deep lying on the surface of the water pumped in by firemen.' The victims are melted into a kind of human memorial. As the CNN-watcher Saddam knows, al Amiriyah has already become exhibit **A** for European and American opponents of the war. Christopher Hitchens, before his conversion, does the Sunday morning chat-show circuit sounding off Nahum-like, telling of Iraqis 'rendered into soap.'

The Mother of All Battles—it becomes Iraqi existence itself. War in the south, war in the north, war above. American jets menace the skies. Signs and portents everywhere. The Kurds revolt, then the Shia. The Shia clerics in Karbala and Najaf assure their follow-ers the Mahdi is near, the end is close, the tyrant must be toppled to prime the ground for the millennium. Two million people flee Iraq. Saddam coopts the Shia apocalypse, he doubles down on it. He attacks nature. He gasses the mountains. He drains the wetlands. Utility workers killed by Marsh Arabs while pumping swamp water are proclaimed martyrs in 'The Jihad of Rebuilding.' In Baghdad he breaks ground on what will be the largest mosque in the world. He produces documentary proof of his descent from the Prophet Muhammad. He adds 'Allahu Akbar' to the Iraqi flag. He commis-sions a Koran written in his own blood. Piety and savagery prog-ress in lockstep. His Islamic revival must be accompanied by death. Apostates must die. Infidels must die. Spies must die, and skeptics, and questioners, and onlookers, and others, and friends, and family, must die. And more than die, they must be tortured, dismembered, disemboweled, flayed, beheaded, for their own good, for their souls, so that they may be reconstituted into his sacred realm. It is out of his love of the Arab nation, of the true Islam, Saddam knows, that he must carry on this bloody work.

In Tikrit he goes the full Ashurbanipal. He turns it into a temple to his power over life and death, a city-size sepulcher-in-waiting. Sanctioned, unable to buy weapons, he buys marble. He builds a pal-ace for his mother, a palace for his own birthday, palaces for his sons Uday and Qusay. The rumored scenes of sex and carnage in the last are beyond Assyrian. While Saddam's corps of body doubles circu-late the country like drones, waiting for assassins' bullets, he is in his salon. Why? What is he doing in there? We convince ourselves he is building a demonic arsenal. He is sinking a nuclear silo beneath the settees and wainscoting, we become convinced. To Tikrit weapons inspectors are dispatched. They are turned away, return, are turned away again. Finally admitted, in 2002, they are amazed by what they find but they find no warheads. What they find: books. Books upon books. A vast library. What is he doing in there? Writing. For years, the secret bibliomaniac has been writing.

On Saddam Hussein's shelves are the collected nonfiction works of Saddam Hussein: *On History, Heritage and Religion* (1981); *Our Policy is the Embodiment of the Nation's Present and Future* (also 1981, the same year he has published his uncle Khairallah's philosophical treatise *Three Whom God Should Not Have Created: Persians, Jews and Flies*); *Thus We Should Fight Persians* (1983); and *America Reaps the Thorns its Rulers Sowed in the World* (2001). Perhaps more interesting is the late fiction of Saddam Hussein. In the novel *Zabiba and the King,* which he begins in 2000, a brutal pagan king who 'wanted kings who ruled in the far reaches of the world to submit to him' meets a beautiful, poor young woman while out riding. He is entranced and invites her to his palace, where they talk for days. The king tells Zabiba that he is the way he is because of his boyhood. He was kicked out of his mother's home and sent to live with an uncle. Zabiba teaches him about Islam. When a foreign army invades, Zabiba hurls herself in front of a sword thrust meant for the king. The people rise up and repel the invader. It is said Saddam was inspired by the daughter of one of his advisers, whom he made his fourth wife. That is followed by *Walled Fortress* and, finally, *Get Out, You Damned One!,* which Saddam completes only in the spring of 2003, as the Americans prepare to invade.

A coalition converges on Iraq, not as diverse as the coalition of Babylonians, Elamites, and Medes who converged on Assyria, but enough. His sons flee to Mosul. There they are killed. He returns to the countryside, to boyhood. Again he is a Son of the Alleys. He sleeps on a dirt floor in a village.

When the Marines arrive at Tikrit, that May, a captain tells Dexter Filkins of *The New York Times*, 'Wow, this looks like Las Vegas.' The palace compound contains a hundred and thirty-four buildings. It is only the most magnificent of eighty such compounds of Saddam's around Iraq. A monumental bronze statue of Saddam is dismantled and shipped to the U.S., where it is melted down and recast into Operation Iraqi Freedom commemorative medals. The Marines don't stay long. They hand the complex over to the Army 4th Infantry, who name it Forward Operating Base Ironhorse, and they to the 1st Infantry, who rename it Forward Operating Base Danger. The Big Red One moves into Saddam's fantasy with apparently no more self-consciousness than it carries on its faintly perverse nickname. The 1st had fought at Cantigny, at Kasserine Pass, in Sicily, Normandy, the Ardennes. It secured Nuremberg during the trials and Tan Son Nhut during the Tet offensive and blocked Highway 80 so that it could be turned into the Highway of Death. Now its engineers, having nothing better to do, install in the vast corridors plywood bedroom dividers and particle-board office cubicles, fiberoptic cable and dumbbell racks and basketball hoops. When the inventor of the combat-aerobics exercise craze Tae Bo, Billy Blanks, visits the Big Red One during a morale-boosting tour, he says of the soldiers, 'They're changing people's lives and sacrificing their lives, like Jesus did, to set people free. I just hope they see it. Being in a place for so long, sometimes you get blinded.'

Actually, it's not fair to say they bear no self-consciousness. Just not enough to notice that, in the estimation of the people whom you claim to be liberating, occupying the palaces of the oppressor you're liberating them from takes some of the charm out of the liberation. The Americans at least recognize the sinister campiness of the place. 'There is much within the complex that would delight the kitsch-loving tourist,' writes a peculiarly silver-penned reporter with *Stars and Stripes.* 'Brass and glass chandeliers drip from the ceilings and sconces. Nearly every horizontal surface is coated with a thin veneer of marble. Twisting marble staircases lead to endless marble hallways, which lead to cavernous marble rooms (not to mention small, poorly functioning marble bathrooms with toilets inlaid with gold leaf).' The palaces, it turns out, are a shambles. Marble veneer falls from the walls like dry flypaper. 'It's a façade,' a major tells the *Stripes.* 'It's flashy, but nothing works.'

When I arrived at Tikrit, in the summer of 2016, the yellow and green banners of the Shia militias who had occupied the city hung from the fences around the palace compound. A militia commander was called and I waited for an hour at the northern gate while his proxy was sent. All Iraqi fighters, regular and irregular alike, took liberties with their battle dress, but the Shia militiamen were in a category of their own. They looked as though they'd been kitted out at some urban unisex martial athleisure boutique. It was a sartorial riot of dozens of different patterns and shades of camouflage and denim and tactical gear and gym wear and footwear of every description, and they paid as much attention to their hair as any Prussian cavalry officer. They may have had no training on their weapons, they may have been committing human rights abuses, but their heads were marvels of trimming and mousse. As I stood there admiring a few exemplars, and they stared at me in hardly less wonder, a pickup arrived at the gate and out stepped the commander's man. He wore forest camouflage whose deep green would have served him well in a Congolese war but had no place in this one, blue felt Adidas sneakers, and a keffiyeh wrapped rakishly about his neck though it was over a hundred degrees out.

'What are you doing in Iraq—it's dangerous!' he demanded with a simpering grin.

I looked down and saw what the grin was about: in his palm was a grenade. He jiggered his wrist as though the thing were dice and our suddenly entwined futures the craps table. Before I could frown he exclaimed, 'A picture!' He drew out his cellphone and handed the grenade to the gate guard. The guard puzzled over it and handed it to the driver of the pickup. The driver looked at it neutrally and set it on the passenger seat.

After the photo shoot, I was led to a building of mock-Mediterranean white masonry on the riverbank escarpment. It was here, from the long stone terrace, that the jihadis had kicked the corpses of Speicher cadets into the turbid current. The terrace was now hung with portraits of the victims and draped with a black banner of Koranic verse. Walking on, we passed handwritten signs on low stakes: MASS GRAVE NO. 1: MARTYRS OF TIKRIT MASSACRE. A middle-aged militiaman in a sweat-stained tank-top who'd given up on trying to compete for grooming points with his younger comrades walked around the graves, worrying his prayer beads and clucking his tongue in theatrical disapproval. I wondered how many visitors he'd done that for.

The grandest of Saddam's palaces was on a promontory, surrounded by villas and chalets in various architectural styles—New Islamic, Neo-Assyrian, Brutalist-Baathist, Fascist-Floral. The years of war had made it all feel somehow less obscene. All the rents in the cheap masonry, the rebar hanging from fake cornices, the craters, the sheer windswept bleakness, gave the place a kind of gravity in death it had never possessed in life. Most of the jihadi signage remained. Across the length of a lintel, on a villa, was the most lovingly painted Islamic State standard I would ever see in Iraq. The jihadis had evidently been as bored living here as Saddam's family had been, as the Americans had been, as the militiamen were now. Looking at the calligraphy, the expanse of buildings behind it, the Tigris beyond, it was as though you were looking at a tableau vivant of history, watching the sins of the centuries accumulating, melding, the crimes of Mesopotamia and its many invaders, of the Ottomans and the British and Saddam and the militias and the Americans flowing into the crimes of the Caliphate, past and present running together, being forgotten, being repeated, being written about, in this preposterous declawed cut-rate Nineveh.

———————

In Abu Omar's tent, the conversation about history continued. It hadn't escaped his notice that that battle for Mosul was joined in 2016, the centenary of Sykes-Picot. He placed no numerological significance in this, I was glad to learn, but he liked the symmetry of it. So did I. So did the jihadis. After they seized Mosul, the al-Hayat Media Center released a video called 'The End of Sykes-Picot.' The host of the video wears a black baseball cap over long, stringy hair, a pinstripe dishdasha, and an AK slung on his back. He raises an Islamic State flag at a Syrian checkpoint on the border with Iraq. 'Right now we're on the side of al-Sham,' he says, in slightly accented English, walking along like the host of a BBC documentary. 'As you can see, this is the so-called border of Sykes-Picot. *Alhamdulillah*, we don't recognize it and we will never recognize it. *Inshallah*, this is not the first border we will break, *inshallah* we will break other borders also, but we start with this, *inshallah*.' He walks over a hillock and crosses into Iraq. 'This is the so-called checkpoint of the soldiers of *Maliki-stan*.' He walks among the American-made Humvees and jeeps that had belonged to the Iraqi army and border patrol and are now part of the Islamic State fleet. 'Look how much money America spends to fight Islam and it just ends up being in our pockets, *alhamdulillah*.'

When Abu Omar brought up Sykes-Picot and Turkey's role in the rise of the Islamic State, I asked 'So, you think the Islamic State was conceived a century ago?'

'No,' he said. 'I am saying this has all been planned. I cannot explain to you how, exactly, because it's a very deep scheme. Bigger than me, bigger than you, bigger than all of us. Very deep politics. But it was all planned. And in the end they will divide Iraq.' Sighing, he continued, 'I don't know. But I know the main reason for Iraq's destruction is America. Honestly. During Saddam, you wouldn't hear a single gunshot. Not one. America brought all of these thieving politicians. All they do is steal. They brought militias who kill millions of Sunnis. Who brought those? America! Politicians like Maliki. America brought them!'

He did not add that America was backing both Iraq and the Islamic State, but many soldiers and Moslawis I knew had.

During the night I spent in Tahrir with the assault team, they had kept me awake with proof.

'I saw Americans with the jihadis,' one man told me matter-of-factly. 'They spoke English very well and had American faces and beards.'

'Zarqawi worked for the Americans, but they killed him before he could reveal this,' said another. The same was true, he went on, of Baghdadi. 'American forces are protecting him, hiding him. Why?'

'I don't know,' I said. 'Why?'

'You're American, you should know,' he said. 'Osama bin Laden too. For four months before he was killed by the Americans, they were watching him. But they didn't capture him. Why?'

This time I just raised my eyebrows in desperation and shrugged.

Another man cut in. 'There are Americans in Daesh, it's true, but not just Americans. People from many countries have joined. It's said the Americans gave the jihadis their weapons. No, those were weapons the Americans gave the Iraqi army. When the army left Mosul, Daesh took them.'

I nodded gratefully. He went on.

'But Americans did send supplies to Daesh in Ramadi. And their airstrikes there didn't hit the jihadis. The supplies they dropped weren't dropped in civilian areas. They were dropped in Daesh areas.'

When I first began hearing these stories, I attempted to counter them. One's feelings about the American invasion of Iraq aside, I would say, the U.S. had rebuilt the Iraqi military. It had specially created CTS to combat jihadis. Washington still armed the Iraqi military. Thousands of American servicepeople were in Iraq as we spoke, aiding the Mosul offensive. Billions were being spent on the effort. Why would we also be backing the Islamic State? What could we have to gain?

This was the wrong logic, of course. That was all true, they would say—and that's precisely what made America so brilliant. It controlled both sides of this war, just as it did every other war. Eventually I learned to shut up and just listen, to try and discern the conflicting sentiments beneath the conversation. There was respect and suspicion, betrayal and gratitude, grievance and awe. The longer and closer I listened, the more I saw the opposing strands had fused. Respect and suspicion were one, grievance and awe inseparable. Iraqis believed America was betraying them because that's what a power worthy of reverence did. It betrayed, ally and enemy alike. You venerate those who do you great violence. As Samir al-Khalil wrote, Saddam had taught Iraqis to be 'a populace to whom strength of character is invariably associated with the ability to both sustain and inflict pain.'

But Iraqis were never remonstrating with me, not even protesting. They were just trying to help me understand how America worked. They were amused, and a little touched, that, as a person from this omnipotent place, I couldn't see the truth. There was no way to react but with tangled feelings of my own. I wanted to apologize to them, to slap them, to hug them, to yell at them. It was a terrible, a sublime intimacy, and in the midst of it I came to feel a shameful and a belligerent nostalgia for a world I had never known but in which they were sure they lived, a world managed by ingenious, pragmatic, victorious Americans.

And of course there was no putting the American invasion *aside*. What a stupid thing for me to think much less say. The American war now defined Iraq. Iraqi history since 2003 could only be understood in the context of the war, in its baneful shadow and blinding light. In the new Iraqi cosmology, the invasion was genesis and apocalypse. America had the power to ruin or to save Iraq, as it wished. It was Ishtar, creator-destroyer, loathed and loved. Coming to understand this, I finally saw what Michael Herr had meant in *Dispatches* when he'd written that, as an American journalist in Vietnam, 'you were as responsible for everything you saw as everything you did.' A more awful understanding followed. In the minds of many Iraqis, I realized, America and the Islamic State were equal in this crucial sense: they were invaders. No matter what they claimed their intentions were—liberation, salvation, modernization—they were both invaders. When you're invaded, the difference between a democratic utopia and a religious one is immaterial.

Yet most Iraqis I came to know well, civilians and soldiers, claimed they wanted to move to America. The psychology was complex. For obvious and unassailable reasons, Iraqis hate America. For less obvious ones, they admire it, even love it. They love America and hate it for some of the same reasons, chief among them its strength, a strength they conceive of as second only to God's.

Sometimes their hatred was plainly expressed, as when a refugee who was living on the floor of an abandoned hotel in Anbar, on the other side of a tarp from an open toilet, glared at me and asked, 'As an American, could you live in these conditions?' Sometimes it came with unconscious irony, as when a general, sitting at his desk, told me, 'America is responsible for this war,' as he pressed the channel buttons on his satellite TV remote, flipping among American programs, from one about fishing to another about hunting rifles to a third whose content was unapparent but which involved very large breasts. Sometimes it was just a look, like the look General Abdulwahab gave me in Fallujah when he said, 'Americans took Iraq in twenty days.' It was a look I received many times, a look that said 'You invaded and crushed this place, and now it's fallen to us to face the consequences. But in spite of ourselves we find we still like you. So welcome back and go fuck yourself.'

In this country vastly older than mine, this civilization that gave us civilization, Iraqis had long since learned what I was just coming to see: the histories of our two countries, of Iraq and America, were entwined. Fourteen years before, having been attacked by nineteen men, not one of them Iraqi, America, in its fear, in its shame, in its belligerent nostalgia, had attacked Iraq. But in attacking Iraq, America wasn't just attacking a country. It was attacking history. In Mesopotamia we had sought our retribution on the past itself. For once and all, the New World would tear the curse of war from the Old, impose order upon chaos, we pledged, and the future had answered not with order, but with more chaos, with the Islamic State, with that fever dream of the American mania. Now the two countries were bound together in a death embrace, ally and enemy, our resentment-filled and respect-filled eyes locked, our teeth sunk into one another's flesh. The history of neither country any longer made sense without the other, and nor did our mutually twilit futures.

The most shaming and the most sublime part of this new understanding: no matter how much resentment they felt, Iraqis expressed their thoughts about America to me with a warmth and a curiosity and a clemency that only left me loving them the more. They were always careful to say they knew a man was not his government. They always wanted to know how, as an American, *I* felt about all this, what *I* thought, not in the hopes of getting an apology, but of gaining some mutual comprehension, of forging a connection with a person from the place that had made their lives a hell. It was the very meaning of forgiveness. It was humanity itself.

And they always had stories about Americans they'd loved. One morning, I was with a squad in a requisitioned house next to the Tigris. A young soldier said, 'I want to tell you a story.' When he was ten years old, he said, the Americans invaded. Between his school and his home in Baghdad sprang up an American checkpoint. At first he was scared of them. But then he found they were friendly. Every day after classes he'd go there and spend two hours with the soldiers. They fed him, played with him, showed him pictures of their children. He taught them Arabic words, they taught him English words. He loved them. They loved him. Even now, he thought of them every day.

I looked at him expectantly.

'That's all,' he said. 'That's my story.'

I asked whether he was glad America had come all those years ago. The stupidity of the question occurred to me only as it left my mouth.

'No,' he said, smiling.

The conversation about history brought Abu Omar and Omar back around to the subject of the imam Abu Bakr. The imam had come to be known to the residents of Zahra as 'Little Abu Bakr,' to distinguish him from Abu Bakr al-Baghdadi. (Abu Bakr was the Prophet Muhammad's father-in-law and his closest companion, and it is a common jihadi nom de guerre.) Like other Islamic State higher-ups, the imam often moved and sermonized with a videographer in tow. Like big Abu Bakr, he believed he was instrumental in history—or, more to the point, in the end of history.

'I didn't like him from the first time I saw him,' Abu Omar told me. 'His eyes shone with evil. They looked as though they'd explode from malice. You could find no mercy in his face. . . . He was a big, rough man with a huge belly. He loved to eat tashrib, the lamb stew. These fatties, they're like vampires. Sucking people's blood to the last drop.'

I pointed out that I too loved tashrib. It was my favorite Iraqi dish. Abu Omar and Omar laughed.

'Tell him they were monsters, monsters,' Omar said to the translator. 'Excuse me, but Abu Bakr, he was a dog. A son of a dog.'

'He had no morals,' Abu Omar said. 'We were not raised with such morals. To kill this and that!'

'He considered everyone an infidel,' said Omar.

'He told sons to attack their fathers,' his father said, 'if they didn't allow them to go on jihad. He instigated women against their husbands, if their husbands didn't allow it. He gave them the right to beat their husbands, or kill them, and to leave the house to go on jihad. This isn't right.'

Omar admitted, 'In the beginning I believed them. It made sense to me. Later, when they started killing Yazidis and Christians and making them flee from their homes, I stopped believing them. You know, our prophet had Jewish neighbors, and they were his friends.' But, he went on, 'I want you to record this: When we go back to Mosul, if Christians or Yazidis attack us, I will be the first one to slaughter them.'

Ignoring his son's comment, Abu Omar said of the jihadis, 'These are not Muslims. They came with the name of Islam. They didn't enter any place without destroying it. They came only with the name of religion. When I saw Abu Bakr al-Baghdadi, he was wearing exactly what Iranians wear. That long black shirt. And once I saw the Iranian television channels, I noticed they were exactly like the Islamic State's channels.'

I asked if he thought Baghdadi might be Iranian—he certainly wouldn't have been the first to voice this theory to me.

'Yes, I think so. I think so. They claim they're Sunnis, but what have they done for Sunnis? You tell me. Did they help or destroy us? And compare that to how Shia are living.'

As we talked, Omar became more candid, and Abu Omar allowed him to say more.

'If it wasn't for my father,' Omar said, 'I would have joined them for sure. I swear to God, they would have been able to fool me and brainwash me.'

'Do you know what they do?' Abu Omar said. 'They tell you, Son, you are doing jihad for God, you will be martyred and go to heaven. There are mermaids in heaven. You will eat lunch with the Prophet. Through jihad you will defend your pride, your house, your money.'

'They told me jihad was mandatory,' Omar said, 'as mandatory as prayer. They said if you didn't wage jihad with them, you'd be tortured in hell. They were saying it was mandatory for everyone, even little kids and women. They said our enemies were attacking Muslim houses. We had to defend Muslim lands. They said that if we were in the infidel's territory, you could choose whether to wage jihad or not. But since we were in Muslim territory, there was no choice, it was a must.'

'All these things are mentioned in the Koran, by the way,' Abu Omar added. 'It says kill the infidels and be merciful toward each other.'

A gun was fired outside, somewhere in the camp. Abu Omar sat upright and his face tightened in fright. I told him I thought the Kurdish guards were probably just dispersing a crowd.

'I'm worried to go to sleep tonight,' he said. 'Imagine if we wake up and Daesh is here. I swear to God, I'm afraid that will happen. It could happen. Why not? Don't you think?'

3

Historians aren't certain from which ancient people the Kurds descend. One theory is that they come from the Medes, who helped sack Nineveh in 612 B.C. For centuries the Kurdish tribesmen left the ravines of the Zagros mostly for the purposes of embarrassing larger armies, fending off Arab tribesmen, or sacking some village or monastery. They were among the most feared of Ottoman janissaries—it was Kurds who in many instances carried out massacres of Armenian and Assyrian Christians before WWI—when they weren't fighting the Ottomans. They also fought the British, and then almost every government of independent Iraq, most bitterly that of Saddam, who killed between fifty thousand and two hundred thousand Kurds, it's estimated, including with chemical weapons. Some consider it an attempted genocide. They fought each other, too, in a three-year-long civil war in the '90s.

'More an attitude than an army,' is how one Kurd described the peshmerga force to me. It is a diffuse institution which contained, by the time of the Mosul offensive, anywhere from several tens of thousands to a hundred thousand fighters, depending on who was counting and how proud they were feeling that day. Many were volunteers. Only a few had training that would warrant the name in a serious, or even an unserious, military. But if their tactics were negligible, and occasionally as suicidal as those of the jihadis, their courage certainly was not.

In 2003, the peshmerga fought alongside the Americans and were rewarded when Iraqi Kurdistan became semiautonomous. They assisted in the occupation of Mosul. After Petraeus left the city, they were given more or less free rein. Some Moslawis will tell you that's when the real trouble began, before Maliki showed his fangs. Kurdish soldiers were accused of looking for vengeance and enrichment after all those years of oppression, and doubtless some were. Abu Fahad said it was peshmerga and American soldiers who killed his first wife at the checkpoint.

After Iraqi troops took Fallujah in the summer of 2016, they spent the next two months making their way north along the Tigris, taking more cities and villages, closing in on Mosul. By the autumn, they were ready to move on the city. On the morning of Monday, October 17, the Iraqi prime minister, Haider al-Abadi, sat down in front of the television cameras, wearing a black military tunic and flanked by generals. He said: 'I announce today the start of these heroic operations to free you from your terror and the oppression of Daesh. And, God willing, soon we will meet on the soil of Mosul to celebrate liberation and your salvation, and we will live, once again, with all our religions and our sects, together.' A little prematurely, he added 'The hour of victory has arrived.'

Before CTS, the 16th and 9th divisions could breach Mosul, however, the peshmerga had to extend a cordon around it in the northeast, to prevent the jihadis breaking out in this direction and to protect what would become the rear of the eastern front. Over the previous year, the peshmerga had pushed the Caliphate from much of the Nineveh plain between Irbil and Mosul. They had halted on a ridgeline that ran parallel to Highway 2 and overlooked Mosul. Now it was time to finish the job. The peshmerga were to move from the ridgeline and advance on Bashiqa, a small city about six miles from east Mosul. To get to Bashiqa they would have to first take a series of villages ranged on either side of the highway. Once done, the main assault on Mosul could begin.

At dawn on the Sunday after Abadi's announcement, I joined a battalion of peshmerga—about five hundred male soldiers, along with a few women—gathered in the shadow of the ridgeline. They were sons, fathers, grandfathers, daughters. They were shopkeepers, mechanics, clerks, teachers. They wore an assortment of camouflages, beige, green, gray, or traditional Kurdish billowing pants and jackets, waist sashes, headscarves. Some carried antique Kalashnikovs, others new assault rifles. Though few had helmets and fewer body armor, strapped to backs and belts and legs were daggers, revolvers, axes. Many had received the call to duty only the day before and had been driven to the front by proud and worried family members or in overnight taxis. They were accompanied by a column of vehicles new, old, and very old: armored personnel carriers, Humvees, SUVs, ambulances, Soviet tanks, backhoes, bulldozers, long-suffering sedans, and a procession of retrofitted pickups and battlewagons whose tenuous welding and argumentative suspensions told of the years Kurds spent fighting Iraqi forces with hand-me-down and homemade hardware. The war against the Islamic State had improved their lot. Also in the column were American commandos, sequestered and in a tight wordless cluster of JLTVs and MRAPs with remote-controlled machine-gun turrets that looked, in this cortege, imported from some future conflict in space.

At 7 a.m. exactly, the idling engines came to life and cries went up. 'Long live peshmerga!'

'Death to Daesh!'

The troops started down an unpaved track that led through the Nineveh plain toward Bashiqa. As the march went on, villages receded into abandoned farmhouses, crop fields into dunes, and the sun made itself felt. A miles-long dust cloud rose above the column.

The first enemy mortar shells arrived with whizzes and thuds. They were off-target, and the soldiers looked on at the dirt plumes with indifference. The first bursts of incoming gunfire soon followed, and these were cause for more alarm. The bullets flew from a compound on the crest of a slope at a bend in the track. In the compound were several outbuildings and a rambling, two-story cinderblock home. The column slowed. With each group of vehicles that went around the bend and out of sight on the far side of the compound, a ferocious small arms volley could be heard, followed by a ferocious reply.

The Islamic State fighters had evidently chosen this as an ambush spot. After several exchanges had rung out, the enemy riflemen started shooting in our direction, at the approaching vehicles. Their fire control, if not their aim, was sound, and within minutes they had managed to split the column. The back portion of the column stopped behind a berm about twelve feet high and about five hundred meters downslope from the compound. A few soldiers climbed to the crest of the berm and took aim. The rest got out of their vehicles and pulled out their phones and cigarettes. Group photos and selfies were snapped.

'Let's use the cannon,' a commander suggested.

A pickup mounted with a SPG-9 antitank gun pulled in front of the berm. The first shot fell short but rattled eardrums impressively. A second went into the main house, leaving a disappointingly small hole in the façade. I was in a group of trucks that emerged from behind the berm and raced up the track then turned right and sped up a hillock overlooking the compound. They parked, and a cadre of peshmerga jumped out and gathered on foot. They didn't appear to mind that they presented a plum target for snipers and artillery. They chatted, laughed, smoked, checked their phones. More group photos, more selfies. Two shells landed in quick succession on either side of them. They remained unconcerned. It was pointed out that they were being bracketed by whoever was firing the mortars, and that the next one might well land on their heads. Unhurriedly they got back into their vehicles and, amid a hail of gunfire from the house, headed straight for it.

The jihadis had built their own berm, we found, outside the compound's exterior wall. The Kurds backed their trucks up to it. A gunner opened up on the house with a 50-cal. Others peeked over the dirt and got off the sporadic potshot. One walked up to a gap in the dirt, and, with no cover or helmet but with a cigarette dangling from his lips, emptied a magazine. More rockets were sent into the house. The jihadis returned fire. The firefight lasted several minutes. Then, as they had been doing all morning, the gunmen in the house suddenly went quiet. The Kurds' 50-cal jammed. Seeing this as a cue to take a break, they reclined on the base of the berm. Out came the phones. More selfies. Texting. A man called his mother. Another watched a video of a firefight that had taken place on some other front around Mosul. No one was interested in storming the house on foot.

'You are welcome here,' a soldier said to me. 'You can come any time.'

'I'm deaf from that cannon!' said his comrade.

'Did you take any photos of it being shot?'

The gunner got into an argument with another man over whose responsibility it had been to make sure the 50-cal was working properly before they'd headed out.

'You were supposed to fix it!'

'It's not my job!'

'It's not like you had to build an airplane. It's simple.'

'You came all the way to the front in a taxi, and now all you do is talk. You just talk.'

The antitank cannon was reloaded and fired, the back blast shattering the windshield of the pickup I'd rented and sending its air-conditioning dials flying from the console. The soldiers reclined again.

'Bazan, where are your cigarettes?'

Bazan ran to a truck and returned with a pack of cigarettes.

'Who wants a cigarette?'

The group lit up.

'Everyone here talks like a man,' a soldier said to me, 'but no one fights like one.'

Two days later, the peshmerga prepared to take the village of Omar-qapchi. In the intervening forty-eight hours, four thousand peshmerga had marched into the plain. They now occupied roughly a hundred encampments and posts, surrounded by trenchworks, all of which had been made in a few days by the drivers of earthmovers, perhaps the bravest soldiers in the entire war. An unarmed vanguard, they toiled mere meters from Islamic State positions as they dug and piled. They were bombed, mortared, rocketed, and sniped, all the while doing astonishingly fast and effective work.

The call to move came in, and the APCs and tanks and trucks filled up in moments. Far more soldiers wanted to take part in the assault than there was space in vehicles. An old fighter in traditional garb tried to climb into my truck.

'Let me in!' he insisted, his eyes flashing with anger.

A spot was found for him in the general's truck, which already contained a scrum of infantrymen, assorted hangers-on, and who knew how much ammunition—a tinder box on wheels.

A commander got hold of some villagers on a cellphone and was telling them what to do when the fighting started.

'Stay together, don't separate,' he said. 'If you see any Daesh, call this number. Take care of yourselves. We're coming.'

Omarqapchi, spreading about a half-mile down a slope ending at a road that ran along the foot of a hill, was made up of tightly packed one- and two-story homes. Near the village's western gate, the column broke into three convoys. The general's convoy, which I was in, cut across a field and barreled down toward the road. Though the ground was thought to be full of mines and I.E.D.s, the drivers cut one another off as they careered over suspicious patches of dirt and objects, racing to get into the action. When the convoy reached the road, muzzle flashes appeared in windows and rounds whizzed by and hit the sides of the vehicles. The peshmerga raked the buildings with machine-gun fire and grenades while they kept moving. At the eastern gate, the convoy hooked into the village. The streets were empty. The villager whom the commander had talked to said there were about a dozen jihadis here. The convoy raced into the village center and suddenly found itself in a firefight with an enemy contingent, who, surrounded, had taken a stand at one end of a short, wide alley. The soldiers, on the other end, jumped from their vehicles, piled into the alley, directly in the line of fire, and began shooting back. There was little aiming but a lot of yelling. One man stepped into the alley with a grenade launcher. He pulled the trigger. Nothing happened. He lifted the launcher from his shoulder, brought it parallel to his person, held the rocket inches from his nose, and looked at it quizzically. As enemy bullets hit the dirt at his feet, he slowly peeled off a piece of plastic wrapping. He lifted the launcher back onto his shoulder and tried again. This time it fired.

The jihadis took to their heels, and the soldiers gave chase, eventually cornering several in a mosque. One jihadi detonated a suicide vest; another was sheared in half by a rocket. By the end of the day, eight of them were dead, three had escaped and one was captured. Three peshmerga sustained minor wounds. Rather than going on foot from house to house to make sure the village was cleared, they gathered outside it and celebrated, blasting peshmerga anthems from their Humvee loudspeakers.

'I think I killed someone,' the older fighter who'd tried to get into my truck told me. 'It would be a shame if I shot my rifle and didn't kill anyone.'

The wind at their backs, the battalion next moved on the village of Faziliya, connected to Omarqapchi by the same road. The road was littered with I.E.D.s, which went off one after another as a tank at the head of the column rolled forward. The bombs sent up showers of gravel and tarmac but were too small to damage the vehicles. By the time we reached the entrance of the village, eight of them had exploded. On the wall of a kiosk was spray-painted: 'Every Islamic State man who dies goes to paradise.' A black flag fluttered on a fence post, but the roofs of the houses of Faziliya, which ranged steeply up the hillside, bore newly hung white flags, signs that its residents were eagerly awaiting the peshmerga's arrival and that the jihadis had probably mostly fled. An old man in a white dishdasha shuffled from an olive grove waving his hands. The soldiers took aim and he sank to his knees. Sensing he wasn't a threat, they lowered their rifles, approached him, patted him down gently, and led him to safety. From a spire came gunfire, then a rocket. The tank reduced the spire and the building below it to smoking rubble.

As the convoy rolled up into the village's narrow streets, people streamed from their homes. They patted their heads, a gesture of welcome. 'Long live peshmerga!' children chanted, 'Long live peshmerga!' In the village square, a group of boys tore down a Caliphate billboard. Soldiers shot off celebratory rounds.

'Who has cigarettes?' a man asked the soldiers. 'We want to smoke!'

The next day, those residents of Omarqapchi who had remained in it for the battle were gathered outside the village next to a caged soccer pitch. Kurdish soldiers and intelligence agents watched over them. The women sat with their children on the ground in one group. The men, sitting in a separate group nearby, waited to be interrogated. A grandmother, her son, and grandchildren were sitting in a car, not wanting to join the groups. The jihadis had warned the villagers that they would be raped and killed by the liberating forces, not liberated. The grandmother wanted to know where her brother was. A shell or airstrike, she didn't know which, had destroyed his house, and he was nowhere to be found.

'He's dead,' a neighbor of hers whispered to me, 'but she hasn't found out yet.'

An intelligence agent scrutinized the group of sitting men. He pointed to one whom he believed was with the Islamic State. The man was dragged from the group. His hands were bound behind his back with a scarf and a green knit facemask was pulled backwards over his head so that his eyes were covered, but bunched below his nose so that his mouth wasn't. He was forced to the ground. As he pled his innocence, a soldier menaced him with his rifle.

'Shut up you imbecile!' he yelled at the prisoner.

'It's obvious he's Daesh,' another soldier said. 'Just look at his color. He's taken on the jihadis' color.'

'I'm not Daesh, I swear!' the prisoner said. 'I'm a Kurd!'

'Shut up or I'll stuff this down your throat!' the first soldier said, jabbing the rifle's stock at his face.

The intelligence agent told me that he was from Omarqapchi and had fled the village as the Islamic State approached two years before.

He had managed to stay in touch with friends there, and they told him which villagers sided with the jihadis. This prisoner had driven an ambulance for them, the agent had been told. The prisoner's son, he'd heard, was also allied. The agent joined the soldiers who were guarding the prisoner.

'You're all fools if you don't believe he's Daesh,' he said, though they seemed as convinced as he of the man's guilt.

'I haven't done anything,' the prisoner said. 'I was just told to drive somewhere.'

The soldier with the rifle repeated his threat to feed it to the prisoner.

'You keep saying that,' his colleague said. 'Hit him already.'

More soldiers and a commander congregated around the prisoner.

'Stop yelling, you're confusing him,' the commander said. And to the prisoner: 'Calm down, we're just investigating.'

The prisoner's son, his hands also bound and face covered, was brought over and pushed down beside his father.

'Where should we take them?' a soldier asked. 'What's the procedure?'

'My son is a student in Bashiqa,' the prisoner said. 'I'll tell you anything about him. Please don't put a gun to his head.'

'I'm just following orders,' the soldier with the rifle said.

'Everyone says my son is Daesh and hits him. He'll lose his mind!'

'Don't worry,' the commander said. 'We don't know if he's Daesh. We have to investigate.'

'You've humiliated my son!'

'So are you saying your son is Daesh or not?' a soldier asked.

'He's a student!'

They were bundled into the bed of a pickup and driven away.

The main peshmerga encampment outside Bashiqa was presided over by Barham Areef, the Kurdish general whose convoy I'd been riding in. Tall, soft-spoken and young, with pitted cheeks, Barham led his men into battle in a jaunty black-and-brown-painted MRAP with a Go-Pro camera duct-taped to the hood.

'Daesh is not smart and not brave, but they wash the minds of stupid people,' Barham told me. 'They give drugs to their fighters. They fight for twenty minutes and then run away.'

A cult of personality had formed around the general. His camp was home to a bizarre assortment of foreigners drawn to the romance of the Kurdish cause. There were the American volunteer medics, the most flagrant of whom belonged to a group that was led by a wiry, loquacious middle-aged man who said he was a former Special Forces officer and Ranger. He inserted himself into various conflicts around the world, often dragging along his wife and children, and insisted on saying prayers for you at every opportunity whether you wanted him to or not. 'Can I say a prayer?' he'd ask, and, without waiting for an answer, would grab your shoulder and any other shoulders near him and bow his head and thank god for everything. He also said prayers over the corpses of Islamic State fighters, some of which he claimed to have shot himself. Unlike the other volunteer medics, his group all carried rifles, and it was clear from their behavior they had only the barest interest in doing medical work. They were there because they wanted to kill jihadis, though, aside from the leader, none of them appeared to know their way around their weapons. He told me, after a prayer, as breezily as you like, that he had no formal medical training.

There was also a videographer couple, the man Brazilian, the woman Czech, the both of them always much too chic, with their tight-fitting designer fatigue pants and perfectly wrapped keffiyehs, and, constantly at Barham's side, a chain-smoking Scotsman in spectacles who claimed to be a sniper. In every village the peshmerga took, he would leap from Barham's MRAP and, standing entirely in the open, would lift his rifle and bring the scope to his eye and pivot and swirl dramatically, apparently expecting to find an enemy standing on a rooftop waiting to be shot. On his Facebook page, under employer, he listed 'Peshmerga.'

Generations of Kurds converged in the camp, too. The youngest soldiers were in their twenties. Most were in their thirties, forties, and fifties. Out of pride or lack of work opportunities or both, men admitted into the peshmerga tended to stay. The oldest soldier in the camp, as far as anyone knew, was Jamil Rashid, the man who'd tried to get into my truck before the Omarqapchi assault and who had thought it would be a shame if he hadn't killed someone. When I first asked Rashid his age, he told me 'a lot.' Later offerings from himself and others ranged from sixty-one to seventy-eight. I asked how many children he had. 'At least nine.' How many grandchildren? 'More than I can count.' How many battles had he fought in? 'That notebook does not have enough paper to write them all down.' Five sons were likewise in the peshmerga. One had recently been killed.

'The Islamic State is nothing, they've been around for two years,' said Rashid, who was fond of listing, in the profanest terms possible, the Iraqi premiers whose regimes he'd fought against. 'Abdul Karim Qasim? I fucked his mother. Then there was Ahmed Hassan al-Bakr. Then Saddam. Then Maliki. He was a bad guy. And now—what's his name?'

'Abadi,' a young soldier said.

'Right, Abadi. I fought all of them on this holy ground. For this holy ground. Our mud is holy. Whoever doesn't fight for his land gets fucked in the ass. This land is so precious.'

'We're honored to be fighting with you,' a soldier said to him.

'Why are you talking about history, Jamil?' asked another. 'We're supposed to be discussing now.'

'So what if I talk about history?' Rashid said. 'It's all the same, history and now.'

One day I found Rashid sitting with an old friend. They'd fought

. against al-Bakr, against Saddam, in the Kurdish civil wars, ıst Saddam again.

'Where do you sleep?' his friend asked.

Jamil Rashid pointed to a ditch.

'It's good. It's very natural.'

His friend approved.

'This is our land,' Rashid said, taking up a handful of dirt and pebbles and kissing it. 'Every single night I'm here. I'll never leave until I finish my job.' He looked at a group of young men. 'They're very courageous. Now it's their turn to keep the revolution going. We're old now. These are our new men.'

I asked Rashid how often he spoke with his family.

'They call me. I don't call them.' He frowned. 'My relationship with my family has expired. Those days are gone. It doesn't make any difference if I'm at home or not.'

'How can you say that?' a young soldier asked. 'If I don't speak to my family for a day, I can't bear it.'

'You're young, I'm old.'

Gunfire sounded.

'This is nothing,' Rashid said. 'It's air. I like the sound of it.'

'You're such a good protector,' a young soldier said. 'We've never seen anyone like you.'

'When have you ever seen me let my guard down?' Rashid said. 'I'm very excited. But we want to fight before the rains.'

My favorite of General Barham's band was a shopkeeper named Kaefe. I'd first met him up on the ridgeline over the summer. He'd shared his rice and cigarettes with me. Ahmed's father, a peshmerga, had been killed by Saddam's army when he was four. Ten other family members had died fighting the Iraqis or other Kurds. Kaefe always wore traditional Kurdish dress into battle. He refused to wear a uniform because, he told me, 'for decades the Iraqi army destroyed our land in those uniforms.' He'd fought in Sinjar and Bashiqa before they'd fallen to the Islamic State. He'd always fought alongside his cousin, who was with him still. Kaefe was thirty-seven years old and had already been fighting for more than twenty years. This war, however, was unlike anything he'd seen. 'They're suicidal,' he said of the jihadis. Though the Kurdish approach had its own faults, he conceded. 'Here, when it comes to fighting, it's like a competition.'

The peshmerga was nominally commanded by Masoud Barzani, the president of the Kurdish Regional Government. When the Islamic State took Mosul, Barzani offered his help to Maliki, who snubbed him. Maliki worried Barzani intended to annex whatever land his troops took, including Mosul, and it wasn't an unreasonable suspicion. Some Kurds consider Mosul a Kurdish city. (Most I know don't.) Abadi may have delayed the invasion of Mosul for the same reason. But the Kurds, the Iraqis, and the coalition came to an agreement that called for the peshmerga to stop its advance at Bashiqa. Many peshmerga worried they would be attacked by Iraqi soldiers when the two forces met on the frontlines—speculation about a sequel war between Kurdistan and Iraq was commonplace, and, if history was any indication, a decent bet—but so far the Kurds had been pleasantly surprised. Relations were cordial, even comradely.

'This war is very different for us Kurds,' Barzani's brother, Sehad Barzani, told me. 'This is the first time we've seen airstrikes that we're not afraid of. This is the first time the Iraqi army is not trying to kill us and we're not trying to kill them. We hope it stays this way.'

Barzani and I were speaking in a large abandoned house on Bashiqa's periphery that the peshmerga had commandeered. Masoud and Sehad's father, Mustafa, the patriarch of the incipient Iraqi Kurdish republic, led its revolution against Iraq until his death in 1979. It's common to meet peshmerga with tattoos of Mustafa's portrait. They usually occupy upper arms but sometimes are more grandiose. As Sehad and I stepped from the house, a soldier lifted up his shirt to reveal Mustafa, with thick black mustache and checkered red headscarf, covering his entire back. This soldier would have been a decade from existence when Mustafa died, but in Kurdistan youth culture and historical homage complement one another. (Tattooed on his stomach was *Thug Life*.) Sehad looked on the portrait of his father approvingly. I asked him how many of his own family were fighting.

'They're all my family,' he said, gesturing at the soldiers gathered in the courtyard, who crowded round him and asked for his blessing.

'Daesh has no escape,' he told them. 'They will have to die now.'

After leaving Barzani's company, I found an entire village on the roadside of Highway 2. As the peshmerga pushed forward, the jihadis tried to bring villagers to Mosul. One night, they told the residents of Bujarbuq, a village near Bashiqa, to be ready to leave at 6 a.m. the next morning for the city. The point of this forced exodus didn't have to be stated: they would be used as human shields, like the people in the ugly apartment complex in Gogjali. Anyone who refused would be killed on the spot.

Instead of submitting, the villagers had fled en masse in the middle of the night. A caravan of eighty or so cars and trucks was now stretched along the highway. Into them the people of Bujarbuq had stuffed everyone and everything they could: children, mattresses, sheep, blankets, grandmothers, pots, buckets, chickens. One truck contained a mechanized wheelchair, another seven newborn lambs. The women were still fully covered in black, as per jihadi regulation, not knowing whom they might encounter in their flight. Kurdish intelligence agents had met the villagers on the road with a fleet of buses that would take them to a refugee camp. There had been suicide bombings at such gatherings, and so the agents patted down each person before ushering them aboard. A soldier pulled up with a freight truck full of crackers and water. Women crushed sleeves of crackers into their handbags. Others waited in line in front of the buses, speaking while slowly, thoughtfully munching cracker pieces.

'All of our life is wasted in this Daesh mess,' a woman said to her husband. 'I feel a hundred years old. I hope Daesh goes to hell, then rots in hell.'

'I'm so tired,' her husband replied.

Though the jihadis had confiscated cellphones in Bujarbuq, these villagers, like everyone else, had managed to secrete theirs. They had called relatives and friends outside the Caliphate who were now arriving. The roadside turned into a scene of heartsick reunion. Two old classmates, one a Kurd who'd fled Bujarbuq, the other an Arab shop owner who'd stayed, hugged for the first time in two years.

'Life was very bitter,' the shop owner told his friend. He pulled from his pocket a thousand-dinar note, less than a dollar. 'This is all my money.'

A young man found his mother. She clung to his neck and wept and kissed his face again and again.

'Thank God,' she muttered. 'Thank God.'

Two weeks after the Bashiqa campaign had commenced, President Barzani still hadn't given the order to attack the city of Bashiqa. At General Barham's camp, the berms had grown taller and the foxholes deeper. The jihadis weren't giving up. They attacked on foot by night and by day they lobbed in shells and handcrafted missiles. Ten had already landed within the walls of the camp, Barham told me. A shell exploded nearby as we spoke. He didn't flinch. He had been collecting the unexploded ordnance. He waved a dismissive hand at a trio of rockets with cartoonishly oversized nose cones that looked as though they came from a science fair.

Finally, the order was given. Barham's troops collected on a road outside Bashiqa. Sehad Barzani arrived to wish them luck.

'We must move,' he told the general, 'but slowly.'

For six hours, the column crept towards the city, while airstrikes and artillery pummeled buildings within. As they waited, soldiers checked for news of the American election and of the war on their cell phones. The lead headline on the website of Rudaw, a Kurdish news network, read, 'Iraqis wake up daily to selfies of soldiers on the battlefield.' Word came in that a very accurate sniper was holed up somewhere inside Bashiqa. He'd already killed one soldier and wounded four.

Finally the column was cleared to move in. Entering the city, we passed a peshmerga bulldozer in flames. It had been hit by a rocket. The driver appeared to have been incinerated in the cab. As the column passed a small park, a rocket-propelled grenade was shot straight towards my truck. It hit the low cement wall of the park, about twenty feet away. Its orange fireball, visible for less than a second, was terrifyingly beautiful. Another exploded nearby.

The column made it to a central plaza. A handsome old church with a suspicious tower was peppered with machine-gun fire and grenades. Jamil Rashid hopped from a truck and took up a position outside the church. Standing in the open, his rifle dangling, he looked around and breathed in the smoke, beaming.

In an effort to move farther into the city, the column turned back onto the road on which it had entered. But now there was an empty white sedan in the middle of the road. It had appeared out of nowhere. Had some innocent tried to flee and suffered a breakdown? Was it a car bomb? The prelude to an ambush? The pilot of the lead tank stuck his head from the turret hatch. A shot cracked the air, its tone higher and sharper than that of a Kalashnikov. Blood sprayed from the pilot's head and he slumped from the turret. Panic passed down the line. 'Sniper! Sniper!' The column reversed course, honking and rear-ending, and labored back to the plaza.

The tank sped from the city by a different route. I followed it. At the staging point, the pilot was lifted out and put in an ambulance. He was dead. His crewmates bent over the tank's side skirt and knelt in the dirt, weeping.

Kaefe and his cousin and the rest of their detachment had descended into Bashiqa from the hills to the north on foot. They came under fire, retreated back up a hill, and took up a position. Another high-pitched crack. Kaefe's cousin lurched forward, falling over Kaefe's leg. He thought his cousin had tripped. Then he saw the blood.

Three days later, Kaefe was worrying a string of wooden prayer beads in a mosque in their hometown, Rawanduz, in the eastern mountains of Kurdistan. He sat by the muezzin, who sang a death prayer, a Koran open before him on a stand. Old peshmerga in sashes and headscarves and younger ones in suits and jeans filed in. They greeted the cousin's father and Kaefe, their hands to their chests, saying 'May God forgive him his sins.' No one cried.

After the service, long rugs were spread on the floor, and Kaefe and the men from his unit sat down to lunch. Their part in the fight against the Islamic State was over, for now. Bashiqa was taken. The invasion of Mosul was about to begin.

'It will be a heavy fight,' one man said.

Kaefe and his friends would help the Iraqi troops in Mosul if they were ordered to, they agreed, but they wouldn't like it.

'Is it fair that a Kurd should die for an Arab?' Kaefe asked.

Anyway, history had taught them that another war would be along soon enough.

'Once you finish one fight, they prepare another one for you,' a man said. 'It makes you tired.'

III

THEY WILL HAVE TO DIE NOW

We also knew that for years now there had been no country here but the war.

—MICHAEL HERR

Combat in east Mosul came to an official end in the third week of January 2017, though for months afterwards there were bombings and the odd gunfight. The casualty rate among frontline troops in the east was about forty percent. Hundreds of soldiers and no one knew how many civilians died. Yet the high command considered the fighting there, like the peshmerga's fighting, 'shaping operations'—mere preparation to the assault on the west. The Islamic State had always been less popular in the east, Mosul's more diverse half, home to its minority populations and the university. West Mosul, larger and more populous, was the Sunni inland of the city, where discontent with Maliki's government had run the highest and where the Islamic State's precursors, al Qaeda and ISI, had been the strongest. It was also home to the government quarter and the major transportation hubs. The Islamic State had based itself there.

Combat in the west began in the third week of February and within days it was clear that, indeed, this latter half of the battle would be vastly worse. Already whole neighborhoods were devastated. A major told me, 'Any creature, when you corner it, gets more aggressive. They know they're going to die.' The destruction was the more upsetting because the west was also home to most of the city's past. Outside of the ruins of Nineveh, the east had built up largely since the Baath. The west, by contrast, contained Mosul's old city and mosques, shrines, churches, and monasteries going back to the Abbasid Empire, and the Mosul Museum. Much of this the jihadis had already destroyed.

In the old city was the Grand Mosque of al-Nuri, the center of spiritual life in Mosul and the spiritual center of the Caliphate. Zarqawi claimed it was Nur ad-Din Zangi, the beloved Abbasid atabeg who supposedly endowed al-Nuri, who inspired him to conceive of the Islamic State. And it was at al-Nuri that Baghdadi had summoned the Caliphate into existence. So closely was the grand old place now associated with him that Moslawis, even those who hated the Caliph, referred to it as 'Baghdadi's Mosque.' Its famous leaning minaret could be seen from all over the west side, as though monitoring each skirmish, pulling jihadi and soldier alike toward it. Not until the minaret fell—and everyone knew it must fall, by one hand or the other—would the battle be over.

At what remained of the Mosul Museum, once the finest repository of Assyrian art outside Europe, a single glimpse into the galleries was enough to bring you to tears. The way in was no longer through the entranceway but rather through a hole blasted into the exterior wall. Once you climbed inside, you were confronted with part of a cuneiform tablet. It was the largest thing in sight. The rest of the artifacts were chunks, shards, dust. A lone policeman stood watch over the building. He led me through the corridors quietly. He picked up a wedge of carved stone and handed it to me, appearing to think I might know how to decipher the broken tendril of cuneiform inscribed on its flat side.

In the stairwell, the walls darkened steadily and the scent of recently extinguished flames increased until, in the basement, I found myself in carbonic, nostril-filling black. The fleeing jihadis had attempted to set this level alight with some kind of accelerant that had produced an extremely hot but short-lived conflagration, cauterizing the walls but extinguishing before it could reach the desks and filing cabinets and map shelves, which were left unsinged. The Caliphate had turned this into a printing office for public notices and propaganda, and it was the leftover material they presumably wanted to destroy. It told of the regime's farcical last act.

From the Islamic State Committee of General Oversight, a handbill dated October 2, 2016, and entitled *Announcement of punishment for those who steal money from the house of Muslims*: 'God commands that we should not spend money frivolously. He requires that we spend it wisely. If money goes missing, whether accidentally or intentionally, it must be reported, especially if those who've lost it work in the budget departments. . . . Whoever is corrupted in this world will either be crucified or lose their hands and feet and will be punished in the next life. God loves the believers and hates the ones who don't work.' A postscript adds, 'The Islamic State is very careful about the spilling of its own blood but it is also careful about how its money is spent. We would not have issued this statement if we did not expect a budget shortfall.'

From the Ministry of Prayer and Mosques, a laminated motivational placard, the type set against a soothing image of a palm frond and beads of light: 'Brother of the mujahideen, remember: You are not in governmental duty, you are in jihad. In jihad, you don't have to wait for a salary check at the end of the month. You are doing this for the sake of God. You are not to boast about being a jihadi, but you should fight to kill the unbelievers. Remember: You are doing jihad for your own salvation. Remember: Victory doesn't come from sitting in a chair in an office. It comes with the spilling of blood, with dismembered limbs, with injury, with fear. Remember: Keep your faith, that you may have an afterlife.'

The least amusing specimen was also the most impressive, a poster printed on glossy stock that appeared to have been produced for the religious police. Titled *Introduction of limits*, it described the 'solutions' or 'limits' for certain grave crimes. It was an illustrated guide to the *hudud*, essentially the sharia punishments for society's worst infractions, in this case interpreted from the maximally sanguinary Salafi perspective. The difference now, the poster advised, was that the limits no longer had to be prescribed by a judge. Any Moslawi with sufficient conviction could punish a fellow citizen. The poster was large, about four feet long and three high, and appeared to be meant for prominent public display. It wasn't dated, but apparently, at some point late in the day, the higher-ups had come to feel they could no longer rely on their local judges to enforce the level of brutality required to keep Moslawis on the path to paradise. The sins addressed were homosexuality, fornication, theft, killing or frightening people, and consuming alcohol. Given over to each was a panel containing Koranic citations and commentary, and then a photograph of how to administer each 'limit.' The images, like the images in all the best Islamic State propaganda, were of professional quality—perfectly cropped, in dramatic shallow focus, as suggestive in what they didn't show as they are shocking in what they did.

In the photograph in the fornication panel, you see men in fighting dress hurling stones at a mass on the ground. You stare for some moments before realizing this mass is a person. Of indeterminate sex, his or her hands are bound and upraised in a futile effort at self-protection. From the victim's head blood leaks onto a pile of already-thrown stones. The photographer catches the punishers winding up, pitcher-like. There are at least ten of them, standing only a few feet from the victim. In the panel to do with killing and frightening (the latter isn't explained) you see two decapitated corpses attached to either side of a crucifix. The bodies are tied to the cross with cloth straps that bear the colors, bizarrely, of the Iraqi flag. One disattached head is tied to the right end of the transept, while a barely visible tuft of hair peeks out from behind a handwritten sign of warning on the left end—the other head, you conclude.

The image in the homosexuality panel is the most affecting. You see, from behind, a man who's been thrown from a building. He is in mid-fall. The photographer has positioned himself on a high floor, within a gap in the building's façade, above the falling man, his lens angled downwards, so that the falling man is framed on either side by cinderblock and on top by the crowd of Moslawis on the street who've gathered, or been corralled, to watch the execution. The photographer knows to choose a fast shutter speed, so that while the falling man is in nearly perfect focus, the onlookers are blurred.

I shouldn't have, but I folded up the poster and hid it under my flak jacket, and gave the policeman a remorseful wave as I left the museum. Later, back in the comfort of Irbil, I pulled it out and gazed at this vertiginous image, with its flattened depth of field. The odor in the museum basement of incinerated paper and plasterwork and chemicals was still in my nose, and I had one of those moments of intense time-collapsing recollection that only the olfactory sense can bring on. I remembered being at the World Trade Center on September 11. I remembered the infernal smell. I remembered the people leaping and falling from the towers, some turning or jerking as they fell, some just sailing. That brought to mind the iconic Falling Man photograph from that day. The image on the poster suddenly felt like an answer or cruel rejoinder to that earlier image. The World Trade Center falling man, who leapt, presumably, is seen from outside and below, from the perspective of a bystander standing at the foot of the towers. He goes down headfirst, arms straight by his sides, plunging with a grace that beggars description. You know he is on his way to his death but you are allowed to admire his poise, to share in his volition and his dignity, to connect your innocence with his. This is not a victim but a person bravely meeting his end. In the photograph on the poster, by contrast, you look down upon the condemned, whose legs are bent and arms spread in terror as he tries to push against the air—what most falling people instinctively do. You are not below but up in the building with the executioners. You are inculcated. You are the executioner. The image tells a Moslawi, 'You are the Islamic State and the Islamic State is you.' Propaganda doesn't get much more effective than that.

As to how the citizen executioners of these ad-hoc revolutionary tribunals could be sure their victims were guilty, the authors of the poster required 'A confession by the perpetrator or others. Pregnancy of an unmarried woman. Breath or vomit smelling of alcohol . . . Or any suspicion.' As for the wisdom of calling on people to police themselves in this way, they added, 'No one should think that God has given us a choice in this regard. The solutions must be implemented and anyone who doesn't implement them is an unbeliever. God would not prescribe these limits if they weren't good for us.' In other words, if you don't kill your neighbor on the strength of the barest suspicion of impiety, you ought to be killed yourself. To be a true Muslim, you must kill, kill not just infidels, not just apostates, but kill other Muslims, kill any Muslim whom you feel is a lesser Muslim than yourself. This is Paris in 1794. This is the Moscow of 1937, Berlin 1945. Seeing this poster, you realize that, much more than homicidal, the Islamic State was suicidal. 'Because of these limits and solutions,' the authors concluded, 'crime rates are much lower in the Islamic State than in the United States, may God vanish it from existence. The FBI published an estimate that in America, every 27 minutes there is a murder, every 7 minutes a rape, every 30 seconds a burglary, and every 10 seconds an incidental petty theft.'

This kind of thing was common. Caliphate propagandists loved to cite figures to support their ongoing argument that their state was safer, saner, and more fiscally responsible than the United States—as though prospective jihadis might be deciding between Mosul and Chicago. One of the great joys of walking around recently freed neighborhoods in the city was that you occasionally came upon copies of *al-Naba*, the Islamic State newspaper, which excelled at such temporizing. The News, as *al-Naba* translates, came out every fortnight or so and was distributed gratis, and I was always thrilled when I found it. True, it didn't have the panache of *Dabiq*, the Islamic State's impeccably produced digital magazine, so good that international news agencies used its images. But it had more heart. *Al-Naba* was the *Village Voice* to Dabiq's *Vogue*. Black-and-white, produced with the most rudimentary publishing software and printed on cheap stock, usually about a dozen pages, *al-Naba* had an indomitable enthusiasm which, if you couldn't believe, you also couldn't help but finding somehow bracing. If the Islamic State was losing this war, you would never have known it from the pages of *al-Naba*, the season of whose jihad was ever spring.

In the museum basement I found an old issue, dated, in the Islamic calendar, February 30, 1437—December 13, 2015. It made no mention of the fact that the Islamic State had just been defeated in Ramadi. It did however announce the retaking of Mahin, a town south of Homs, in Syria. That Mahin had a population of eleven thousand people—before the war—did not dispirit the *al-Naba* editors, who'd made the victory their lead story. It was accompanied by a photo of a tank barreling up a track on a rocky hill. Presumably jihadis are driving the tank, though you can't tell, and there is no caption. Really it could be anywhere. On page 2 was a map of the world with those

Google-style upside-down-teardrop things stuck in the Arabian peninsula, Africa, and South Asia. Each corresponded to a recent jihadi attack—in Yemen, Pakistan, Nigeria, Bangladesh, and so forth. A story describing an Islamic State suicide bombing at a 'temple,' i.e., a Shia mosque or shrine, in Baghdad, had this to say about the perpetrator, one Abu Salam: 'With God's approval he went into the crowd and detonated his suicide belt. In this way, the Islamic State kills and maims those who refuse to believe.' On the editorial page was an essay about the corrupt ideas that have emanated from Europe over the years—colonialism, communism, Zionism—and their deleterious effects. Another editorial, entitled 'The Cost of the Jihad,' said: 'On the tenth anniversary of September 11th, *The New York Times* reported that all the attacks committed by the mujahideen between 9/11 and 2011 cost about $500,000. But analysts estimate that since then America has spent $3.3 trillion on the War on Terror, or $7 million for every dollar the jihadis have spent.'

The longest and most moving piece in this issue was what the *al-Naba* editors might have called a human-interest story. It recounted the life of a young Libyan man who, while studying journalism at university, heard the call. 'He knew he was late for jihad,' the author begins. The boy drops out of school. His friends tease him. You shouldn't go off to fight, they tell him, you should marry, finish your degree, find work. He scolds their frivolity. 'We are meant to be warriors of God!' He gets himself smuggled into Syria and finds an Islamic State training camp. He undergoes the medical examination required of all new recruits. He is told he has bad ankles and is turned away. Indefatigable, he goes to another camp. Here he is accepted, but falls ill. From his sickbed, he writes to his mother:

> Dear Mom, only God knows how much I miss you. You will not understand how much and maybe you will blame me and claim

I never loved you. Because if I loved you, how could I have gone off on jihad and hurt you so? But let me tell you, from my heart, nobody loves their mother like I love you. But I must meet my jihad. With God's approval, you and I will meet in heaven. God gives mujahideen special treatment in heaven. I want you to be proud of me and happy and laughing. I don't want you to cry and be sad.

To his father he writes. 'With God's approval, we will meet in the next life.' He arises from his sickbed and 'He went to his first and last battle, where he was killed. His family remembers the last look he gave them before leaving. It was a smile.'

The story had been gussied up, clearly, but it may well have originated in truth. The Islamic State was full of real stories like it. They made for good propaganda. But they were also essential to the movement's identity and its self-mythologizing. The Islamic State's most famous 'fighters,' online at any rate, were in fact useless as fighters but invaluable as storytellers, with their personal variations on the journey from callow youth to warrior of God. That so many of them ended up like the Libyan boy, as cannon fodder, of no more consequence to Baghdadi than the unarmed Iranian boys with the plastic keys around their necks were to the Ayatollah, didn't diminish the stories' appeal.

Individualist expression comes naturally to young jihadis. To those of bin Laden's generation, however, it must be baffling, like a Vietnam veteran seeing the 'Army of One' advertising campaign the Pentagon used to recruit for Afghanistan and Iraq. Baffling, though they have themselves to blame. The movement toward the hyperpersonal began with the theologians and theorists of jihad in bin Laden's orbit, who became fixated on exploring the individual Muslim's personal relationship with God. The crux of that relationship, they deduced, conveniently, was jihad. Destroying those who were trying to destroy Islam (more or less every non-Muslim) was as sacred a duty as Islam's five pillars, they came to believe. One of bin Laden's favorite theorists called jihad 'the most excellent form of worship.' Jihadis, he wrote, 'are the ones who keep the tree of this religion from wilting and drying up, because the tree of this religion is watered only with blood,' and 'Every Muslim on Earth bears the responsibility of abandoning jihad and the sin of abandoning the gun.'

He was writing in the context of the Soviet war in Afghanistan, the catalyst and crucible of late-twentieth-century jihadism. Over the years his ideas passed through the hysterical alembic of jihadi thought, so that by the 2000s one famous preacher could write 'Jihad is the identity of the Muslim in his existence.' Anwar al-Awlaki, the American-born cleric whose online sermons have been so important to young jihadis, and who was killed by an American airstrike in Yemen, went further, declaring that, contrary to centuries of teaching, no religious authority was needed to sanction jihad. God could summon a jihadi with one direct deity-to-person call. For a holy warrior as bumptious as Zarqawi, this was the revelation he was waiting for. Like a Martin Luther or a John Wesley, he ran with it. 'Jihad will continue until the Day of Judgment whether or not an imam exists,' Zarqawi wrote in *Our Creed and Methodology*. 'Next to faith, there is nothing more important than repulsing an assailant enemy who ruins the religion and the world.' He concluded: 'There is no condition to jihad.'

A personal line to God and no check on violence save your own spiritual ambitions—it is a shift whose significance cannot be overstated, a shift comparable in its way to the Protestant Reformation or the Great Awakening, but one that could have taken hold so quickly only in the age of the Internet, with its power to instantaneously make the personal social and the social personal. It was only the first of two great shifts between the al Qaeda and Islamic State eras.

Bin Laden's circle were not career millenarians. They may have believed the end of the world was imminent, that is, as many Muslims, Christians, Jews, and others do, but they did not base their exhortations to jihad on the belief. In fact, most of them studiously avoided the topic of the apocalypse. The Islamic State is different. Its jihad is saturated in apocalypse, thanks in large part to the war in Iraq, catalyst and crucible of twenty-first-century jihadism. The scholar Jean-Pierre Filiu writes in *Apocalypse in Islam* that 'the Anglo-American invasion of Iraq in March 2003 changed the very nature of apocalyptic propaganda in Islamic nations,' which 'now became an obsessive style or paranoid interpretation, an irrational technique for making sense of a world in which hostile and infidel forces ran wild.' But the Islamic State's apocalypticism reaches further back than that war. We can't know what each member really believes, but if its most plangent rhetoricians are to be taken at their word, they live in constant expectation of the end of the world. They understand their mission to be to build the Islamic State precisely that it might be destroyed, along with everything else. And, sadly, we must take them at their word, at least on this point, because it is only with it that their insistence on killing and torture and destruction, that the death cult at the core of the Islamic State, can be fully understood. Baghdadi is said to be steeped in the apocalyptic literature of Islam, the Koranic passages, Hadiths and commentaries on them in which the Day of Judgment is accompanied by global holy war. According to some of those texts it is also accompanied by God's destruction of cities, specifically of beautiful architecture, more specifically of beautiful places of worship, and most importantly mosques, which for certain Muslim apocalypticists came to symbolize false faith, as beautiful cathedrals would for Protestants. All of these texts were written in specific historical circumstances like the Mongol invasion and many for unique political purposes such as dynastic power struggles. Despite his university education, however, the finer details of context appear to have been lost on Baghdadi, who, if he was as thoroughgoing a millenarian as he was reputed to be, believed that by killing and destroying he was preparing for the apocalypse, even helping to bring it on—ensuring that Time would end on time, as it were. It is a bottomlessly convenient pretext for cruelty: when you claim to know the end is nigh, and what's more to be its usher, you can also claim any wreckage, however depraved, is preparation, that every killing, no matter how sadistic, is a beneficence.

Yet a bloodlust as insatiable as his reaches further back still, you sense. You sense that for Baghdadi, as for the Assyrian kings, war didn't seem to sow chaos, as it does for the rest of us, but instead seemed to impose order. You sense he saw violence as ritual, a means by which he communicated with the divine, connected reality to myth, present to past, man to God. He tortured with such aplomb, with such attention, such invention, such *care*, you can't help sense that, like Ashurbanipal, Baghdadi looked on torture as a favor, considered dismemberment and stoning and flaying and beheading—especially beheading—acts not of hate, or not just of hate, but of grace. *I behead Moslawis to make them as pious as myself. I behead you because I love you.*

Baghdadi mainstreamed not just jihad but also Armageddon. He portrayed himself not just as a theocratic populist but as your average apocalyptic Joe. And, here, too, his genius as a pitchman surpassed. He knew from history that those jihadis who'd claimed to be messiahs, such as the Mahdi in Sudan, had usually died young and disproved, and he saw that his immediate predecessors made much too much of themselves. Jihadis got sick of seeing bin Laden, the supposed face of the movement, with those rheumy doe eyes and cupidinous lips. Zarqawi too just had to be a star, uploading videos of his scowling self shooting machine guns at sand. Baghdadi realized that while his followers must be encouraged to celebrate their individualism, he must not. The Caliph didn't appear in Caliphate propaganda. He didn't send out public messages to the faithful or warnings to the enemy. He kept in the shadows, encurtaining himself in history's wings, enshrouded in black, a digital shimmer, intimating he was undergoing some kind of occultation, that he was some kind of Hidden Imam. His absence made his aura grow. Mosul had an emir, as every Islamic State holding did, but you never heard his name. Only the Caliph mattered.

Not that Baghdadi deserved credit for inventing a revolutionary charisma, or an original eschatology, any more than Ashurbanipal did for inventing beheading. The Hidden Imam is, after all, a Shia messianic figure. Indeed, so much of the apocalyptic lore Baghdadi called on is Shia in origin, as is the fetish of martyrdom he relied upon to recruit his army of suicides. But, then, Sunni holy warriors from the Abbasids to Saddam have been cadging Shia traditions, not least in order to kill Shiites, for a thousand years, just as Christians and Muslims have long cadged the apocalyptic postures of the ancient Hebrews to justify killing Jews. All of which Baghdadi knew if he was as versed in the literature as his followers believed. An historical ironist with no sense of irony, the man was not even original in his hypocrisies.

His highest hypocrisy: the religious insurgency from which all of those above in some sense descend, and which the Islamic State, out of the entire contemporary jihadi bestiary, evokes most vividly, is the Sicarii. The Sicarii, along with their more famous compatriots the Zealots, arose out of the paranoid apocalyptic ferment in the Levant in the first centuries B.C. and A.D. It was a time when almost every event was seized upon, writes the historian Hugh Schonfield, 'to discover how and in what way it represented a Sign of the Times and threw light on the approach of the End of Days.' The Sicarii believed their Roman rulers were preventing them from living by the law of God. Not incidentally, they didn't like the taxes levied on them to pay for pagan buildings. But the Sicarii's main targets were the priests, officials, and others of their own faith whom they believed were complicit with the Romans. The group graduated from hit-and-run attacks to outright war. The Romans responded by massacring the Sicarii's coreligionists in Egypt and Cyprus. Though the movement prefigured the rise of Christianity, it degenerated into brigandage. The Sicarii closed out their revolution preying on their neighbors around Masada. They were last heard from flinging themselves from a cliff there, in a self-pitying suicide that today is remembered as a heroic self-sacrifice.

Baghdadi's band evoke the Sicarii vividly, but they cannot do so consciously, because of course the Sicarii were Jews. Their movement led to the expulsion of the Israelites from Judea, making exile the central theme of Jewish life for the next two millennia. Is it any surprise, then, that today Islamists purport to blame Israel for every misfortune since—or that modern-day Zionists countenance their every incursion as a genocide-defying move against Islam? Is it any wonder that the militarized berserks on either side are indistinguishable from one another in their grievances, in their wailing over lost empires, their obsession with time's justice, their endless retributive-theorizing of history? These are foes driven by the same shame, the shame of abandonment by their maker; bound by the same nostalgia, the nostalgia for a time when they ruled, a time none of them knew and which they all secretly suspect—most shameful of all to admit—their prophets were lying about anyway; foes impelled by a resemblance so elemental it dare not acknowledge itself.

Interestingly, though, one of the few places in the world Jews remained and remained welcome was Iraq. Until it finally disappeared under Saddam, Iraqi Jewry represented the oldest continuous religious community in the world.

Today Iraqi Sunnis worry the Islamic State will end as badly for them as the Sicarii did for the Jews. In a 2012 Pew poll, half of Muslims surveyed said they believed the end of the world was imminent. In my experience, rates are much higher in Iraq. Can you blame them? Are they not, in a sense, right already? What else to call forty years of wars and invasions, the death and displacement of millions, the atrocities, the massacres, the suicide bombings, the black flags fluttering across the landscape, if not portents of the Day of Judgment? Or, fucking hell, the Day itself?

Finally, the difference between Baghdadi and the ancient holy warriors whose violence he carried on is that, for Baghdadi, the world was not a *creatio continua*. It will end. It *must* end. Why must it end? Because it is bad. Because he is bad. Because Muhammad's descendants have failed their Prophet, Islam has failed God. Time has taken a wrong turn. The Americans, the Jews, the Persians, they have exploited this turn, they have hijacked history, but it is Muslims who, in abandoning jihad, lost history. By pronouncing himself Caliph, you sense, Baghdadi was putting the capstone on a palatial shame. He was really saying *I kill you because I hate you, hate the world, but not half so much as I hate myself.*

2

Before the fighting in west Mosul began, I got a call from Abu Omar. He was in the infirmary at the Khazer camp. He was upset. He and Omar had got into a fight. I went to the camp. As soon as I got through the gate, I saw Omar with two friends, ambling along the main road by the bazaar. He smiled and greeted me warmly. I asked what had happened.

'Oh, nothing important,' he said. 'My father and I had a disagreement is all.'

We walked back to the family tent. Three Kurdish intelligence agents were speaking with Abu Omar, whose head was wrapped in a bandage soaked through with blood. The residents of neighboring tents were standing about pretending not to watch. As we approached, an agent stepped forward and grabbed Omar by the arm. Another agent said a few more words to Abu Omar, and then the trio led Omar away. Omar didn't object, didn't even look surprised. He said goodbye, still smiling.

Inside the tent, Abu Omar told me what happened. That morning, he'd asked his son to fetch some water. Omar went into a rage. He took hold of a rock and bludgeoned his father's head. When it flew from his hand, he grabbed another, and did the same again. Abu Omar recounted this to me in a hushed, hurried voice, as though assuring himself it had really happened.

'This is the blood,' he said, pointing to the stains on his shirt and pants and head, 'and a lot more on the way to the hospital.' He added, 'Now I'll tell you the worst part.'

As Amina screamed, and some men rushed over to keep Omar from killing his father, Aya ran to the camp's administrative office. There she blurted out everything the family had been trying to keep from their neighbors, from the camp authorities, from me.

'Omar was Daesh,' he said.

I'd suspected, of course, that Omar had had a good deal more to do with the Islamic State than his father and he let on to me, but now I tried to reply to Abu Omar with as much surprise as possible.

'He was?' I said. 'Do you know for how long?'

'A month only, maybe two months at most,' Abu Omar said.

He explained that when they'd arrived in Gogjali, just before I first met them, Omar had been with them. At the way station where refugees gathered, Abu Omar informed a soldier that his son was caught up with the Islamic State. Omar was taken away.

'I was afraid of telling you about this before,' Abu Omar said. 'Poor Omar, he's a good kid, but he was brainwashed. They brainwashed him when I was in their prison for a month. There was no one to advise him, so he joined Daesh. I hope they rot in hell. I hope God takes his revenge from them.' He added, 'When you arrived with Omar at the tent a few minutes ago, what that Kurdish agent said to me was "Don't talk to this American journalist. Don't tell him anything."'

Omar's calmness in my company was rare, apparently. He was violent with his family, his father said, had been for years. Abu Omar thought maybe it began at the orphanage. Omar had taken the separation worse than his sisters. Over the years of the American occupation, as Mosul worsened, so did his temper. When he was large enough, he began beating his father, then his sisters. He'd beaten Abu Omar in the street one day, in front of the people of Zahra. On another occasion he'd thrown Amina against a wall with such force she was in bed for days afterwards.

As we spoke, Aya listened intently, eyeing her father. Finally, she cut in.

'He wasn't just with Daesh for a month or two,' she said. 'It was seven months.'

For once, Aya did not want to be silent. The words came tumbling out. Omar was not just violent, she said, but crazy. He'd wanted to join Daesh from the beginning. After they took over, he spent more and more time at the mosque, more and more time with the imam Abu Bakr. One day he came home in a uniform, carrying a rifle. He threatened his father and sisters with death. 'I'll behead all of you right here in our home,' he told them. His attacks on Abu Omar and his sisters got worse. After Omar hit Aya one day, Abu Omar kicked him out of the house. Omar reported his father to the Caliphate. His father was dragged before a judge. The judge told Abu Omar that if he mistreated his son again, he'd have the entire family aside from Omar executed. Omar was brave enough to hit his little sisters, she went on, but too craven to fight with the jihadis. When he heard gunfire, he'd hide. When the troops approached Mosul, he said he didn't want to be in Daesh anymore. As Aya told me all this, Abu Omar nodded in agreement.

'We got rid of his rifle and burned his uniform,' he said.

But when Abu Omar again insisted that his son had only been with the jihadis for a short while, Aya insisted back that, no, it had been seven months. Lowering his voice, but not so low that my audio recorder didn't pick it up, he hissed at her 'Why are you revealing your brother like this?'

'When you have a son like Omar,' she answered, louder, 'do you know what you should do with him? You should just kill him. Kill him and be done with him.'

They'd hoped CTS would keep him for some months, maybe imprison him long enough to scare him straight, put a real fear of God in him. But he was quickly released and sent to Khazer, where the threats and violence resumed. You never knew when it was coming, Abu Omar said. One moment the boy was sweet and docile, the next he was slamming you in the head with a rock.

'You saw him, he looks old but he has a little brain,' Abu Omar said. 'The kid needs to be put in a mental asylum. Today, when he hit me, I went to the infirmary. When I came back, he was crying—crying for me.'

'Those were crocodile tears,' Aya said.

That afternoon, I walked to Abu Fahad's tent. The brothers still weren't talking, but Abu Fahad had heard about Omar's arrest. Word travels fast in a refugee camp. I asked if he planned to go see Abu Omar. He said he didn't. I asked why.

'We have some problems, that's all,' Abu Fahad told me. 'We have different mentalities.' But he loved his nephew Omar, as did everyone in the family. He was a good-natured kid. Abu Omar treated him terribly. Not only did he deride him in front of everyone—he beat Omar, had done since he was a boy. It was disgraceful. Unsurprisingly, Abu Omar had not mentioned this to me.

'I always advised him not to do that, but he would never listen to me,' Abu Fahad said. 'Omar did listen to me and the other relatives, so he continued to be a good boy. I don't know why his father treated him so badly.' His voice grew sadder. 'Poor Omar. He is naturally a calm kid. But because of his father's violence and the pressure on him, he's been badly socialized. He doesn't know how to talk to people.'

'Omar is an angry guy now, because of his father's pressure,' Abu Fahad's son Hamudi said.

'But Omar is a good person,' his daughter Maha said. 'He's calm, he likes to help others, is very nice to everyone, even strangers. His father and sisters are no good to him.'

'The anger is a permanent part of Omar's mind now, I think,' Abu Fahad said. 'There's every chance he'll continue to beat his father, even though I advise him against it, just as his father beat him. His father doesn't know how to treat him. They might kill one another one day.'

Abu Fahad blamed the jihadis, too. They had turned many young men in Mosul against their fathers, not just Omar. This was how it had gone, he said. Their revolution had gone the way of every revolution. The Islamic State had come in promising to restore peace and dignity to Mosul, and he'd welcomed them, but reality proved otherwise. They made things not better, but worse, then much worse.

He could see the decline in every aspect of his life. Hospitals, for instance. The jihadis had made a point of keeping them open, including the one where Abu Fahad worked and where he stayed on under the Caliphate. With the city cut off from the world, and no funds coming in from Baghdad, the hospital's new administrators devised a system whereby patients, instead of receiving free healthcare from the state, as they normally would, paid a small fee, which went mostly to the staff salaries. Abu Fahad and his colleagues were paid through profit sharing. It was clever and, like many of the Islamic State's municipal innovations, equitable, and he saw in it evidence of their good intentions. The problem was that his take-home pay went from seven hundred fifty dollars a month to eighteen.

'It was not enough for anything at all,' he said. 'Not even my cigarettes.'

The new courts, too, were fair but futile. Shortly before the

Islamic State had come in, Abu Fahad had sold one of his cars. After they were in, the buyer stopped making payments. Abu Fahad asked him again and again for the money but the man claimed that, with Mosul's economy tanking, he was broke. They met, got in an argument, and Abu Fahad struck him. The buyer took him to the Islamic State court. The buyer admitted he hadn't abided by their contract, and the judge, while reprimanding Abu Fahad for resorting to violence, also found in his favor. The judge ordered the buyer to pay Abu Fahad a hundred dollars a month. Abu Fahad didn't like this and told the judge if this was all that could be done, he'd take his payment out of the buyer's hide. The judge responded that if Abu Fahad did, he would have to be beaten in turn. With nothing else to do, Abu Fahad waited for his hundred dollars. The man didn't pay. The judge jailed the man briefly but released him. Abu Fahad went to the judge and told him he wanted the man jailed for as long as it took him to pay.

'You want us to put him in prison over some money?' the judge answered. 'The city is being attacked every day with airstrikes. What if he died in prison because of your money?'

'I don't care,' Abu Fahad told the judge. 'I have rights, too. How about this—if he's killed in prison, I'll pay for his grave.'

There were more absurd degradations. At first the religious police didn't bother men about their beards. Then beards became mandatory. Then the regulation beard was lengthened. Then lengthened again. Then mustaches were forbidden. Then the religious police began confiscating IDs from any man whose facial hair was deemed incorrect and the scofflaw was told to report for inspection in a month. If by that time the beard wasn't adequate, he was given twenty lashes. Hamudi, sixteen, had been cited for his beard. In fact, his ID was still sitting in some Hizbah station. Abu Fahad wouldn't let him go to retrieve it, afraid his son would be whipped.

But for Abu Fahad, it was the smoking ban that most typified the

Daesh's hypocrisy. Cigarettes were important to him, as they were to almost every man I knew in Mosul, civilian and soldier, and in Iraq generally. Smoking is not considered an addiction but rather a matter of independence, an index of defiant spirit and tragic sensibility, a Bogartian dispensation. Of all the things the Islamic State banned, cigarettes were the most galling. The worst part is that it wasn't really a ban but a way to corner the market. As everyone, even nonsmokers, knew, privately the jihadis sold cigarettes. They had a line on an Armenian brand, called Akhtamars, smuggled in from Turkey. They were terrible cigarettes but they were all you could get. The Akhtamars came to be known as *Daeshi*s. For a month's salary or more, you could buy a carton from a religious policeman, the same one who might arrest you tomorrow for smoking.

The Islamic State began in corruption and ended in corruption. Baghdadi may have been a pragmatist, he may have been a millenarian, he may have been both, but what he was beyond question was a thief. His new constitution for Mosul, in addition to all its talk of fairness and justice, laid claim to all public monies, and, true to its word, the group stole $425 million from Mosul's Central Bank, according to a U.N. report. This even while it imposed a mandatory 'charitable' tax on every citizen and ramped up duties on all commerce and consumption. The jihadis confiscated and rented and resold homes and commercial properties and forcibly took over farms and granaries. *The New York Times*'s Rukmini Callimachi found Caliphate receipts for grain sales in one day in 2015 totaling nearly $2 million. This money very clearly wasn't being put back into the land. With no export or import economy, Mosul's public works and private construction projects came to a halt and factories and stores closed. As they did, the Caliphate dismantled them and shipped off the equipment to its territory in Syria or for sale abroad. By 2016, the U.N. report found, as much as three-quarters of Mosul's industrial enterprises were destroyed, as was a comparable share of its government infrastructure. The Caliphate bunkered millions of barrels of oil and gasoline and smuggled them out of the country, driving up prices.

The planning department director whom I knew recalled being in his office when a bunch of bearded, rifle-toting heavies came in. They told him, 'Close everything, give us your keys, go home. We'll call you if we need you.' One of them saw a satellite-image map of Mosul on his office wall. He asked, 'What's that?' The director realized these people had no interest in planning anything. 'It's all a lie,' he remembered thinking. 'We thought the Americans were their target. But they weren't. We were their target. Our money was their target.'

With Mosul cut off from all external power sources save one, the decrepit Mosul Dam, electricity and water service were reduced to a few hours a week. The government in Baghdad ceased paying salaries to its employees in Mosul and benefits to the needy. Abu Fahad lost his job. So did Abu Omar. Food markets went empty. The airstrikes began. The sadism increased. Lists of executed people were posted at mosques and medical centers, like the proscription lists pinned up on walls in ancient Rome, except in this case the people on the lists were already dead. Public executions and tortures were not just performed publicly, but also broadcast on plasma-screen TVs mounted at intersections and in plazas. Once a matter of theological law or propaganda, violence became a civic entertainment, the jihadi coliseum. Anyone who wanted to, including children, could go to a religious police station with a flash drive and download the videos, free of charge. Maha watched some. 'They were cutting throats halfway in order to increase the torture,' she told me. 'They were hanging them like cows and chickens, one beside the next. They called it "the art of beheading." They were being creative.'

The Islamic State's reign came to remind some Moslawis of a folk-tale about the city. The Moslawi novelist Mahmoud Saeed retells it this way in his book *The World Through the Eyes of Angels*:

> One harsh winter the river water froze, and people and wagons and even buffaloes could move around on the ice in the day-time. The poor wolves, however, couldn't find anything to eat and almost starved to death. And so one day at dawn the guard who was opening the gate—here the Sheikh pointed at Bab al-Jadid, only a couple of hundred meters away—was attacked by hundreds of wolves who devoured him in the blink of an eye, and then rushed howling through the alleys of the city, looking for more. People cowered in their homes. They stopped going to the dawn prayer and stopped going to their work.

Abu Fahad's eldest son, Loy, was a furniture maker by trade but no one was buying furniture. He turned to piecemeal construction work until that dried up. His wife's family lived in west Mosul and Loy moved there. Abu Fahad knew his son was friends with jihadis and that he supported their goals of wresting Iraq from the control of the Maliki government and reintroducing Islamic morality. But when they began abusing Moslawis, Loy told his father, he turned against them.

Abu Fahad worried what would become of him. No one will ever know how many Moslawis joined the Islamic State, how many worked for it in one way or another, how many were true believ-ers, how many casual abiders, how many begrudging accepters. Those Moslawis who were truly in the Islamic State, who'd fought and killed for it, were on the west side now, too. The hardcore and the periphery were pushed together and they were all as good as dead, he believed. 'Let me tell you something,' he told me, 'those who joined Daesh, they can never escape. You can't undo what's been done. Either way, they'll die. If they fight the army, the army will kill them, and if they try to leave Daesh, the jihadis will kill them. There is no way out of it.'

It was a gray afternoon in the Khazer camp. His life was becoming a blur, Abu Fahad said. War after war, disaster after disaster. 'Each day you receive a call, and you don't know if it's just a call or if someone is calling to tell you your brother's died, or your uncle. We haven't found comfort or peace in our entire lives. We've spent all our energy on misery. It's like being back in the army. You can only take a few days off, and then you must go back on duty, back into the misery. I am a little over fifty years old, and if you compare me to a European person my age—you see him traveling, swimming, enjoying life, while I am always tired. I'm tired all the time. Our existence has become tired.'

'Even before Daesh came to Mosul, I was so tired,' Hamudi agreed. 'I already have gray hair.'

'I wish youth could come back to see what age has done to me,' said Abu Fahad, quoting a poem.

———

During the combat on the east side, the jihadis and the coalition had, between them, managed to destroy all five bridges on the Tigris, including one originally built of boats that had been there in one form or another for nine hundred years. This meant the troops had to approach west Mosul from the south. The road in passed the Assyrian city of Nimrud, bulldozed by the jihadis. It continued through what had been two bases, Camp Diamondback and Forward Operating Base Marez, and an adjoining airport, occupied by American troops until 2011, when they were handed over to Iraqi forces. After seizing Mosul, the jihadis had dismantled all of it—not just dismantled, but razed it, razed with an occult fury. Where there had once been buildings and blast walls and a runway there were now acres of obsessively chunked concrete. They had left intact only a mosque and a group of bunkers built by Saddam. The bunkers, capped aboveground by hulking trapezoids of pebbledash, the sort of comically hideous architectural feature that could only exist for a military purpose, combined with the rubble and the long, drooping branches of the tall trees—like taller, thinner weeping willows, their dust-caked leaves rustling in the faint wind—to give this entire corner of the city a bygone funereal feel. It was like an ancient burial ground set upon by grave robbers.

With no base left them, and with operations on the west side beginning, the American forces backing the Iraqis requisitioned the compound of a sheikh who was said to have thrown his lot in with the Islamic State. The compound was so immense it fit a detachment of the 82nd Airborne, which had replaced the 101st, one of Special Forces, a group of military contractors, and the CTS generals and their retinues. Of the six homes on the property, which were arrayed in an L shape along the north and east sides of a sprawling garden, the construction of only three had been completed, but those three all qualified as mansions. The Americans had turned the ground floor of one into a command center, larding it with banks of computers and gadgetry. On the front terrace they'd erected a carpentry and machine shop, while the rear terrace they'd outfitted with treadmills, a rowing machine, kettlebells, and a squat rack. This gym was for Special Forces only. Not to be upstaged, the 82nd had assembled their own weight room in one of the unfinished houses, from which they could look onto the rest of their handiwork: the garden, probably an acre in size, was covered over with prefab bunks and offices; a battery of 800-kilowatt generators the size of Manhattan studio apartments, along with various massive radar dishes and antennae; a bank of portable toilets, impossibly clean, never smelling of anything but disinfectant, and piled with roll after roll of soft American toilet paper; and a tented chow hall, air-conditioned to frigidity, though it was winter, and stocked day and night with coolers of sodas and juice, palettes of potato chips and individually wrapped cake slices. Those were the snacks. At mealtimes there were chafing dishes of French toast and pancakes and hash browns, of beef stew, sliced ham and scalloped potatoes, of hamburgers, enchiladas, mashed potatoes, meatloaf, and boiled vegetables. If you got up before dawn, you could watch the night-raid helicopters come in and then find the commandos in the mess, loading their plates with scrambled eggs and Pop-Tarts.

Though they were allowed to dine with the Americans, the Iraqi generals and colonels preferred to stick with the roast lamb and chicken and salads turned out by a Kurdish chef who cursed his Arab bosses once they had finished eating and were out of earshot. The Iraqi bodyguards and soldiers, not welcome at either buffet, ate mostly rice and beans, scrounging whatever meat the generals didn't finish. The Americans had erected for the Iraqis a shower block in the garden. On its exterior were the masking-taped letters C-T-S. On the exterior of the American showers next door were signs in English and Arabic reading US MILITARY AND COALITION PARTNERS ONLY. Whoever had put up the signs had apparently forgotten that Iraq was a coalition partner—the lead partner, indeed, whom the Americans were there to support, as the Army public-affairs people never tired of reminding me.

A reporter friend, a former Marine, pointed the shower signs out to me. We were sitting one morning watching the scene in the supercharged garden. The paratroopers marched to and from the showers in their matching black Army running shorts, black T-shirts, clean white towels folded over their shoulders, dopp kits under their arms. They would climb into their new MRAPs, then spend the day firing the occasional shell, then return to lift weights and watch movies and listen to music and play with their phones. My friend had pulled two combat tours in Iraq in the mid-2000s, during the civil war, fighting insurgents and watching friends die with the proud Marine frugality.

'Fucking *Army*,' he said, shaking his head in disgust.

At night, the more garrulous Americans gathered around a fire pit, smoking cigarettes and dipping. One night, a young Dominican-American man from the Bronx struck up a conversation with me. This was rare. American servicepeople are taught early and often not to talk with journalists unless ordered to. We got on the subject of the enemy drones. The fighting in west Mosul had just begun with a flock of bad omens: the jihadis had figured out how to rig 44-mm grenades to the undersides of their drones with a catching mechanism that connected to the headlamps. When the pilot turned on the lights, the grenade armed and released. As the troops progressed north toward the city, quadcopters came over them, dropping the small bombs. The better drone pilots could put a grenade into a Humvee turret. Then, almost overnight, the attacks stopped. Everyone suspected the Americans had employed some wizardly technology but no one could say what exactly it had been.

I told him about a drone episode I'd seen. Even before the jihadis turned them into bombers, the Iraqi soldiers hated the drones, these cowardly little machines, hated them almost as much as they hated the VBIEDs. I had been standing in a front yard of one of the requisitioned homes in Zahra when I heard a demure whir overhead. This was soon followed by what sounded like the opening notes of a gun battle. The fire thickened. I rushed out expecting to see the soldiers shooting down a street. Instead I found them gathered in the plaza, their rifles angled up at the clouds. Scanning above, I finally noticed a floating cross. I mistook it for a long bird before noticing its wings didn't move. More men appeared on the street and on roofs. They emptied clips. A man leapt onto the hood of a Humvee and climbed into the turret, where he racked the 50-cal and shot wildly at the sky. He wasn't using his sights. Nor were most of his colleagues. But they fired with expressions of concentration which turned into expressions of exultant release. The drone was far enough to make the chances of hitting it remote even with superb aim, but hitting it wasn't the point. The point was to shoot at something in the open, something they could identify, unlike this spectral immanence the Islamic State. They didn't hit it.

I asked the young soldier if he knew how the recent drone-grenade attacks had been stopped. He did. He'd done it. He described how he'd disabled them, jamming the radio frequencies and then hacking into the controls, taking the things over long enough to land them somewhere absent of people, where bomb techs went and disabled the grenades. He offered to show me the next day. I wanted to see, of course, but worried he'd get himself in trouble.

'You may want to ask your CO,' I said.

'I don't have a CO,' he said.

He was not a soldier, it turned out, but a contractor. He'd recently graduated from an electronics trade school in Connecticut, got a job, and been sent to Iraq. I asked how he liked it.

'I like it all right. I like this operation. We're part of history.'

And no doubt we were, though it was interesting to consider where his bit of history fell. He wasn't old enough to have understood most of what had led up to it. Twenty-five, he hadn't been alive for the Gulf War in 1991 and was barely conscious when the next one began. Many of the paratroopers were even younger. Some had been in grade school when America *pulled out* of Iraq.

Unlike the contractor, the commander of the 82nd detachment, a colonel, had seen the history, had been part of it, and he was not so sanguine. 'It will be decades before this place is rebuilt,' he told me in a wearied voice that suggested he might as well have said 'generations,' or 'never.' The madness of the Islamic State's losing stand here was his ostensible subject, but in his voice you sensed a cognizance of the madness of the invasion fourteen years before. Americans and foreigners who've never interacted with American servicepeople often assume they are unthinkingly combative, always spoiling for a fight, or that they all supported the invasion of Iraq, all thought like an American infantryman in Iraq in David Finkel's *The Good Soldiers* who told the author, without a hint of irony, 'I hate the way these people don't care about freedom.' This is not true. Many did not support the invasion, especially in the officer corps. Many thought it lunacy and said so. Some generals told the White House as much, among them James Mattis, Trump's first defense secretary. Today, speaking with Americans of a certain age in the military, you can usually tell, without their having to say, who felt this way. I got a strong sense this colonel did. I also got the sense he felt the way many American commanders did about the American departure in 2011—that it was a betrayal of the Iraqis, an abandonment of them to the worst of their possible fates. And yet, like so many colonels, he had been made by Iraq. He owed his career to this place he'd helped destroy. This knowledge seemed to weigh on him. Anyway I hope it did.

Around the fire, the paratroopers compared stories of what all grand inspired nastiness they'd seen the enemy get up to that day. On the night the contractor and I spoke, they were talking about the resourcefulness of the Islamic State bombmakers. A soldier described one munition he'd seen, a missile with an oil barrel for a cone.

A sergeant recalled his first deployment to Mosul a decade before. Zarqawi was still running the insurgency then, and his guys sent a propane tank rigged to a parachute into an American outpost.

'They must play a lot of video games,' the sergeant said, with begrudging respect. He spat out some tobacco juice.

In the sergeant's right eye the fire produced a red gleam, as though there was an ember in his pupil. When a soldier who was sitting next to the sergeant got up, I took his seat. It was then I saw the sergeant had a prosthetic eye.

'Want to know how I got it?' asked the sergeant, whose name was Cavazos.

I said I did.

His platoon had been in the initial invasion force in 2003. They'd fought the Fedayeen Saddam in Samawah and Diwaniya, then al Qaeda in Anbar, then the Shia militias in Baghdad.

'What's so funny is this,' Sergeant Cavazos told me. 'The way we're being treated now? It's the way we were being treated when we first came in. We came in and we were liberators and it was a good push and they loved us, you know? And then it went to—it went bad. Both sides. The Shia, the Sunni. It was bad on both sides.'

On New Year's Day, 2005, the 82nd arrived in Mosul. Zarqawi's people had just bombed the dining facility at Diamondback, killing fourteen Americans. Al Qaeda in Iraq had got to be very bold. 'They were really ballsy. There were a lot of engagements with them. But they found out we were pretty persistent. Day and night.' Zarqawi was said to be spending a lot of time in Mosul. The sergeant's platoon was chasing a particularly vicious contingent of his men whom they'd nicknamed the Santa Fe Gang. 'One day we ended up killing four of them. It was simple. We parked two Humvees by the road. We picked up the hood, made it look like the vehicles were damaged. We had set up the night before. They circled around twice, then attempted an ambush. We ambushed them. We ended up killing all four of them. Some of the key guys were smart. A lot of their cronies weren't.' One of the smart guys was a world-class sniper. Everyone was afraid of him. They had intelligence that he was foreign, possibly Chechen. 'He was out there and he was good. He had tagged a lot of people. He almost got me before. He was really close. But he was always covered by a personal security detail. So he had to be pretty important. He would take a shot and then his PSD would engage us, and then he'd disengage.'

Sergeant Cavazos was on a street in west Mosul, not far from where we were now, with his platoon, inspecting possible polling sites for the upcoming election. He was near his Humvee, thinking what a good place they'd finally found—a school where voters could safely form into queues—when the hairs on the back of his neck stood up. This was not a figure of speech. The hairs literally lifted off the skin. He could feel himself standing on the wrong end of a rifle scope. 'I knew someone was glassing me.' He was turning his head to address a soldier when his Oakleys flew from his face as though of their own volition. He thought he'd been hit on the temple by a ball. Then he heard the report from the rifle. 'I thought, Oh shit.' He didn't black out. He wasn't in pain. He never even got very dizzy. He suddenly couldn't see out of one eye, was all. A scratch, he thought. The main problem was he'd swallowed his dip. The wad of tobacco had gone down his throat and was nauseating him. Other than that, he was all right. He was rushed in a Humvee to the base, where he stepped off the stretcher himself and stripped, knowing the doctor would have to cut off his clothing anyway. No need to waste a good uniform. The doctor looked at the wound. He told the sergeant he'd have to be flown stateside at once. 'Why?' Cavazos demanded. He hadn't even lost consciousness. How bad could it be? He wasn't going back. No way. The doctor took the sergeant's index finger and gently moved it towards the sergeant's cheek. The finger didn't stop at the skin. It just kept going. That was because there was no skin. The sniper's bullet had blown a hole through his face below the eye, entering the nasal cavity, and then exited from the eye socket, taking the eyeball with it. 'It found the cavity, boom, straight out.'

Now he has a collection of prosthetic eyes. Before a new private or specialist comes into his office at Fort Bragg for the first time, he likes to remove whichever one he has in and place it on the prosthetic-eye stand on his desk, pupil out, so that it's looking right at the young buck. The one he had in at the moment was the one he was known for. Within the milky black orb was painted the claret red skull insignia of The Punisher. The same insignia was painted on the passenger-side door of his MRAP.

This was Sergeant Cavazos's fifth deployment to Iraq. It was twelve years almost to the day after he was sniped. It was not a bitter memory. On the contrary, he told me, he called the day his eye was shot out his Born Again Day.

'It's like a career of playing football. You have some great games. You remember every stadium you've played at. To come back to this stadium again, that you hadn't been to in so many years. That was pretty awesome for me.'

3

Before the young contractor figured out how to disable the drones, an Iraqi journalist was killed by a grenade. She was one of several local journalists to die. Foreign journalists had been shot and hit with shrapnel. The generals were fed up with the press by this point. They didn't like that we were getting hurt. They also didn't like that we were reporting on military and civilian casualties. Like most generals, they seemed to believe the role of the media in wartime should be restricted to cheerleading the troops and decrying the enemy's bad sportsmanship. Reporters were doing themselves no favors, meanwhile, running amok on the frontlines, barreling around in unarmored vehicles, endangering themselves and the troops and Moslawis. It was a poor showing by my compatriots, whose presence already felt slightly obscene to me. With a few exceptions, I felt, news organizations had sent reporters to Iraq because of the Islamic State's luridness. They didn't betray much interest in understanding the history or nuances of this conflict, let alone of Iraq. Most of their shallowly shocking coverage existed somewhere on the same spectrum as the Caliphate's own blood-porn. Maybe mine was no better. I got the sinking sense that where American editors were concerned, there was a certain crowing beneath the fascination with the Islamic State. American newsrooms had been hoodwinked in 2003 and the editorial class felt lingering guilt and resentment over this. A lot of editors and journalists, most of them mediocrities, but also some very good ones, had seen the wisdom in the war to topple Saddam, though he and al Qaeda had been demonstrably irrelevant, when not hostile, to one another. Iraq had become a locus of jihadism only after the invasion, as we all would learn. But now these editors could point to the Islamic State, with its undeniably Iraqi pedigree, and say 'See, I knew all along there was something horrible lurking in the desert there.' If they knew even enough history to say that.

I knew the sharper generals, like Abdulwahab and Riyadh, sensed this prurience, too, and so I couldn't blame them for what they finally did, which was to expel journalists from Mosul, regardless of who they were or who they worked for. Even people who'd spent months with the troops were told to get lost. Ayman Oghanna of *VICE*, who'd been cheating death with the CTS since Ramadi, was barred. *The New York Times Magazine* was accorded no special treatment. The expulsions began in late November. By February it was almost impossible to report in Mosul. I was kicked out more times than I remember. I'd sneak back in, be noticed by some general or colonel, and be told to leave again. Soon corporals and privates were yelling at me to get away. Any man caught so much as talking to a journalist would be disciplined.

But there was one commander who always allowed me to stay with him. Major Hassan was the company commander whom I'd seen carried into the triage station in Gogjali, at the beginning of the battle, with a gunshot wound to the leg. It was Hassan who, though writhing in agony, had shouted at the medic for trying to filch his watch when the man rolled up his sleeve to put an IV in Hassan's arm. I found him by chance one morning in early March in a CTS command post in Makhmour, a neighborhood near the southwest edge of the city.

Physically, there was not much about Hassan that you would call exactly commanding. He looked like someone's chipper younger brother, short, chubby, with jolly cheeks like big ripe apricots. He smoked his cigarettes from a long, dandyish plastic filter tip. But his eyes made up for any deficit of bodily authority. They were remarkable, mesmerizing, had the umber of Venus. Their composition seemed to change with his moods, like the sulfuric acid clouding around that planet, growing browner and murkier when they flashed with anger, which was common, more golden and limpid when he smiled and laughed, common too.

They were golden and limpid now. By his smile and easy manner, you'd never know that Hassan had just recovered from a grievous wound, one of many he'd sustained in this war, nor that the jihadis were at this very moment hurling their homemade 60-mm shells at his position with devilish abandon. A burst rocked the walls every few minutes, at certain points more often. It was an astounding rate of fire, especially considering that the coalition had become expert at tracing the trajectory of enemy shells with radar acquisition and blasting the positions from which they were fired in a matter of seconds. The artillerists were either really well hidden or equally expert at changing positions very rapidly—or simply ready to die.

At first it seemed they were trying to land a bullseye on Hassan, and they were getting close enough. But as the morning progressed, and more and more refugees poured in from the neighborhoods to the north and east, where the fighting was heaviest, it became clear the jihadis were, in fact, sending this tremendous fusillade our way not with the goal of killing soldiers, but rather civilians. They had their sights on a few chokepoints through which the crowds of refugees were passing and which happened to be near the command post.

The Caliphate could claim it had warned Moslawis this would happen. In October, after the ground invasion began, announcements were posted: 'Not one of you will be unaware of the size of the Crusader conspiracy in all its forms against the Islamic State,' they read. 'But no, by God, they have failed, lost and their appointment is Hellfire in this world and the Hereafter.' Just in case Moslawis were not aware the Crusaders had already failed in their conspiracy, and were tempted to protect themselves or leave, a new raft of rules was introduced. It was forbidden to go to Caliphate military installations or to the front lines; to park or gather in front of hospitals; to purchase heavy weaponry whose caliber exceeded 7.62 mm; to breach the dress code even in case of emergency; or to flee Mosul, except in the case of medical emergency, 'under penalty of Sharia reckoning.' That some of the refugees fleeing through Makhmour now were desperately ill or injured didn't appear to bother the enemy artillerists. Nor, probably, did the commonly known fact that, until the ground invasion began, and very likely even after it did, the jihadis themselves ran an exorbitant people-smuggling racket, secreting Moslawis out of their own city.

One of the chokepoints was an intersection onto which an overpass had collapsed. There the civilians, themselves moving with astounding speed considering their state, had to slow down to climb over the rubble. With each new group, a shell would come in. After each burst, the plume would lift, a few seconds would pass, and the families would dash into view and up the street toward us, the men in sweatpants and blazers and sandals, the women in abayas and impractical footwear, the children in anything. And while the intersection was taking direct hits, I saw not one person hit that morning. Mortars are fickle that way. Some days the shells land on a dime and hurt no one; others they land nowhere and hurt everyone. The frag holes in a body could be so small and bloodless that it was impossible to see how the person had died. If the victim were close enough to a big enough blast, the blast wave could rupture their organs even as the shrapnel and frag missed him, and he'd die without a mark on him.

As we watched this scene, Hassan told me his leg had taken two months to heal. It might have been longer, but there was only one bullet. That is what the doctors said, anyway. He wondered. Hassan knew the government needed to rush men back into combat as quickly as possible. Experienced fighters couldn't be spared, and men were fighting with ill-set bones, discolored limbs, inflamed scars. The generals needed their best field commanders in the field, and Hassan was one of the best. He didn't trust the generals any more than he did the doctors, but this was his job. And, besides, he told me, he liked killing jihadis.

The wounds hadn't been quite so straightforward the previous three times he'd been hit. In Ramadi, several pieces of shrapnel had gone into his arm and chest. Near Baiji, he was sprayed with metal and glass from a car bomb. After each surgery, he returned to his family in Baghdad. Each time, it got harder to leave.

'Every minute is like one year for her,' Hassan said of his wife. 'She doesn't want me to fight. Of course women don't want their husbands to go to battle. She doesn't say quit, but she's not happy that I'm here. I didn't think about quitting after getting shot. My wife is a PhD student. She's smart. She understands my situation. When I left the house, I left early so my children wouldn't see me so they wouldn't be sad. I wish I didn't have to leave them like that. But they understand that this is my life, that I have to be in this war.' Hassan had lost four of his men in Anbar and, so far in Mosul, eleven. 'The hardest part is when a man from my division dies. I cannot do anything. It's very hard. I cry.'

But his men were glad he was back, every time more than the last.

They adored him. A young private who had been serving under Hassan for four years told me that the year before, he (the private) had been arrested for 'a problem with my girlfriend.' He had spent seven months in prison. Hassan helped get him out.

'He's the best. He's golden,' the private said. 'He's very brave.'

Though Hassan had only just set up this command post, the enemy had already sent in a VBIED to try to blow him up. Not just any VBIED, but a bulldozer bomb. A BBIED, if you like. The suicide-driver had burst through a cinderblock barrier and then detonated amid some of the major's Humvees. The blast had rent off building exteriors and shredded vehicles. The body of a Humvee rested on one side of the street, by the façade-less houses, while its turret lay on the other side, next to a mosque. Strangely, the mosque appeared to have sustained no damage save one felicitous augmentation: the metal crescent moon–shaped finial atop the dome had been bent in a perfectly gentle curve, so that its tip was now directed not skyward but to the northeast, where the fighting was headed, as though ushering the troops onward.

On the metal gate of the mosque were taped a pair of flyers from the Islamic State Inspector General for Mosul. One was a reproof of Moslawis for 'taking advantage of the situation,' i.e., the battle, and 'massively manipulating' the market for foodstuffs. 'The people's money must be earned honestly. Merchants or consumers should not cheat or abuse one another.' Included was a list of price caps for flour, sugar, cooking oil, tomato paste, fat, Basmati rice, Thai rice, Vietnamese rice, Pakistani rice, chickpeas, red beans, and milk. Below the list, a postscript: 'You have to adhere to these prices and don't raise prices. Those who disobey will be punished.' The other flyer announced that Moslawis who had been displaced by the coalition bombing and who hadn't yet registered for aid could do so now.

While Hassan and I talked, his phone rang. He answered it. It was his mother. My translator and I could hear her over the speaker.

'Are you at the front line?' she asked Hassan.

'No, no,' he said. 'I'm not even outside. I'm in a room. I've shut the door.'

'Don't go to the front line. Please. Have you had breakfast?'

'Yes I had breakfast. Now you should have breakfast, too. Please relax. Don't worry about anything. Be comfortable.'

Covering the phone, he told us 'If I don't answer, she thinks I'm dead.'

'You're lying to me. You're injured. That's why you didn't answer the phone before.'

'No, no, I just don't have a signal sometimes.'

He rang off and told me, laughing, 'She calls every day.'

To meet the Islamic State's redoubled aggression, the air war had, as the flyer on the mosque suggested, been escalated, and the results were impossible to miss. Looking around Hassan's position in Makhmour, I saw demolition in every direction. In addition to the raids by winged aircraft, there were now constant helicopter sorties by American Apaches and Iraqi Hinds. Few jihadis in Mosul were old enough to have fought in the Soviet war in Afghanistan, but those who had would have to remember the Hind, the ghastly Russian-made gunship, seventy feet long and capable of doing two hundred miles per hour, looking like a great winged lizard chewing through the clouds. There was a lot of noise in Mosul but nothing so head-rattling as the arsenal of the Hind, which carried a twin-barrel cannon that put out 3,400 rounds a minute. When fired overhead, it was as though the earth's atmosphere was a closet and you were trapped inside it with a crazed timpanist, and the Hind's rockets gave the aural effect of tearing the sky in two like a canvas. Terrible as these sounds were, though, and try as I might to stay fair-minded about the death I knew they dispensed, it was impossible not to come to find them reassuring; and, eventually, deeply comforting. The enemy had nothing nearly so terrible, I knew, while also knowing not only enemy fighters were dying in those sorties.

One morning I stood on a roof and watched as a Hind made rounds above. Each time it came overhead, a jihadi gunman shot at it—not with anything that could have had some effect, but with an AK. The Hind would approach, the gunman would fire, the Hind would glide off, seeming almost amused. From his fire control, it was clear the gunman was aiming, not shooting wildly. He was doing his level best. You really had to credit his gall. I watched this for what must have been an hour, marveling at the gunman's persistence, until, on its last round, the Hind fired a rocket. A plume went up. The corrida came to an end.

During operations on the east side, the Iraqis had left open a narrow corridor between Mosul and the border, giving jihadis the chance to flee to Syria, in the hopes of minimizing civilian deaths and damage in Mosul. The corridor had been cut off for weeks now, so any new munitions the jihadis were using they were making themselves—and yet they seemed to have more munitions now than ever. They'd standardized, on an industrial scale, the manufacture of bombs and bomb parts, from the shell casings to the charges to the fuses to the triggers, as well as shoulder-fired rockets, mortars, and the kind of wondrous beastly creations the paratroopers liked to puzzle over by the fire. Near Makhmour I inspected one of their mortar shell factories. It appeared to be a former cement plant. There were hundreds of metal molds for producing 60-mm shell casings, packets of German-made forging clay, furnaces, tongs, hammers, equipment sufficient to furnish a small battle. There was a 9th division colonel who kept a collection of the Islamic State's most malign innovations: bombs built into cooking pots, teakettles, vacuum cleaners, computer consoles, space heaters, fire extinguishers, light switches.

CTS had already taken far more casualties than it could replace. The 16th division was busy patrolling the east side. The 9th had shown itself unequal to this fight. This meant the federal police had to do much of the fighting in the west. Until recently, many of the federal police had been Shia militiamen. The Shia militias had played a necessary if controversial part in the war. They had fought bravely in many engagements, and because there weren't nearly enough regular troops to occupy all the newly liberated parts of Iraq, the militias had done it. But they were feared by Sunni civilians. In Tikrit and Fallujah and many other places, there were reports of Sunni men being rounded up, tortured, disappeared by the militias. By the time of the Mosul offensive, it was widely understood that, beneath the war against the Islamic State, there was another, unofficial, quieter war going on, a dirty war of sectarian revenge. There was no question the Caliphate had held genocidal intentions toward the Shia, nor that they had acted on them at every opportunity. Now many militiamen felt it was only fair they should take some flesh as recompense. It was never clear to me how extensive this campaign of revenge was, but it was obvious the militias were acting with the backing of the government in Baghdad, which was still dominated by Maliki's Dawah party, and which eventually went so far as to formalize the militias as part of the Iraqi military. By the time fighting in the west got underway, the revolving door between the militias and the federal police was in constant motion. Meanwhile, funding, equipment, and fighters were pouring in from Hezbollah and Iran. I arrived at a checkpoint in a militia-held territory one day and didn't recognize the language the guards were speaking.

'That's not Arabic,' I said to my translator.

'No, it's Persian,' he replied under his breath.

Unsurprisingly, the federal police in Mosul fought sloppily. This was partly because many of them didn't much care what happened to Moslawis, partly because they were barely trained—three weeks of basic training for new recruits, then into the field—and partly because they were, despite the foreign help, badly provisioned. In late March a federal police unit I was with had liberated the stately central rail station, in the process shooting the beautiful stone building to bits. Now they had taken up positions by the tracks, from which they were trying to dislodge a nearby enemy contingent. Having nothing better at hand, they had up-armored their APC with sandbags, fastening them to the vehicle's sides with chicken wire. Their artillery was similarly do-it-yourself. The prize item was a multilaunch system consisting of a trio of immense handmade mortar tubes welded onto an open-back Humvee. It looked like something the jihadis would have made.

The men parked the Humvee facing vaguely toward the enemy. One man made some cursory calculations with what appeared to be a hand compass, while another lit a tail fuse. From a tube launched a rusty projectile the length of a man and the width of a pine trunk. It hurtled a high arc, wobbling like a poorly thrown football, and exploded a few blocks away with a dismal rumble. Four of these bombs were launched, each time an officer yelling 'Blasting in the name of the Prophet!' I didn't know whether he was serious or glib until I noticed that there was a Shia prayer ceremony being conducted near us—in the open street, in the midst of the fighting. If there were civilians in the vicinity of the detonations, there was little chance they were alive. I asked one of the men how the aiming was done.

'I don't want to talk to you,' he said. 'I don't want you shouting about this and saying bad things.'

He was referring to an incident that had occurred a few days earlier. An airstrike had killed as many as a hundred fifty civilians who'd gathered in a building in a nearby neighborhood, Mosul al Jedida. Reporters flocked to the scene (before being expelled) and it became an international news story. A coalition investigation would later find that the Islamic State had probably forced the civilians to stay put as they invited the airstrike by launching projectiles from the building. The jihadis were trying to provoke such massacres by proxy. It was obvious to anyone who looked around that their aim now was to destroy as much of the city and kill as many as they could, to close the door of history, as Goebbels had put it, with a slam. But some locals claimed that, on the contrary, Moslawis had gathered in the building precisely in order to hide from airstrikes. The bombing of the al Amiriyah shelter in 1991 came up, inevitably. Every time the Americans claim they care about Iraqi civilians, people said, and every time this happens. An awful cycle took hold. The more Moslawis were killed, the more they resented the soldiers, and the more soldiers were killed, the more they resented the Moslawis.

After the incident in Mosul al Jedida, I was with some of Hassan's soldiers, sitting in a Humvee, listening to a local call-in radio show. Already Mosul radio stations were up and running again, amazingly.

'What I'm hearing about what's happening there makes me very sad,' a man calling from Palestine said to the host. 'May God be with you and protect you. I hope Daesh all dies and burns in hell. But it doesn't make sense to destroy an entire neighborhood because of one Daesh dog. It doesn't make sense. It's not acceptable. Ten thousand people are dying because of this. They're making a second Aleppo in Mosul.'

'You're right, it has become another Aleppo,' the host said. 'Houses are destroyed. The city is destroyed. This is very bad politics. It's a very bad plan if they want to restore Mosul.'

The next week, I followed the convoy of a CTS general as he went to a command post on a compact residential street in Mosul al Jedida, a few blocks from where the civilians had been killed. The neighborhoods of west Mosul had evolved over the centuries in the same fashion, which was that a mosque would be built, then commercial spaces would be built around it, which would pay for the building of schools and other institutions, and finally houses and streets would radiate out around the center. Mosul al Jedida had evolved this way, and it was a very pleasant place, even in wartime, with narrow tree-lined streets, plazas, and stately homes. The general I was following always traveled in a Humvee nested with sofa cushions and tasseled pillows and made himself otherwise conspicuous, always moving in a large convoy, lingering unnecessarily in crowded areas which the jihadis could easily target. He got out of his Humvee and entered the command post, which was near a food distribution that CTS was overseeing. As always, a crowd of several hundred had gathered around the trucks. On a side street across from this, a mother who'd fled the fighting elsewhere with her children had found refuge in an abandoned house. Her husband had been killed in crossfire. Outside the house she and her two sons had set up a small grocery. After getting their ration boxes, people came over to supplement them with a few tomatoes and onions. The family was happy to have the business.

A shell whistled in. I was sitting in a car about fifty meters away, on the far side of a block of homes, but the impact was enough to send a hail of pavement chunks onto the windscreen. I jumped from the car and went toward the blast as the crowd bolted from it. Within seconds the street with the aid trucks was empty. The shell may have been meant for the general, or the trucks, but it had hit the grocery. The side street was enshrouded in smoke. Out of it came two civilian men carrying a soldier, one pantleg of his fatigues already soaked with blood pumping from a shrapnel hole in his thigh. As he was lifted into a Humvee, another man, conscious but the color of death, his chest a confusion of entry wounds, was carried out and laid on the curb. Beside him was set down a boy whose injury was unapparent but whose face suggested something dreadful.

A flatbed truck raced up. The walking wounded climbed on. By the time the man with the wounds in his chest was lifted up, he was already dead. As the boy was handed on, his insides spilled from a hole in his abdomen.

An old man held another boy in his arms amid the melee of soldiers rushing about. Blood dripped down the boy's face. The old man walked back and forth, murmuring, approaching soldiers beseechingly, trying to get someone to help him, but in the chaos none took notice.

On the side street, in front of the grocery, lay a lone sandal, loose tomatoes, bags of chips, a pool of blood. The shell crater was minuscule, barely the size of a pothole. In the home where the family was living, behind the grocery, the kitchen windowpane had been blown out and its pieces lay on the floor. The mother and three girls stood in the kitchen, screaming. The man who had died was the woman's eldest son. She didn't yet know he was dead. The doorstep was pooled with his blood.

His younger brother, her last living son, stumbled into the kitchen, ranting and pulling at his hair with bloody hands, cursing the army. First his father was killed, now his brother. His mother begged him to lower his voice.

'Let them hear it!' he said. 'Let them hear it!' He went outside and crumpled onto the doorstep, his feet in the blood. Hyperventilating, he keeled forward.

In the command post, the general had heard the shelling and the commotion. It was one of his bodyguard who'd caught the shrapnel in the thigh. But the general was not overly concerned. He stayed inside. After learning his man had been taken care of, the general sat down to a catered lunch of kebabs, salads, fruit, and baklava.

This was how he ate most days, no matter where he was, no matter what the people around him were eating, or weren't, or how many of them were dying.

Around the time of the dessert course, the dead man was returned to his mother in a military body bag. It was opened. She glimpsed his face.

'God avenge us!' she yelled at the soldiers who carried in the corpse. 'I want my son!'

While the general smoked, shrieks came from another direction, up the block. I went toward them. A woman stood in the entranceway of her home, her hands to her face. Her shrieks had turned into gasps and tears. In front of her was her son. He wasn't dead, nor even injured. He looked just as hale as you'd want a sixteen-year-old boy to look. That was why she was gasping. She'd given up hope he was alive.

The boy kissed his mother and hugged his uncle.

'I can't believe it,' his mother gasped.

'I'm not that young anymore,' her son said.

'You've grown up. You're a man now,' his uncle said, smiling lovingly but standing at a distance from the boy, whose name was Muhammad, so that he could size him up properly.

'I can't believe I'm seeing him again,' his mother said through her hands. 'I don't remember the day he left.'

They went into a sitting room, its only adornment the grill of a cargo truck. The family owned a small trucking business, or had before the Islamic State. After a jihadi shot dead his father in front of him, Muhammad had escaped Mosul. That had been a year and a half ago. Since then, he had been on an odyssey around Iraq which he recounted as his younger brothers and sisters crowded into the room and kissed him. That first night, after the murder, he had fled Mosul by car, though he'd never in his life driven. He learned fast. He got as far as Shirqat, a town on the Tigris seventy miles south of

Mosul. It was still under the Islamic State. Petrified, he hid for days in an abandoned factory. Shirqat was soon liberated. He came out of hiding and made his way to Tikrit. Along the way he made friends, worked odd jobs to buy food. From Tikrit he hitched a ride to Baghdad. He found some distant relatives. When he'd heard the troops had reached Mosul al Jedida, he set out for home. As he talked, his mother held her youngest child, a developmentally disabled baby boy. He'd never set eyes on his father. The boy lay slumped in his mother's arms, his head lolling and tipping. Listening to Muhammad, she kept her eyes on the floor and put her lips to the baby's cheek. Occasionally she glanced at Muhammad, beamed, and then averted her eyes again, as though he was too much to take in.

Muhammad opened a black plastic garbage bag, his only luggage, and removed from it toy cars, handing them to his siblings. To the baby he gave a plastic red bull painted with blue flowers. To his uncle he handed a thick roll of dinars and a carton of cigarettes—the horrid Armenian Akhtamars.

'Daeshis!' his uncle said.

He told Muhammad how difficult it had been to smoke in Mosul. Not because the Islamic State forbade it—they ran the cigarette trade, after all—but because they charged so much for them.

'They wanted fifteen thousand dinars for a pack. One cigarette was a dollar!'

His uncle lit up. So did a younger brother.

'Don't smoke in front of the adults,' Muhammad scolded. 'It's not polite.'

His uncle said it was all right, so Muhammad lit one himself.

'Mom used to tell me, 'If you ever start smoking, I'll disown you,'' he said, laughing.

His mother smiled.

'I don't mind so much anymore,' she said.

When I next caught up with Major Hassan, in late April, his company had fought its way to the far eastern edge of Mosul al Jedida. His eyes were dark and murky. His men were being hunted by a sniper, he was convinced of it. Two had been killed instantly by head shots the day before. The young private whom Hassan had helped get out of prison was wearing a ring that had belonged to one of the dead men.

'I mean, this guy is a fucking *professional*,' Hassan said of the sniper. 'He always has two Iraqi fighters standing behind him, watching his rear, so he can focus. Just focus on anything that moves in front of him. He doesn't leave his rifle, and he doesn't miss. He only needs a second. I saw a person run across the road. In a second, he'd been shot in the neck.'

The next morning at dawn, Hassan's men were lined up, their backs against privacy walls, on either side of a street. The day's mission was to move on the neighborhood immediately to the west, called Thawra. The winter months of cold rain had been hard to endure, but they had one nice result—on clear mornings like this one, in which the imminent spring suggested itself, the battle dust was gone from the atmosphere and you could see for miles. The street on which we stood sloped steeply downwards, affording a view onto the old city, then across the Tigris, on to east Mosul, and beyond that to ridgelines of the Zagros. It was, technically, a beautiful vista, but also infernal. Black smoke rose from the car fires; the unfinished concrete hide of a soccer stadium hunkered before us, seeming to wish everyone ill; and the minaret of the al-Nuri Mosque was in full view now, leaning balefully toward the mountains. To a man, the soldiers were all wearing flak jackets and helmets. It could have been that Hassan had forced them to put on the protective gear, but something in their faces said that they wore it because they wanted to. Their faces also said they had not the slightest desire to move on Thawra. They were younger than the soldiers with whom I'd begun the battle. Many of them appeared to be in their very early twenties. So many experienced men had been killed and maimed irreparably and had to be replaced, and they were replaced with these boys, boys who'd never fought al Qaeda, never fought the militias, hadn't fought in Ramadi or Fallujah or Hit or Baiji. They were fresh and petrified.

Inside a requisitioned home, Hassan sat in an armchair, eating a breakfast of fried eggs and an Iraqi crepe, a glorious thing slathered with honey and tahini. His mother called.

'No, mom, there's nothing wrong. . . . No, no, we're good. Everything is ok. No, no, no, the opposite, mom, I swear! I just woke up and now we're drinking tea. . . . No, we're sitting! We don't have anything to do today. . . . Thank you, thank you. . . . No, no, there's not even a single bullet flying.'

He rang off.

'No matter how bad it is, I don't tell her what's going on,' he told me. 'I don't want her to live with the worry. I will not let my family know anything. Men were created to live difficulties, but I don't want to worry the people around me.'

'Does she believe you?'

'No, she doesn't believe me. But I try to soothe her.'

Hassan's commander radioed. The mission was pushed to tomorrow. The men outside were told. Their faces lit up. They walked up the foreboding street holding hands and singing. Hassan's column made the short trip back to the group of homes serving as barracks. When it arrived, a young soldier was standing in the street, kitted up and holding his rifle. Hassan stepped from his Humvee.

'Where were you?' he demanded.

The soldier explained that in the morning the column had filled up and there was no space for him. Hassan wasn't having it.

'There is never enough space in the Humvees. Your brothers saw this and what did they do? They jumped onto the tops of the Humvees! Your brothers went in to die. How do you feel when you know all your brothers are going to die, and you stay here and hide? How could you live with yourself if any of them died?' The company had a break coming up, but this man wouldn't be going anywhere. 'You had your vacation here.' Two comrades came to the young soldier's defense. He was new. He was young. He hadn't learned yet. Hassan calmed down. 'I'm kind to you and your brothers. Don't take advantage of my kindness. Tomorrow I want to see you the first man on the front line.'

A caravan of local well-wishers drove through. From the bed of a pickup a man tossed gray polyblend tracksuits and boxer-brief underwear in plastic bags to the troops, who were delighted. They changed out of their uniforms and for the rest of the day lounged in the sun or in their rooms in the fresh-smelling matching leisure wear. Hassan's driver, a compact man, dozed like a gray squirrel, his body folded into the driver's seat of his Humvee, not an easy thing even for someone of his stature. I spent the afternoon sitting on the floor with the soldiers, smoking and drinking tea. I asked what they would do after Mosul was taken.

'Go to Hawija, I guess, or Tal Afar,' one man said, referring to the Islamic State's last urban strongholds in Iraq. 'When you sign the CTS contract, you sign up to die.'

The conversation came around to the newly inaugurated President Trump. In one of his first executive acts, he was attempting to ban citizens from seven Muslim-majority nations from entering the U.S. One of them was Iraq.

'Before he came into office, I knew he didn't like Muslims,' a soldier said. 'But I thought he'd take care of the nasty Muslims. Instead, he came for us.'

Hassan's barracks was in a three-story home whose rooms formed a quadrangle around a central atrium courtyard. Some Moslawi homeowners had taken precautions before fleeing. It was common to find pieces of paper on credenzas or side tables in foyers printed with a particular Koranic verse meant to protect one's home. *God is one*, it read. *He is the uppermost of everything. He never tires. No one can have mercy without his sanction. He knows what is before you and what behind.* And, at the beginning of the battle, the soldiers had treated the homes they requisitioned as respectfully as they could. But by now, six months in, such scruples had passed. Hassan's house was a wreck: piles of empty water bottles and other garbage; ransacked bed linens; uneaten, rotting food; toilets flowing over with shit. In the evening, the men built a bonfire in the courtyard with sticks of furniture and told stories of the previous days' combat. Hassan joined them. One man recalled watching his comrade, who had never been trained to run a proper zigzag, fleeing from a sniper.

'He ran in a straight line but like this,' he said, wagging his head wildly from side to side. The laughs resounded through the atrium and up into the night.

After telling some stories, Hassan went to bed. Sometime later, the fire had burned down to embers, but a few men were still talking. Hassan bolted upright, turned on the flashlight on his phone and, in his long underwear and socks, went out onto the landing overlooking the courtyard.

'Get to bed, goddamnit!' he yelled.

He got back into bed and turned off the light. A few minutes later he sat up again.

'I forgot the RPG-7s!' he exclaimed.

He ran off to remind his driver to stow the launcher and rockets in his Humvee before they left. When he returned, Hassan explained to me that he'd taken up the habit of blasting open suspicious doors in the Mosul streets with RPGs.

'They're putting a lot more bombs in the houses. They're using home products like gas canisters. We're finding wires everywhere. They're even putting triggers in the cracks of the doors. When you open the door, it explodes. We have to be careful with every door.'

During the night, a battle between federal police and the enemy raged in a nearby neighborhood. I went to the roof to watch. A hellish glare rose above the houses, strands of red and yellow, tracers. By now I was used to this, and I had stopped trying to deny I saw beauty in it. I did. I found these streaks of violence beautiful. Fleeing residents made their way onto our street. The number of people was astounding. Some east Moslawis had fled, but nothing like this. From the west there was mass exodus, day and night. You watched lines of marching refugees miles long. It put you in mind of Malcolm Muggeridge watching Neapolitans fleeing in 1943, 'a vast concourse gathered on the hills around the city, like a vision of the Last Day, when all the dead arise.' That night, their chatter and moans and footfalls filled the night, echoing against the cobblestones and façades. I found that beautiful, too.

At dawn, Hassan's men climbed back into their Humvees and drove back to the mission staging area. A father with his family on a roadside tried to flag down Hassan's Humvee.

'Keep moving!' Hassan said through the window. He added, rhetorically, 'Where would we even put you?' He turned to his little driver. 'Where do they want me to put them? Up your ass?'

Back on the foreboding downsloping street, the men lined up as they'd done the day before. The sun wasn't yet visible but already firefights echoed up from Thawra. But the mood this morning was brighter. The day off and the banter at the bonfire had lightened spirits. It was another beautiful day. Overnight, spring had arrived. A small forward detachment set out down the street. Hassan took by the arm the young soldier who'd missed the convoy the day before and fairly swung him into the group of departing men, yelling 'Go!' The other soldiers smiled at this but didn't laugh.

Hassan marched the rest of his company into Thawra, down barren streets and onto a long commercial avenue. It was a picture of ruin. The wrecked shops and office buildings looked as though they'd surrendered, casting out their contents onto the street. There was not a soul anywhere. The whole city felt hollowed. The pavement in every direction was cratered, every wall pitted, every surface marred. We kept out of the open, weaving among and scrambling over the furrows and hillocks of rubble, ducking through the jihadi-made wall holes. Where we had to expose ourselves, at intersections, we dashed madly, leaping in and out of the craters, concentrating on nothing but the kicking of our legs. The man in front of me carried the RPG-7 rockets in a drawstring canvas bag on his back. Shredded aluminum panels and sticks of wood hung down from the blasted-out security grilles and doorframes and window casements, and the cones of the rockets knocked lightly against them as he ran.

We entered a destroyed room and came to a gate whose metal doors were shut save for a two-inch gap. A man took from this pocket a small shard of mirror and slowly moved it through the gap until it could reflect the other side of the doors. He rotated the glass, looking for wires. He found none, and opened the door. We came to an empty lot with a chicken coop. Somehow, the animals were still alive. Their feathers were sooty but otherwise the birds were in improbably good shape. It seemed miraculous. These wonderful, resilient animals. Then, wait, it seemed sinister. Who had kept these filthy birds alive?

'Daesh chickens,' a soldier said.

As though hearing this and wanting to prove his patriotism, a rooster left the safety of his mates and hopped into formation in our rear. He followed as we ran through the next intersection. He hopped through a crater. We lined up along a wall on the fire side. The rooster arrived. He crowed inquiringly. We looked at him. He gave us a once over, apparently feeling the gallantry he'd shown during the recent affair of the crater had won him this right. He jerked his head, turned on his heels, and hopped out of sight.

We moved back towards the commercial avenue. The reports of a lone rifle rang out. Single shots, unhurried. Across the avenue, a group of civilians came into sight from behind a colossal mound of rubble. In this lifeless landscape, they looked even more out of place than the chickens. They climbed down into an immense crater. The last in the group was an old man. He stopped in the crater's nadir. The group moved on until a young man turned around and looked back. He rushed to the crater and climbed down. The single shots continued. He folded the old man over his shoulder and carried him out. With each discharge I winced, expecting to see the men go down. But they got away.

We arrived at another intersection, and Hassan sent a squad to take up a position in a house on the far side. A few men dashed across and inside. An enemy shooter sent a round into the masonry in its doorway. In groups of twos and threes, a dozen of us dashed across the street and into the house. We went to the second floor. As we stood in the hallway there, the shooter put bullet after bullet into the façade, as though daring someone to engage. A request for air support was radioed in.

A tall, thin soldier, carrying a belt-feeding SAW machine gun in his hands and an M4 on his back, sat down across from me. On his flak jacket he'd sown a circular patch with a skull and crossed sabers that had apparently not been made by a native English speaker. SPE-CLAL FORCES, it read. Another man noticed a wooden palette in the hallway. This reminded him of boot camp, he told me. He'd had American instructors. They were fair but firm. When they wanted to penalize a private, he was made to run on a track with a plywood frame on his shoulders. If he was really punished, he had to try to run with the frame on his shoulders and another man sitting on top of it. He didn't resent it, the soldier said. On the contrary, he was glad of it. The flak jacket and extra magazines and the rest of his gear—it felt like nothing by comparison. Outside, the shooter kept firing tauntingly on our position.

'Fuck this sniper, fuck Baghdadi, fuck Daesh,' a soldier pacing the hallway said.

'I'm fine with liberating Iraq,' another said. 'But I'm worried they'll send us to Syria with the Americans.'

Finally we heard the blades of a helicopter overhead, then the comforting din of its guns.

We had been back at the staging area only a short time when the air and ground shuddered and a tremendous blast roared out. I looked up to see the cloud of a VBIED rising above the roofs. What sounded like a firefight immediately followed. I ran several blocks to the scene. The car bomb had hit a federal police position and with it an ammunition cache. The cook-off went on and on, exploding thousands of rounds, sending them flying everywhere as everyone ducked behind walls and cars. When the bursts finally ended, fifteen minutes later, and I could approach the blast scene, I saw, on a wall coping, the VBIED's steaming, charred chassis. The façades of the surrounding houses were pitted and splattered in motor oil. On the sidewalk and pavement were bits of the suicide-driver's skin and organs and bones, charred and coated in oil. A good fifty feet from the explosion lay part of his spinal column. I climbed to a roof overlooking the scene, its deck also coated in oil. A burly federal policeman was yelling the name of a friend who'd been near the blast.

'Hazzam! Hazzam!'

Others joined in.

'Hazzam! Can you hear us! Hazzam!'

'I'm down here!' someone finally called back.

The policeman, burly though he was, swung himself over the parapet and lowered himself onto a water spout, then leapt to the ground. There he found Hazzam, holding his head, walking in circles, barefoot—the explosion had blown his sandals off.

On the street, three mangled Humvees were in flames. A man lay between them, dead, his body blackening and cooking in the heat. A group of three civilian men walked toward the flames at the same time that two army medics, in their scrubs, approached from the other direction. One carried a pistol in a shoulder holster. 'Get back!' a medic yelled at the civilians. They kept walking toward the burning Humvees. The medic reached over to his friend's holster, wrenched the pistol from it, racked the chamber and aimed at the men. 'Get back!' he yelled again, and the men retreated around the corner.

When the medics had gone, the three men returned. Two were young, the third middle-aged. They were all very tall. One of the young ones approached the flames. He was crying. Even from a distance, even through the fire and smoke, he could tell that the man lying there was his father.

'I can't,' he moaned, turning back towards his brother and uncle. 'I can't.'

His uncle yelled at him. The brother and uncle took hold of him, and slowly they walked to the body. They laid a blanket on the ground and attempted to lift their father onto it. But the heat had already done a lot of damage. Trying to take his father's arm, one of the brothers came away with a long strip of skin instead.

They finally managed to wrap their father in the blanket. His foot and ankle, barely attached to his body, hung from the hem of the blanket precariously until the burly policeman took up the unmanned corner. They carried the body away.

I last saw Major Hassan in Thawra in early May. He was stationed on a comely street, or what would have been a comely street if there weren't at its end the blackened carcass of a tank and along its curbs the husks of cars that had been either burned by the Islamic State or shot to ribbons by soldiers worried that in the cars were bombs. We were on the edge of the old city, and you could look directly onto the leaning minaret of al-Nuri Mosque. But from this vantage the minaret was not leaning; its curve went outwards on exactly the axis of your line of sight, so that it appeared to be standing straight. It was a marvelous optical effect. Where a few days before the tower had looked sinister, now it looked plumb and strong, as though it had switched sides from the jihadis to the inevitable winners. Hassan had undergone a similar transformation. In the few weeks since I'd seen him, he'd lost probably fifteen pounds. He explained that in all that time his company hadn't stopped moving. Every day they'd pushed forward, meter by meter, block by block, and every day they were met with engagements. While we talked, a man and his young son approached. The man smiled amiably, as though they were just out for a walk.

'What are you doing here?' Hassan asked.

'What should we do about our cows?' the man responded.

'You can't just walk around in a combat zone,' Hassan said impatiently. 'If something happens, it's possible you'll get hit.'

They walked off as blithely as they'd arrived. Hassan turned to me with an expression of disbelief. 'I face difficulties with these civilians,' he said, fitting a cigarette into a filter tip and lighting it.

'They have very limited minds. They don't understand. It's a battle! They don't care. They just come here and walk around. He came here to ask me what he should do with his cows. In a war! We try to be patient with them, but sometimes they ask very stupid things. A woman came to me and said, "I left my favorite earrings in my house. Can I go get them?" When I tell them they're in danger, I try to be respectful. I'll say, "I respect you like a son." So she said, "If you're like my son, then go get the earrings for me."'

'Yesterday I saw the most difficult situation,' he went on. 'We entered the area. Seeing us, civilians came out of their houses. Daesh shot at them. They didn't shoot at us, they shot the civilians. They killed a lot of civilians yesterday. Shooting anything.'

He couldn't figure out Moslawis' attitude toward the Islamic State. It seemed to vary from person to person, family to family. Some were delighted to see the jihadis die. Others showed an odd inclination to protect them, whether out of fear or pity or attachment, he could not say. The day before, for instance, he'd witnessed two contradicting scenes. After a firefight, he saw a young jihadi crawl, injured, into a house. When the fighting was over, Hassan went into the house. He found a family. He also found the jihadi, wearing a fresh dishdasha. A woman claimed the militant was her son. 'This kind of situation really bothers me. He's not only our enemy, he's the enemy of the civilians. But we have human rights. We didn't even argue with the family. We knew. I am sure the mother would have said "My son's innocent." The mothers always say that. So we handed him over to the Diyala Brigade. I said, "You come get him and kill him."'

Soon after, another local family, this one in the process of fleeing, pointed out a jihadi to Hassan. The man, who was wearing combat fatigues and had a big beard, had tried to hide among them as they left. They knew him, he too was local—as were almost all of the jihadis Hassan caught—but they weren't about to protect him.

Hassan collared him. 'He admitted he was the Islamic State right off. But he said he didn't want to be with them anymore. He'd joined a year and a half ago, he told us. You know, anyone who joins Daesh, they have no more humanity. They've lost all humanity. They can't be treated as people—only as examples. They're animals. They don't deserve another chance.'

'So what did you do?' I asked.

'We took him off and shot him,' Hassan said. 'Do you want to see?'

The corpse was in a yard across the street. Lying on his back, his legs bent high like a frog's, was a very short man with a thick beard now sleeked down with blood and brain matter. He wore black combat fatigues and an oddly clean flowing white shirt. His face was blackened with necrosis and in the hole where the occipital bone of his skull once was, flies swarmed.

'I was looking right at him. He was not scared,' Hassan told me. 'Everyone has this thing inside of them, a threshold of fear. I couldn't find his.'

When we emerged from the yard, a soldier motioned silently to Hassan from across the street. He folded his arms in front of his face and then outstretched them, to indicate an imminent explosion. There was a VBIED nearby. An airstrike had been called in. I rushed into a basement with some soldiers. While we waited for the explosion, they confessed that what was really worrying them in Thawra was not the VBIEDs. It was the chemical weapons. I'd told them I'd heard reports but never seen anything. These were more than reports, they said. They'd seen the things. The jihadis were packing chlorine into their homemade shells. When inhaled in sufficient quantities, chlorine asphyxiates you, but even slight exposure can affect the breathing, make you vomit, blur your vision. It hadn't been reported in any news coverage, probably because almost no news was coming out of Mosul anymore, with journalists still barred from the city, and the command wasn't talking about it, but it was happening. A few days before, they told me, they had smelled something weird after a shelling at night. A man who'd been near a chlorine bomb before knew the smell. It was unmistakable. Luckily they were near a house with running water. They'd stripped, showered, and got rid of their clothes. Since then, there had been several more such attacks in the area. At least one soldier had died from inhaling the stuff. The jihadis were also packing some kind of blistering agent, possibly sulfur mustard, into the shells. On his phone, a soldier showed me a picture of the leg of a man who'd been near a fishy burst. On his shin was a ghastly contusion or blister, a bubble of yellowed skin inches long and protruding about an inch from the skin.

The house shook with an airstrike. The VBIED was incinerated. I emerged and found Hassan behind a nearby house, in a rose garden. The flowers were already in full bloom, and they were magnificent, the plumpest rose bulbs I'd ever seen, the size of grapefruit. Hassan's men stood about, burying their faces in the small explosions of violet and pink and blue, inhaling deeply, smiling, remarking to each other on the beauty of the flowers. It was a comical and lovely sight—and oddly fitting, because Hassan had just learned he was being promoted from company commander, a position he'd held in CTS for a decade, to deputy battalion commander. But he was conflicted, he told me.

'I believe that any commander who loves his soldiers shouldn't actually command them. I don't want to be the reason they die. I love them. They are my hands. I cannot achieve anything without them. An officer without his soldiers is meaningless. But I couldn't refuse the promotion. I've been a company commander for ten years. Things must proceed. This is life.'

I asked what he'd do if they wanted to make him a colonel. At this prospect he perked up.

'Why not? My soldiers do so much for me, I suppose I owe it to them, in a way, to accept greater command.'

I asked after his mother.

'Still calling every day. "Have you eaten? Have you had breakfast?" I told her recently, "I'm a man! I'm an officer!" Do you know what she said? She said, "No, you're still my child."'

Another big explosion rang out. It sent a hail of pavement pieces rising above the roofs. Every piece was visible and distinct against the cloudless blue sky, and their oblique trajectory was such that they seemed to be moving in slow motion. They looked like a flock of very small birds winging off. After they had returned to earth, a fine white powdery substance descended from the sky. Everyone immediately had the same thought: chlorine. But we had no chance to act. By the time we noticed it, the stuff was already landing on the rose buds, and then on our arms, then our faces. We looked at each other in a panic. I began furiously brushing it off my skin, then remembered you're not supposed to do that. You're supposed to find water. Instead, I just sat there, paralyzed by fear, staring at my forearm, waiting for it to break out in sores.

Nothing happened. It turned out to be some kind of harmless dust—the missile had hit a nearby construction site, most likely, with cement makings in it. We returned to the command post. I was just starting to laugh off the rose garden fright when I noticed that a bench on the porch of the house was piled with gas masks and rubber gloves. I didn't even know CTS had chemical warfare gear. I asked the soldiers what was happening. They didn't know. A commander came over.

'Everyone, put on your masks,' he said. 'We're expecting a chemical attack any moment.'

Usually I carried my own mask and gloves, but by this point I'd been covering the battle for seven months, and had never until today even heard of a chemical attack. I'd left the gear behind. My translator asked if there were any extra sets. There weren't. We told the commander we had no protection.

'Then I suggest you get your asses out of here,' he said.

We rushed outside and found Hassan's driver. He hustled us into a Humvee. As we pulled away, we could see all the soldiers stationed around Thawra—hundreds of them—jogging toward the end of the block. Some had already donned their masks, others were putting them on as they moved. They were mustering near the destroyed tank.

Hassan walked toward the Humvee and waved goodbye. He had no mask.

'Where's your mask?' I yelled.

He didn't hear me. I put my hands to my face as though putting on a mask. He smiled and shrugged. If it was his day, it was his day. I never went back to Mosul.

4

By the spring, Abu Omar, Abu Fahad, and their families were resettled in their homes in Mosul. Still not talking to each other, they independently both kept inviting me to visit. I wanted to, but there were compelling reasons not to. There was no question but that there was still an insurgency in the east. Shortly after reopening, a popular kebab spot where journalists had been having lunch was blown up by a suicide bomber. Patrolling was minimal. The 16th division was supposedly securing that side of the city, but you could drive for blocks and blocks without seeing a single soldier. There were some local police about, too, but their lack of interest in doing anything other than passing the time and staying alive was obvious.

There was a more vexing problem: I didn't know how far I could trust the brothers. It wasn't just that they'd once supported the Islamic State—so many Moslawis, so many Iraqis I'd come to know and like, to love, to trust with my life, had done that. And it wasn't just that I knew their families were more connected with the Islamic State than they'd let on. It was their circumstances. They were back in their homes, yes, but otherwise they were penniless and powerless. They were between two fires, as the planning department director had put it—between a government that barely cared about them and an insurgency that, though on the ropes at the moment, would inevitably recrudesce. What if one of his neighbors came to Abu Omar and said, 'I know your son is in Daesh, give me X amount of money not to turn you over to the Shiites.' What if someone approached Abu Fahad and said 'We've seen an American go into your house. Give me Y not to tell Daesh, who will blow up your house.' I could no more protect them in such a situation than I could myself. If I was one of the brothers, and a jihadi or a corrupt cop or a desperate relative came to me and whispered in my ear the sum of dinars an American would fetch—would I be able to ignore that sum? Broke and hopeless as I was? Would I be able to ignore that sum *and* risk losing my own life if I refused it? Would anyone? And for how long? Neither Abu Omar nor Abu Fahad, nor any other Moslawi, was foolish enough to think that after the Caliphate was gone from Mosul jihadism would be too. It would go underground, as it had done before. It would morph, find new arguments, new sympathizers, a new name. But it would come back. It would always come back. This violence would always be in us.

The warmth and generosity and protection and candor I had been shown by Iraqis, including by Abu Omar and Abu Fahad, was astonishing, the more so considering I was American—but was I willing to stake my life, or theirs, on it? This calculation made me feel ungrateful, terrible, like an exploitative bastard, but it was a calculation I had to make. I think Abu Fahad, of the two men, must have known this was the calculation I was making, and maybe he thought it wise. Or maybe he said to himself, 'Just like an American: nice to you so far as it benefits him, then he cuts you loose.' I'll never know. Eventually I did take Abu Omar up on his offer, and visited him very briefly at his home in Zahra. It nearly brought me to tears. The small three-room apartment was empty of furniture, appliances, basic necessities. There wasn't even a sink. There were a few sleeping mats on the floor and a small gas stove, not even as good as the one Abu Omar had in the camp. The building was in disrepair. The walls hadn't seen a paintbrush in decades. The place hadn't been shot up but it looked like it had.

One night in April, I got a call from Abu Omar. He was sobbing. Aya had disappeared. He was sure she'd been kidnapped. He'd gone to the police station and they'd told him to shut up and kicked him out. He didn't know what to do.

I went to see the commander of the federal police in east Mosul. He called the station where Abu Omar had gone and bitched them out.

'Don't make me come over there and kick your asses,' the commander said into the phone.

Within hours, Aya was back home. A few days later, I met Abu Omar, Aya, and Amina at a restaurant on Highway 2 outside Mosul.

'Life in Mosul is awful. It was better under Daesh,' he told me, as we sat down. 'During Daesh, there were no jobs, it's true, but now there are no jobs *and* the corruption and stealing is back. With Daesh, there was no such thing because everyone was scared.'

I asked what had happened to Aya. He launched into a frenzied account. She had not been kidnapped, it turned out. She'd gone for a walk by herself and gotten lost. She'd been picked up by a group of militiamen. They'd locked her in a room, insulted her, hit her. Finally they'd returned her, warning Abu Omar not to let his daughter out alone.

Across the table, Amina looked on and listened with her customary patience. But Aya was staring at her father in disgust. I asked her if his version of the story was true. Abu Omar had the endearing habit of never getting angry with me when I questioned his veracity—he sometimes seemed to invite it, as though he was testing me, trying to see what he could get past me—and he didn't get angry now.

'No,' Aya said, without fear. 'It's not true.'

The truth, she said, was that she had run away. In fact, she'd run away three times, once in the camp and twice since they'd returned home. She ran away because she couldn't bear her father, she said, looking him straight in the eyes as she said it. There was more: she'd met a young man in the camp. She was in love with him. Now she and the young man, Barzan, were both back in Mosul. When she ran away she knew where she was going—to Barzan's family's house. He and his brothers were involved with a Sunni militia, but that was the only part of her father's story that had been true.

Abu Omar confessed without my having to ask him that hers was the right account.

'But she is mentally unstable,' he said. 'She doesn't want us.'

Aya thought Barzan was going to propose. She wanted him to. It could happen as soon as tonight. And even if he didn't, even if he didn't love her yet as she loved him, she wanted to live with his family, not her own.

'I want to stay with Barzan's family,' she said. 'I don't want to go home. I don't like it at home. I don't like my father.'

'Ask her why she hates me. Go ahead, ask her,' Abu Omar said to me. But before I could, he blurted out, 'If she runs away again, I'll call the federal police! I have a reputation to maintain. I can't allow my daughter to go live with some boy and his family. What would people say?'

Aya protested that Abu Omar knew Barzan.

'This was the first time I ever saw him.'

'You're lying, you know him.'

'One of my relatives used to work on an oil field with him,' Abu Omar said to me. 'That's how he says he knows me. I don't know him.' He got upset. He turned back to Aya. 'My daughter, why would you do this? Why would you put me through this? It's a shameful act!' And to me, 'Omar, he hits me, Aya, she runs away. I don't know what to do anymore. I will kill myself because I love Aya and she does not love me back!'

Aya was crying. Amina tried to console her.

'Or I'll kill her,' he said. 'If she runs away again, I swear, I'll kill her.'

Aya raised her head and, through her tears, stared at him with the purest hatred I have ever seen a child stare at a parent. She said, still staring at him, but talking to me, 'This morning, at three in the morning, my father woke me up. He was crouching by my bed. He was holding a knife to my face. He said, "If you run away again, I will kill you."'

I turned to Abu Omar and asked if this was true.

He nodded eagerly.

'Yes, yes, it's true.'

When I had last visited Abu Fahad at the Khazer camp, the day before he returned to Mosul, I found him sitting with a friend in his empty tent. He was reclining against a rolled-up tarp, looking dejected. He hadn't the energy left, he said, to tell me anything but the truth.

Kurdish agents had come to the tent a few days before. They had taken him and Hamudi to their offices, and put them in two different rooms. An agent told Abu Fahad that they knew he was a Daesh intelligence operative and Hamudi a fighter. Abu Fahad laughed and asked to be shown the evidence. We have witnesses, the agent told him. Then show me them, Abu Fahad said. We can't, the agent replied, it would endanger them. Abu Fahad said, 'I will not hold a grudge against them. Just bring them here. If they're right about what they're saying, you can execute me here and now, hang me from that ceiling fan.'

Hamudi was brought in. His face was red and swollen from slapping. He'd confessed to being a jihadi. Now he was gone. His father believed he was in Irbil, but there was no way to know. The agents wouldn't tell him anything.

I asked if it was true that Hamudi had joined the Islamic State.

'Yes,' Abu Fahad said.

Having told me this much, he figured he might as well go on. His eldest son, Loy, had been with Daesh since the beginning, since before 2014, in fact. He had probably been with al Qaeda and ISI before that. Perhaps he'd gotten Omar involved, as Aya believed. But it wasn't Loy who had indoctrinated his younger brother Hamudi. Like so many young Moslawi men, Hamudi had been angry and bored to death and desperate for something, anything, to belong to, to believe in. Hamudi had sought out the jihadis on his own, Abu Fahad believed, and had gone in for the monthlong indoctrination course. It was actually Loy himself who brought his younger brother home and told Abu Fahad that Hamudi had no business with these people. He, Loy, had come to hate them—that had not been a lie—but he was also part of them, and there was no hope for him. But Hamudi could be saved.

Loy was still calling his father from west Mosul, even as the fighting went on. Abu Fahad knew Loy had done terrible things. But he was his son. He couldn't not talk to him. Considering how devout Loy had been, his father told me, and how long he'd been affiliated with the insurgency, it wouldn't surprise him if Loy was a Daesh commander by now.

'I can't know for sure, because I haven't seen him in so long, but I am sure he's done wrong,' Abu Fahad said. 'He's caused damage. I have put it in my mind that I will never see him again. I've already accepted the idea that he will be killed and that will be the end of it. If my son is with them, if his actions were damaging and he was torturing people, killing them, then I hope he goes to hell. But if it's a rumor and they're only falsely accusing him, then I hope God takes revenge for him upon them.' For a few minutes, he followed this hopeful logic. 'Loy couldn't even kill a chicken. He's my son and I know him. You know people here love to gossip, to make rumors.' Then he deflated again as he realized he was lying to himself. I asked if he would try to find Loy when he returned to Mosul. He laughed scornfully. 'How could I do that? How could I look for him? He's on that side and I'm on this side. I am telling you, I know he's caused damage. I'm ninety-nine percent sure of it. The last time we talked on the phone, he told me, "Dad, from now on, you have to accept that I will die. You have to try to forget about me." It's hopeless now. He's stuck with them, and there's nothing more he can do about it.'

In early July 2017, Iraqi prime minister Haider al-Abadi pronounced Mosul liberated. For another month, a contingent of jihadis held out in a ruined warren on the western bank of the Tigris. They were wiped out in a final barrage of airstrikes. The comparisons to Aleppo, which had once seemed exaggerated, were now obvious, even inadequate. 'Ruins' did not begin to describe the appearance of the old city and the neighborhoods around it in west Mosul. It looked as though a vindictive god had wiped his hand across the city.

The battle for Mosul, which was supposed to have taken four to six months, lasted ten. Twelve hundred Iraqi soldiers were killed and six thousand wounded, according to the Pentagon. No one will ever know how many civilians died, but it was certainly in the thousands. A *New York Times* report estimated that one in five coalition airstrikes had resulted in an unintended civilian death—thirty-one times the rate the Pentagon claimed. By the end of the battle, according to human rights organizations and news reports, Iraqi security forces were executing unarmed Moslawis en masse. Later, at the trials of suspected jihadis and collaborators, a few minutes of consideration and no substantial evidence could be enough deliver a sentence. Mass graves containing the Islamic State's victims were still being discovered a year after the battle ended.

It was not airstrikes or soldiers but jihadis who finally blew up the Grand al-Nuri Mosque. It was one of dozens of mosques they destroyed in Mosul. Usually they destroyed them on the grounds that the mosques were idolatrous. With al-Nuri, their mosque, the mosque in which the Caliphate had been created, they could make no such claim. They destroyed it because they could. Al-Nuri had stood for nearly a millennium.

A few days after it fell, Abu Fahad was sent a video of Loy on Facebook. It appeared the federal police had shot and uploaded it. In the video he is shirtless, emaciated, bloodied, filthy, his head shaved and beard crudely chopped. His hands are tied behind his back, he is sitting in the dirt, being questioned by a federal policeman. There is a cut in the video. The final frame is of his corpse, curled on the ground.

I last saw Abu Fahad before he received the video, at the same restaurant on Highway 2. His house hadn't been destroyed, he was happy to tell me. Only the windows had been shattered. The day before we met, there'd been a demonstration near Qadasiya, government workers who were protesting not having been paid for more than two years. He hadn't taken part, but of course he sympathized. There hadn't been any bombings in a few weeks, which was nice. Still, he said, 'People are scared, they think they're being watched. Some are scared they're being watched by Daesh sleeping cells, others by the government. Depending on the person, they're frightened of different things.'

He'd brought Maha.

'Mosul is not like before,' she told me. 'We just sit around. There's nothing to do.'

But she hadn't lost her senses of wonder or humor. The last time

I'd seen her in the camp, I'd brought her a biography of Saladin, her favorite figure from Iraqi history, and a leather-bound journal and a silver ballpoint pen. She said she'd been writing in it a lot. She asked me if I could get her an atlas, a thing she'd just learned about.

'There is a book that contains everything! Like animals, outer space.'

I told her I'd try to get one.

We talked about the restaurant she would open.

'I think you should help me open it,' she said. 'Every time you visit, I will host you and make your favorite, tashrib.'

'What will we call it?' I asked.

'We'll call it Tashrib James. Or American Tashrib.'

Abu Fahad's daughter in law, Loy's wife, had given birth during the battle. The little girl was named Zina. She was the second grandchild of Abu Fahad's to be born in the Caliphate. The first, Zainab, Zina's elder sister, was now nearly three years old. Abu Fahad talked to her on the phone often.

'Does she understand what's happening?' I asked.

'She understands everything. She was talking to me about the airstrikes.'

The girls would grow up without their father, very possibly without their mother, probably amid another war.

Abu Fahad brought up a picture of Zainab on his phone and handed it to me. She had transfixing brown eyes and a rose-bulb nose. She was radiant. I couldn't bear to look at her. I handed the phone back to him.

One of the first mosques the Islamic State destroyed after seizing Mosul is called Nabi Yunus. It is a singularly interesting place, with a richer history even than al-Nuri. Built in Ottoman times on the eastern bank of the Tigris, it was once a formidable thing, according to old engravings, with massive exterior walls, a fluted conical dome, and a minaret that, in its day, loomed over what had been Nineveh. It was consecrated to Yunus, as he's known in the Koran, or Jonah as he's known in the Old Testament. It contained bones said to be taken from the leviathan that had swallowed the prophet.

A century and a half ago, a Moslawi man who lived next to Nabi Yunus was digging in the dirt floor of his home, trying to sink a well or make a basement, it is not known, when his shovel hit stone. He tried to dig it out, but the stone was huge. Clearing the dirt as best he could, he found a monumental sculpture. The Moslawis who lived around Nabi Yunus had been coming upon relics for as long as any-one remembered but had never much cared. The leavings of some bygone infidel race, they perhaps thought. Sometimes they used the marble panels or cylinder seals they found as tables or candlestick holders. But by 1852, when the man found the winged Assyrian bull in his basement, excavators were at work in other parts of Nineveh. When the Ottoman pasha of Mosul learned of what was happening in the basement, he threatened to arrest the owner of the house if he dug any further, then sent his own men over to continue excavating. The pasha hoped to beat the British and French archaeologists to the next great find. He bought up the other houses around Nabi Yunus. It turned out the mosque was sitting atop one of Nineveh's buried walls—one of the walls that had supposedly collapsed when the city was sacked in 612 B.C.—and that the sackers had not made off with everything. Riches were being unearthed.

What eventually came to light beneath Nabi Yunus was a great weapons cache, a kingly arsenal that had been attached to the Assyr-ian palaces, though it was big enough to be a kind of palace of its own. In an inscription, King Esarhaddon, son of Sennacherib and father of Ashurbanipal, described this 'palace where all is mustered . . . for setting in order the camp, mustering the steeds, the mules, the chariots, the harness, the battle equipment and the spoil of the enemy, every type of thing which Ashur, the king of the gods, has granted me as my regal lot[.]'

A more pious pasha took over Mosul and the arsenal was reburied so that Nabi Yunus would not be marred. A century later archaeologists returned and found still more beneath the mosque. Saddam Hussein took an interest in the site. Caught between his devotion to antiquity and his desire to show himself to be a devout Muslim, however, he ordered excavations ceased. He had the buildings around the mosque brought down and the gardens around it terraced in his Mesopotamian-hybrid style. There was still much to find, but it would have to wait.

This is how things remained until July of 2014, when Islamic State demolitionists wired Nabi Yunus with explosives and sent the dome and the minaret and much of the rest of the building to the ground. Maybe looking to store weapons or loot, maybe looking for more relics to steal and sell, the jihadis then dug beneath the mosque a tunnel. A little less than three years later, several weeks after the Islamic State had been driven from east Mosul, I accompanied a group of Iraqi and British archaeologists and U.N. officials into the tunnel. We entered through the remains of Nabi Yunus and descended. The rumble of airstrikes faded away as the tunnel went lower and narrowed. A colleague of mine said 'I get claustrophobic' and turned around.

Going farther, we began to find shards of ancient pottery and fragments of tablets in the dirt at our feet. Then whole pots, whole tablets. Then, by our legs, in the wall, an intact row of ancient reliefs depicting women in robes and headdresses. The jihadis hadn't touched the artwork, it appeared. Our flashlights moved up the walls. We were no longer in a tunnel, we found, but in a small room, and the walls were no longer dirt and rock. They were carved lime-stone. The walls were winged bulls. We were standing between a pair of giant Assyrian lamassus. Their human heads were obscured by the ceiling; if they hadn't been, they would have stood at bet-ter than ten feet. The archaeologists knew at once the significance of what was happening: we were looking at an until now unknown trove of Assyrian relics. None except us and a few jihadis and sol-diers had seen these things in centuries. No one spoke. We stood gazing up at these beautiful creatures in awed silence. It was one of those moments you experience only once or twice in your life, if that. The lenses of time collapsed. We were in the fast wind of creation. I could feel history's hem brush my face.

When the lamassus were later excavated, inscriptions were found on them. On the flank of one, Ashurbanipal had written: 'The palace of Ashurbanipal, great king, mighty king, king of the world, king of Assyria, son of Esarhaddon, king of Assyria, descendant of Sennach-erib, king of Assyria.'

As we emerged from the tunnel, the airstrikes faded back in. I asked the archaeologists what more they expected to find in there. They said they didn't know, but whatever it was, it would be of immense historical value. And there wouldn't just be Assyrian rel-ics. The palaces of Nineveh had only been built up by Ashurbanipal and his forebears toward the end of that civilization, after all. Other empires, other peoples, had preceded them. Mosul was one of the oldest cities on earth. It had been battered and leveled and forgotten through the millennia, but never destroyed, never abandoned. It had always found a way to live on. The layers of life went down much further than we could know.

A NOTE ON METHODS, TRANSLATION, STYLE, AND SOURCES

Most of this book derives from reporting I conducted in Iraq in 2016–17. In the field, I worked with what are known by the press as 'fixers,' the indispensable men and women who make their living and risk their lives to provide foreign journalists with access, interviews, transportation, shelter, food, cigarettes, good cheer, and every other necessity. Sadly, in Iraq, being a fixer for a foreign journalist, particularly an American journalist, is still a death-soliciting business. Many have been killed, as have many Iraqi journalists, and while I don't flatter myself the Islamic State will scour this page for the names of potential victims, nor would I put it past them, morally. These friends know the extent of my gratitude, I hope. Also interpreters, they extemporaneously translated between Arabic, Kurdish, and English during the events and conversations described in my articles and this book. While reporting, I always keep an audio recorder on. After returning from the field, I brought my audio recordings to professional interpreters, who translated and transcribed them, usually in my presence, so that we could discuss idiom and such things. For military technicalities, I relied on Master Sergeant Joey Thompson of the U.S. Army 1st Infantry Division and Ellen Pope and Carl Castellano of Talos.

The book's historical passages attempt a jaunty, suggestive, associative tone. You will be the judge of their success. Particularly jaunty is the passage about the life of Saddam Hussein. If it takes a certain poetic license, it takes no factual license. The details of Saddam's life are drawn from his various biographers and from public records, listed below. The other historical passages are based on books, academic articles, reports, interviews with historians and archaeologists, and my own visits to museums, archives, and archaeological sites. In a few instances I've had the space to cite those authors in the text, and in a very few I've had the good fortune to relay my thanks and admiration personally. Most of the scholarship I've relied on was originally published in English or European languages. Scholars working in Arabic and Persian have done essential work on these subjects, too, but, sadly, very little of it has been translated.

Professional scholars are the anonymous inspiration behind much of the best journalism. They deserve more credit. What follows is not credit enough but it is a start. For the history, literature, and art of ancient Mesopotamia and the Levant, including Old Testament and Hebrew matters, I am indebted to Zainab Bahrani, Leo Bersani, C. L. Crouch, Ulysse Dutoit, C. J. Gadd, Paul Haupt, John H. Hilber, Richard A. Horsely, Ali al-Jiboori, Margo Kitts, Mario Liverani, John MacGinnis, Peter Machinist, J. D. A. McGinnis, Scott B. Noegel, André Parrot, Aron Pinker, Beate Pongratz-Leisten, Barbara N. Porter, Karen Radner, David C. Rapoport, Julian Reade, Eleanor Robson, John Malcolm Russell, Yona Sabar, H. W. F. Saggs,

Jonathan Stökl, Geoffrey Turner, D. J. Wiseman, Solomon Zeitlin, and particularly Paul Collins of the Ashmolean Museum and the University of Oxford. For early Islamic, medieval, and Ottoman Mesopotamia, Robert Bedrosian, H. S. Fink, H. A. R. Gibb, Carole Hillenbrand, Percy Kemp, Michael Morony, A. S. Tritton, William F. Tucker, and particularly Dina Khoury of George Washington University, Chase Robinson of the City University of New York, and Sarah Shields of the University of North Carolina. For the translation and discussion of Kharijite verse, Tarif Khalidi of the American University of Beirut. For modern Iraq, Hirmis Aboona, Ali Allawi, M. Awad, Amatzia Baram, Hanna Batatu, Lisa Cooper, Anthony Cordesman, James S. Corum, Warren Dockter, Toby Dodge, David Freeman, David Fromkin, Fannar Haddad, Eric Hamilton, Samir al-Khalil, Berriedale Keith, David Killingray, Dina Khoury, V. O. Lockwood-Drummond, Vali Nasr, Sean McMeekin, Philip S. Meilinger, Vladimir Minorsky, Henry Munson, Robert Olson, Scot Robertson, Priya Satia, Karol R. Sorby, William Spencer, Robert Springborg, Charles Tripp, P. J. Vatikiotis, S. G. Vesey-FitzGerald, H. E. Wilkie Young, W. Thom Workman, and particularly James Barr. For all of Iraq's history, John Robertson. For the life and writings of Saddam, Saïd K. Aburish, Daniel Kalder, Efraim Karsh, Samir al-Khalil, Kanan Makiya, Inari Rautsi, and Turi Munthe. For the history of revolutionary and jihadi thought in Islam and the rise of the Islamic State, Rasha al Aqeedi, John Calvert, Robyn Creswell, Philip D. Curtin, Jean-Pierre Filiu, Mercedes Garcia-Arenal, Fawaz Gerges, Bernard Haykel, Robert L. Hess, Benjamin Isakhan, Hans Jansen, Johannes J. G. Jansen, Jeffrey T. Kenney, Gustav Larrson, Remy Low, Shiraz Maher, William McCants, Andrew McGregor, Rudolph Peters, Sofya Shahab, Emmanuel Sivan, Joby Warrick, Von W. Montgomery Watt, Aaron Zelin, and especially David Cook of Rice University.